POWER AND W
IN THE MIDDLE EAST

Mark Zeitoun has worked as a water engineer, negotiations advisor and policy analyst in conflict and post-conflict zones throughout Africa and the Middle East. He co-directs the UEA Water Security Research Centre, and teaches environmental policy and politics at the School of International Development, University of East Anglia.

POWER AND WATER IN THE MIDDLE EAST

The Hidden Politics of the Palestinian–Israeli Water Conflict

MARK ZEITOUN

I.B. TAURIS
LONDON · NEW YORK

New paperback edition published in 2012 by I.B.Tauris & Co Ltd
6 Salem Road, London W2 4BU
175 Fifth Avenue, New York NY 10010
www.ibtauris.com

Distributed n the United States and Canada Exclusively by Palgrave Macmillan, 175 Fifth
Avenue, New York NY 10010

First published in hardback in 2008 by I.B.Tauris & Co Ltd

ISBN: 978 1 84885 997 5

A full CIP record for this book is available from the British Library
A full CIP record is available from the Library of Congress

Library of Congress Catalog Card Number: available

Printed and bound by CPI Group (UK) Ltd, Croydon, CR0 4YY
From camera-ready copy edited and supplied by the author

For those who struggle to provide water for others.

Contents

Illustrations

Tables

Photographs

Acknowledgements

The ideas that generated this book were conceived during the years spent working with colleagues supplying clean water to people caught up in the centre and in the wake of violent conflicts. Time after time we witnessed our best laid plans and infrastructure deteriorate into disrepair, or be crushed under tank treads. I was forced to question whether the effort was worth it, or if it wouldn't be better instead to address the underlying fundamentals of water and conflict. While I left for this pursuit, my colleagues remained committed to their noble and frustrating profession. I thank for their sacrifice, and the inspiration to write, Adil al Attar, Mazen al Ahmad, Thierry Mayounga, Riccardo Mungia and all other colleagues from the ICRC, UNDP, Oxfam, SNDE, GCWS, PWA, and the employees of the water departments from the municipalities of Abeche, Brazzaville, Baghdad, Basra, Beirut, Dolisie, Gaza City, Jenin, Nablus, Rafah and Tyre.

I have benefited enormously from the extremely fertile interdisciplinary academic environment provided by the London Water Research Group. I thank in particular for their intellectual stimulation from so many in the group Ana Cascao, Joti Giri, Francesca Greco, Dipak Gyawali, Nick Hostettler, Anders Jägerskog, Elizabeth Kistin, Alan MacDonald, Clemens Messerschmid, Naho Mirumachi, Yasir Mohieldeen, Michael Talhami and Melvin Woodhouse. The insight provided by Bazezew Takele confirmed my sense that in the analysis of transboundary water conflicts, as in everything else in life, perspective is crucial. Jeroen Warner has been instrumental in helping me interpret and apply international relations, political science and hegemony theory in a useful way. I am also very grateful to Shaddad Attili, Marwa Daoudy, John Murray, Stephen McCaffrey, David Phillips and Tony Turton for their friendly intellectual force and rigour.

Very special thanks are reserved for Tony Allan, Ehab Shanti, Jon Tunnicliffe, my many friends, my parents, and my brothers. The cerebral stimulation and deep friendship I derive from them has been a source of energy and inspiration.

My appreciation is foremost to Samia el Tabari, for urging me to use the opportunities and voice I have been given for those whose options are closed out and voices muted.

Preface to the Paperback Edition

There have been several developments that might have or may yet serve to open the path to resolution of the Palestinian-Israeli water conflict, in the four years since this book was first published. Israel's astonishing embrace of desalination technology has led to production rates much higher than total Palestinian fresh water consumption (including for agriculture), and may serve to reduce tensions. Also, international norms are maturing, with the Human Right to water recognised by the UN General Assembly in 2009 reflecting a growing global rejection of the denial of basic drinking water services. And two of the three governments that were entrenched in the water conflict have been voted out. Along with the 2011 revolutions in Egypt and Syria, the regional political order established during the previous century has been drastically altered, and the possibility of equitable Jordan River-wide sharing is no longer inconceivable. The Israeli Water Authority has been established, and a new head appointed to the Palestinian Water Authority, leaving open the possibility of improving the hierarchical relationship between the institutions, and a step away from the token cooperation described throughout this book towards effective joint water management.

So some would hope. Indeed, the water conflict was up for termination during the 2008 'Annapolis Round' of permanent status negotiations, and incorporation of desalination technology to create a 'win-win' outcome to the water conflict was the Palestinian side's intention. The rationale of the idea proved unable to overcome internal Palestinian squabbles over tactics, a lukewarm reception from US mediators, and an Israeli water negotiations team under strict orders to discuss no more than data collection unless the status of Jerusalem and the fate of refugees had been agreed.

The water conflict continues to be shaped by the interminable 'Oslo' process, which was given a breath of life from a new US administration and is still clung to by Palestinian and Israeli authorities unable to develop alternatives. In an attempt to wriggle out of the coercive procedures of the Oslo-derived Joint Water Committee (see Chapter 6), the Palestinian Water Authority has created a 'JWC Unit' complete with lawyers. But even as the World Bank and many of those who once praised the JWC now decry the politics behind it, sustainable development of the Palestinian water sector remains constricted, while Israeli construction in the

West Bank continues unabated. Most nascent hilltop outposts are still promptly connected by the state to a water transmission pipeline, the settlement's lifeline.

Generally, things have gotten much worse for the Palestinians in the West Bank and Gaza who rely on water for their livelihoods. The situation has moved from one where the tensions were down-played as the cooperation was celebrated, to one where the conflict is no longer denied and there are few attempts to cover it up. In the language of this study, the Israeli hydro-hegemonic apparatus is currently much more overt, laid bare by unilateral projects throughout the occupied territory. As such, Figure 9.2 should be updated to show a shift around 2007 in 'forms of control', from 'hegemony', back towards 'domination'. Otherwise, the analysis by and large still holds.

The number of people who have welcomed the relevance of the book's frame is encouraging, but it is no comfort to continue to feel the power in action or to ponder the future. The few detractors of the analysis have suggested in a particular way that I do just this, however. Focussed on the details and mechanisms that created and maintained the asymmetry, voices from both left and right decried, I hadn't 'explored the potential for future cooperation sufficiently'. Indeed I had not, for a number of reasons.

First, there have been a number of publications of a bright future of Palestinian-Israeli interaction over the transboundary flows, in the optimistic early post-Oslo days. Those predictions were grounded neither in theory nor on extensive grounded experience, however. The 'glass half-full' positions (taken perhaps by people who may never have been denied water and whose livelihoods are not dependent on it) have in any case proven to be wide of the mark.

Second, my interest is in what prevents resolution of the conflict, and so the analysis remains focussed on facts and events. Having said that, I suggested in the original preface that if the reader still found the analysis relevant a decade on, it meant ideological politics had prevailed. I see they still do, at this artificial mid-way point, and so for a moment step back to look at the bigger picture.

More than ever, it is what's in the minds of those who control the water that counts. Setting aside the slightly different forms of hegemony and resistance employed by Israelis and Palestinians from across the political spectrum, one discerns an outcome darker than just the destruction of people's livelihoods. Chauvinistic forces overwhelm rationale and science to pervert the very essence of the resource. Normally a source of life, water is being used instead for destructive ends.

With monotonous regularity throughout the decades, water has been denied in order to move the wrong people out, and provided to usher the right people in. Witness the current struggle to obtain filling points on Israeli settler lines, by Palestinian farmers in the Jordan River Valley. West of Bethlehem, farmers have to battle an array of army jeeps, zoning regulations, and the Separation Wall – and have been trickling away for years. South of Hebron, Israeli demolition orders served on the most basic of water infrastructure have been implemented in anger since around the time the UN adopted the Human Right to water. Readers are encouraged to see for themselves that these people are prevented even from collecting the rain. No surprise to see that there, too, the families are drifting away.

Even Israeli citizens residing in the so-called 'unrecognised villages' have largely been denied basic water services (not to mention schools) since Israel's establishment in 1948. The recent push to force several thousand (Bedouin) people into a few collective villages will be only the latest in a long chain of transgressions against them. Had proper and safe water been supplied to the communities in the 1950s, it would have been more difficult – if not impossible – to uproot them today. Thus while safe water can cleanse, so can its denial.

But water can still attract, and while the success of the Israeli settler project is driven by political Zionism, credit is also due to the efforts of the Israeli water engineers. Without their pipes, the outposts would be still-born. So the stolen hilltops bloom, as the raw settler sewage flows into the withered Palestinian fields in the valleys below.

Unable to struggle through humiliation to work the land, Palestinian parents scramble to send their children abroad – while Zionist families from around the world are encouraged to settle in. Judging by the rate of replacement since the Oslo process began, there is a generation or two to go. This is where I believe the conflict is heading, and why we should replace wishful thinking with sharp-eyed analysis of the roots of the conflict. And maintain the hope required to fight the racism that perpetuates it.

The final reason I didn't attempt to predict the future of the Palestinian-Israeli water conflict is because I understand that it is determined by – and not driving – the broader political conflict. I find this political ecology approach more illuminating than the environmental determinist approach, which starts with the idea that even minor forms of cooperation over transboundary resources will lead to improved international relations. The determinist 'water leads to peace (or war)' perspective is much more compelling to liberal audiences, and has spawned a number of 'environmental peacemaking' initiatives that claim to be apolitical, on the shores of the Jordan. But searching for evidence, and with senses attuned for covert power plays, I appreciate that resolution of the broader conflict is not that simple. The future of the water conflict is tied-up with the political conflict. This explains why the most effective environmental activists are those who are directly engaged with socio-political forces, as well as with bio-physical ones.

The past year has seen a number of neighbouring dictators fall from decades of dominative or hegemonic rule. This reminds us not only that resolution of conflicts comes with sustained effort, but that it is led by the people, not by the politicians. Thousands of courageous farmers, water engineers, planners, students, lawyers and activists do resist the chauvinism that drives the use of water to replace one people with another in Palestine-Israel, and they will be the ones to revert water back to its life-giving essence. I hope they will find this book of some use.

Norwich, October 2011

Preface

This book documents the role that power plays in determining the outcome of the Palestinian–Israeli water conflict, particularly in the wake of the 'Oslo process', up to December 2005. The story is one that neither the two sides nor the international community that supported the process are likely to boast to their grandchildren about. This is an exposé of coercion and manipulation, of deepened mistrust, and of the failure to manage a precious resource. From this failure, though, we may draw lessons. It is hoped that the analysis may serve as a reference for future attempts to deal with the waters transboundary to Palestine and Israel – at least for what *not* to do.

It would be a good thing if, in a decade from now, the reader finds the analysis simply an interesting account of the way things used to be. This would mean that wiser heads had prevailed. Politicians and the people they are meant to represent would have realised that an equitable and reasonable distribution of the transboundary water resources was not only possible, but was also rational. The transboundary flows would have been managed collectively by Palestinians and Israelis through fair and effective mechanisms of cooperation. The political context would have been set between states that respect each other's sovereignty, but realised that sometimes sovereignty may be restricted for common good. There is no more compelling reason than a wise use of the limited water resources in the tiny land to think about uniting rather than separating.

If, however, you are reading this in 2017 and find its analysis still relevant, you may want to spend considerable effort reflecting on the origins and mechanisms of the conflict. Chauvinistic and ideological politics would have maintained Israel's post-Oslo occupation and siege of the West Bank and Gaza for two decades. Advances in desalination technology would not have led, as they could, to a re-negotiation of the freshwater resources located underground or in the Jordan River; Palestinian water resource managers would still be grappling with basic wastewater re-use technology, Israelis with controlling the deep thirst of their agricultural sector.

This study's exploration of the mechanisms of power behind the conflict is not an academic exercise. An understanding of the links between the conflict's origins and the devices that maintain it can be of direct use to those interested in its resolution. The extreme imbalance in power between the two sides permits a highly asymmetric outcome. Policy-makers keen on effective cooperation would do well to consider attempts to level the playing field.

This book may also be of interest to aficionados of water conflicts around the globe. If power imbalance is simply a fact of life, domination does not have to be. There is a growing body of work demonstrating how the most powerful riparian state on an international river basin may choose to play a dominating or leadership role. The scholars and practitioners associated with the London Water Research Group are pushing this idea to its limits through exploration of the concept of hydro-hegemony. Consideration of the interests of the weaker riparian party is at the discretion of the 'hydro-hegemon'. The statement holds as much for the Nile, the Tigris, the Ganges, the Columbia, Orange or Congo as it does for the Jordan.

Hydropolitics along the Jordan River are fluid. As expected, political and military events have overtaken this study's period of analysis. The Palestinian people's election of a Hamas government in January 2006 has led to a freeze on the limited cooperation that did exist between Israeli and Palestinian water technicians. Most international donors have put their projects aimed at developing the Palestinian water sector on ice. The Israeli assault on the main electrical power plant in Gaza in June 2006 denied tens of thousands of people access to water, and further endangered the highly contaminated sources that lie under the sands. The water towers of over fifty villages in southern Lebanon were crippled by damage inflicted during the summer 2006 war between Israel and Hezbollah. Negotiations over the flows on the Golan appear to be underway between Israel and Syria. Co-existing conflict and cooperation is a chief characteristic of the volatile and ever-changing basin. The consequences of cooperation do not sink as deep as those of conflict, which are felt first and foremost by that group with the least power of all – the people themselves.

Those who live the water conflict generally lack the means to project the voices into the concentrations of power, where national and international policy-makers can – and do – ignore them. It may make little difference to them what framework an academic in London uses to analyse their suffering. Yet we must keep insisting that the impact of destructive power games on water in the region is momentous, and regularly occurs below the radar screen, with superficial understanding and inadequate concern from the international diplomatic, donor and academic communities. It happens and it *does* matter. The myopia that sustains the status quo may be reversed if we keep our eyes and minds open and focused on understanding the hidden politics that lie behind the Palestinian–Israeli water conflict.

London, August 2007

Palestinian students on the Lower Jordan River near its outlet at the Lake of Tiberias, 1935.
The photo was taken three decades before the outlet was dammed to complete the Israel
National Water Carrier in 1964. Followed later by damming on the Jordanian/Syrian
Yarmouk tributary, the Lower Jordan today resembles more a filthy stream than a holy river.
The stream empties into the Dead Sea, which has been shrinking steadily since 1964 at the
rate of about one metre per year (see back cover). *Elia Kahvadjian Photo*, Old City, Jerusalem.

1

Water Wars or Water Conflicts?

TRAVELLERS passing through the new Tel Aviv airport encounter a rather elegant indoor water fountain. The water appears from outlets arranged in a wide circle falling from the ceiling of the large open hall, as rain from the sky. The mood and rain gets heavier, with a loud, soft swoosh as it falls onto the lake underneath, around which people with luggage sip coffee at tables. The downpour then eases up to a light shower and finally stops, only to start again later. The fountain is subtle and graceful. The message it sends is also subtle – to the point that it is probably lost on most travellers, who have yet to become fascinated by hydropolitics: you are arriving in Israel where there is water in abundance; Israel made the desert bloom.

The former part of the message is, of course, simply not true. The region is generally semi-arid and parts of it are desert. The latter part of the message is true, but it should be tempered with an understanding of the wisdom of irrigating a desert, particularly when a large portion of the water used to do so was taken from neighbouring states against their will.

The thoughts evoked by the fountain serve the introduction of a book about the Palestinian–Israeli water conflict first of all by highlighting the ideas, ideologies and tensions that characterise the subject. They also initiate the reader into an understanding of the influence and power of subtle messages. Globally, the management of transboundary water resources is generally kept in check not through efficient water-sharing regimes and proper water resources management, but through silent and invisible processes. Mighty rivers of 'virtual' water (the water used to produce wheat, say, in the US or France) is quietly channelled through the docks in Haifa from the global trade market. Tony Allan – father of the concept of virtual water – usefully points out to us that the region between the Mediterranean and the Jordan River 'ran out' of freshwater about 40 years ago. Despite the fact that few politicians will admit it, there is not enough water for food self-sufficiency. There is in fact a high level of dependency on virtual water. Concerned more about representing the interests of their constituents than understanding the underlying fundamentals of water resources management, the political agents of the dominant discourse would be thankful for the conflict-mitigating effects of virtual water, were they able to acknowledge its existence.

In theory, the fact that both Palestine and Israel depend on virtual water makes the conflict over freshwater entirely resolvable. The limited resources that do exist could be divided equitably according to the principles of international water law, and they could be managed prudently. But the politics hidden from international donor reports and media articles keep this truth out of most people's minds. The forces that 'sanction' the discursive processes which suit the interests of the powerful sustain a silence that is difficult to pin down. Views opposing the sanctioned discourse of the water conflict – such as the book at hand – can be readily discredited or otherwise remain 'unheard'.

This book asserts that the politics hidden from the mass media, donor reports and academic literature are determining factors in both the outcome and perceptions of the Palestinian–Israeli water conflict. More specifically, the book claims that *power* is the primary determinant. We may be deluding ourselves if we think otherwise.

Control over the transboundary flows will be shown to be largely in Israeli hands: while their control was contested in the decades following 1948, it was essentially beyond contention after 1967. It evolved following the 1995 Oslo II Agreement into a pervasive and hegemonic form that endures today, with distinct forms of power enabling each stage in the evolution of Israel's dominance. The account of power and hegemony theory offered here, and illustrated throughout the rest of the book, forms an argument which tests this hypothesis. The reader is invited at the end of the book to make her or his own evaluation of success.

Power is commonly perceived as military might, but this text is not about water wars. As such, this analysis flies in the face of those who trumpet the notion that inter-state violence over water is inevitable. Those readers seeking to reinforce their hold on such notions are advised to stop reading now. It is preferred, however, that these readers will appreciate that the absence of war does not mean the absence of conflict. And that the effects of conflict are no less consequential than the effects of war. Examining the reasons for the confusion is a good place to start the analysis.

Why no Water Wars?

Those analysts interpreting relations over water conflicts in circumstances of asymmetric power relations are immersed in a muddied world indeed. The topic seems perpetually complicated in part by the misunderstood notion of 'water wars'. The undeniable public fascination with war extends to the number of individuals and institutions which have/acquire/invent motives to conduct war. The same public is perhaps less fascinated by water, but this subject too can encourage chauvinistic inclinations. Combined together, the terms water and war immediately conjure images of high-tech fighter aircraft patrolling menacingly over rivers. Readied to blast apart an enemy dam, these war machines are willingly perceived as tools assuring security for the state that has deployed them.

The fighter-jets exist, but realisation of their destructive role in *water* conflicts does not, at least not to any significant degree.[1] The 'water security' expected by the public from the fighter-jet is at once over-stated and insufficiently understood. These are but two of dozens of misperceptions that cloud our understanding of the nature of water and conflict. There are many more.

There is a belief, for example, that in regions with growing populations, unstable governments and dwindling water resources, war over water at some point is highly probable. In semi-arid zones such as the Middle East, the likelihood of a conflict over water is compounded by historic and existing political, national and religious tensions in the region. A water war between Israel and Palestine, Egypt and Ethiopia or Turkey and Iraq – in this simple Malthusian logic – would seem inevitable. There is evidence that tends to support the view that control over the sources of the Jordan River had some (but not determining) influence in the 1967 war between Israel and Syria, Egypt and Jordan. Indeed, there is certainly reason to be concerned over Egyptian threats over the Nile or the effects of Turkey's damming of the Tigris and Euphrates. In the sense that a water war is one fought for control of water, none of these cases prove to be a genuine example. Men find many other reasons to go to war. Extensive research, conducted primarily by Aaron Wolf at Oregon State University, has in fact found no example of water as a casus belli.. Furthermore, even for those states still formally at war with each other, as Israel and Lebanon, there is not likely to be a 'water war' in the future.

There are at least three good reasons that explain the absence of water wars. The first is the economic and strategic value of water. Particularly where water resources are scarce, up to 85 per cent of all water is consumed in the production of food. Drinking water, washing water, water used for industrial processes or swimming pools accounts for less than 20 per cent of water consumed in many parts of the world, including the Middle East. Were the reverse true, we might very well see water wars. Since most states can mobilize enough resources to ensure that at least the basic needs of drinking and washing are met, the flows that are usually contested are used for irrigation. The economic value of 'agricultural water', as it is known, is equivalent only to the value of the food it produces, which in turn is dictated by local or global markets. The value of food is always a fraction of much higher value commodities such as oil, for instance, or natural gas. The latter commodities also carry a much greater strategic value than water does, as they can fuel a war machine or serve to keep others at the mercy of those with a larger share. Men in the capitals of their country can claim a direct link between national and energy security, and be provoked into or find a reason to wage war. They are less likely to pay the same political and economic costs to defend farmers growing wheat, even those who form part of a relatively powerful agricultural lobby (and in many – though certainly not all – places around the world, they do not).

We have already touched upon the second good reason there are no genuine water wars, and this is related to the first. Particularly in water scarce regions, the 'virtual water' imported in the form of crops or livestock acts as an effective pressure-relief valve for governments unable to secure the share of water they claim an adversary is denying them. Thus, while the US states of Arizona or Colorado may have a legitimate grievance with California for its attempts to dominate the Colorado River[2], it is unlikely we will see the citizens of Phoenix go thirsty while those of Los Angeles continue to stride about by their pools. Any 'gap' between the amount of food the state of Colorado could produce and the amount they actually do produce (because of the physical scarcity induced by its downstream and more powerful neighbour) is made up through the import of food. That some of this food may come from the industrial farms of downstream southern California, using so-called 'Colorado' water, is understandably a very sore point of contention between the states. The point is that the virtual water imported in the food back into the state of Colorado relieves the pressure – and saves it from having to engage in outright conflict with California. The conflict exists, but there is and will be no 'water war'.

Power asymmetry is the third reason for the absence of water wars. This concept will be developed at length in Chapter 2, and directly applied to the Palestinian–Israeli water conflict in subsequent chapters. When the imbalance of power is severe, military conflict may be pre-empted according to the rules of realpolitik: the opportunity costs of an attack are too high, in other words. Infinitely weaker states 'know their place' in their regional neighbourhood. Even if Canada and the US were not strong allies and trading partners, for example, we are not likely to see conflicts between them take a violent form (at least not in the current *rapport de forces*). The same applies to water conflicts, even in cases where water is in abundance. The conflict being played out (thus far non-violently) along the Mekong River is a case in point. Cambodia is downstream on the river, and relies heavily upon the river's annual 'flood pulse' for the welfare of its delta ecosystem and millions of its fishermen (Phillips, et al. 2006). The weaker state is not likely to challenge the much stronger and upstream Thailand, which in any case is involved in attempts at basin-wide cooperation through the Mekong River Commission (MRC). Further up the river, China is not part of the MRC, and is currently planning dams that suit its own interests.[3] But will we see Bangkok, Phnom Penh and Hanoi threaten, much less attack, Beijing?

Much of the confusion that surrounds the concept of water wars is driven in unequal parts of misunderstanding, politicking and book sales. Some of the confusion also derives from the fact that water and war *are* intimately related, as will be elaborated in the following section.

Water and Conflicts

While water may rarely be the sole motive for war it is often a victim and target of it. Water resources and water infrastructure are closely associated with all types of military conflict. Humanitarian-aid water engineers committed to mopping up the mess that armies create on behalf of politicians can relate dozens of anecdotes.

Consider the spring just outside of Dolisie, in the heart of the Congolese jungle. It's a rainforest anyway, so freshwater resources abound, but the quality and coolness of the groundwater as it exits at the foot of a hill or a spring is always a spiritual place. The Republic of Congo's third biggest city was completely cleared of people by fighting between warring militias in 1999 (not to mention several times before). The town came back to life slowly in the year 2000, with a trickle of families joining the latest set of presiding militias, with government authorities and water engineers in train. The springs of Dolisie were in desperate shape, contaminated as they were by animal or human carcasses and unchecked growth of vegetation. Springs attract children, like lavender does honey bees. The problem is they also attract armed militias, like flies to dung. Following one spring's rehabilitation by Congolese aid workers, a pickup truck laden with a dozen fighters with Kalashnikovs sticking in every direction like a prickly pear screeches to a halt by it. The local military commander takes a mug of water handed to him by the children, spreads his shoulders back wide, looks up at the sky and drinks. His thirst quenched, he smiles, nods at everyone watching him and proclaims, "*Ah, ca c'est bon. C'est l'eau que je bois, moi*" ("This water is great, safe. This is the water *I* drink"). It matters little that his endorsement comes despite the fact that the water is still very likely heavily contaminated. The spring has been sanctioned by the powerful as a safe source of water and no villager is likely to challenge the discourse. From that point on, all efforts of the villagers (and of international donors) are devoted to turning the declaration into reality.

The event reveals the influence of sanctioned discourse – the politically silent process that serves the most powerful and upon which a large part of this book's thesis is formed. Truth – in so far as it may be proven through experiment and defined by a scientific framework – is subordinate to perception. The story also serves to show that the links between water and conflict are not always evident. The murky and hidden links between the two are normally in extreme counterpoint to the beauty of crystal clear water.

Consider the practice of throwing bodies down wells that became common at the end of the twentieth century in Serbia, for example. The effect of dumping family members down family wells was effective for the murderers. The act contaminated the water along with the memories of those lucky enough to escape and who may think of returning. The response of the Serbian Red Cross employees, who developed broad hooks specially to fish out the bloated corpses, stands in grim contrast with the crystal clear mountain springs nearby. And who can forget the horrible scenes in Sarajevo? The men racing to collect water in the urban jungle were taken down from hundreds of yards away by snipers using high-power rifles. The women were sent instead, in the tragically mistaken belief that the snipers might not cut them down as they filled their buckets. Here water and conflict are at their most lethal combination.

Similar contrasts lie just downstream of the Garden of Eden. Nepalese living along tributaries to the Ganges River know that the meeting points of streams constitute a holy spot, and the confluence of the Tigris and Euphrates rivers was considered by many to be the most spiritual of all. Abraham lived nearby, we are told, and the apple that Eve offered to Adam was grown with the once-mighty rivers' flows. Dammed as they are in Syria, Turkey and elsewhere upstream in Iraq, however, the rivers were quite tame in 2001, obliging Iraqi water engineers working with international aid organisations to keep up with the changes. Much of their work consisted of extending the intake structures of the water treatment units located on the shores of the Euphrates. Because the flows had been dammed, the river had become increasingly shallow, and had begun to pull away from its bank and the original intake structure. The engineers were obliged to extend the intake structure 50 metres in towards the river to find a deep enough spot to draw water off from. The more the rivers dried up, the further the engineers were obliged to extend the intake structures. It is a myopic engineering response to an environmental 'challenge' engendered by an international transboundary water conflict.

The wetlands at the confluence of the Tigris and Euphrates had furthermore been drained by the ruling Iraqi Ba'ath party some time in the 1990s, destroying once and maybe for always the lives and lifestyles of the Mada'an people (the so-called Marsh Arabs). This is a domestic water conflict. Just further down the Shatt al Arab in Basra, the twinned effects of negligent government policy and punishing sanctions imposed by the United Nations unite to create a scene so surreal it is difficult to imagine. Falcon-hunters and salt-gatherers are attracted to a moist spot in the desert just outside of Basra. All three are phenomena consequential of (non-water) violent conflict. Never fully completed due to military campaigning in 1990, the city's sewage treatment remained neglected during the decade of combined Iraqi government and UN punishment. The city's untreated sewage is thus pumped out into the desert. The moist spot there is the endpoint of Basra's near million inhabitants' human, hospital and industrial waste. It's a toxic brew and public-health catastrophe that attracts birds otherwise searching for the dried-up marshes. The birds attract falcon hunters who use their expertise to trap migrating fowl. As the sewage lake evaporates under the desert sun, a crust of salt is left around its edges. The salt attracts the poor, who then sell it on the Basra markets. The whole scene is reminiscent of 'Darwin's Nightmare' – Hubert Sauper's documentary exposing the horrendous effects of the introduction of the Nile Perch into Lake Victoria. But water conflicts along the Nile are a whole other story.

A similar lake of sewage exists in Palestine, in the over-crowded Gaza Strip just north of Beit Lahia. One nomadic group, which has been reined in like most of the refugee inhabitants of Gaza, has been forced to set up home on the only land available – on the banks of the sewage lake. In addition to the constant fear of the lake over spilling the sand mounds shoring it up, the children suffer from a number of water-borne infectious diseases. Efforts led by the World Bank and USAID to address the situation have so far amounted to very little, and the risk of toxic overspill was compounded by Israeli shelling of the area as late as summer 2006, as documented in the literature of the development agencies (see e.g. Oxfam (2006)). When the 'lake' burst its banks in April 2007, five people drowned in the torrent of sewage.[4]

Thus water is an integral part of war – usually as a target, sometimes as a weapon, but seldom as sole motive. Those who have been moved by the evidence that 'genuine' water wars do not exist may be misled in the other direction, however. Since there are no deaths related to water, they concur, there is no problem, no conflict. This book aims to swing the pendulum back somewhere between war and peace, to directly counter such stunted analysis.

Water 'Cooperation'

The outcome of cooperation between an elephant and a fly is not difficult to predict.
Chomsky (1993)

It has been asserted that the absence of war does not mean the absence of conflict. There is ample evidence to support the assertion. The gate-keepers of the resource are found in the more powerful state. The dams are built according to their plans. Deep wells are drilled where the powerful say they will be drilled, and it is usually the powerful who control the valves. The weaker state takes what it is given. There is no war, but there is conflict. And there is no excuse for not understanding and addressing the root causes of water conflict.

There is an extensive body of literature exploring and extolling the virtues of transboundary water cooperation. This includes the brochures and reports of Green Cross International, UNESCO, the Global Water Partnership, the World Water Council and essentially every institution that forms part of the global water community. The community as a whole is progressing slowly in its understanding. The mid 1970s conceptual leap of water management from political to river basin boundaries was incomplete. Even in those places where it did hold, the paradigm of basin-wide Integrated Water Resources Management (IWRM) was found even less effective for managing groundwater aquifers than rivers (see e.g. Wester and Warner (2002)). A trend noticeable in the first decade of this century is to move away from negotiations over sharing water towards negotiating the sharing of benefits provided by the water. The Stockholm International Water Institute's foundational work on the subject has been quick to draw the attention to the merits and limits of the concept, however. Considering the evolution of the process which allows some ideas into the global water discourse, one may usefully take a more critical perspective on what has been developed thus far.

Like IWRM, 'cooperation' over water issues is unquestionably seen as a desirable goal. Of course, cooperation is preferred to conflict. But are the two necessarily incompatible? And what does 'cooperation' mean anyway? The 2006 UNDP Human Development Report states that "given the strategic, political and economic contexts in international basins, it makes sense to promote and support cooperation of any sort, no matter how slight" (UNDP 2006: 28). A group of researchers centred around London – and known as the 'London School' – is calling such assumptions into question. The group points out that cooperation under circumstances of constrained conflict, or instances where cooperation of one party more closely resembles tokenism, or where cooperation is simply at the technical level, are all situations not worthy of the term. Notably, they tell us that 'a treaty does not cooperation make', thus building on the growing body of water treaty analysis founded by the efforts of Aaron Wolf, and extended by Peter Gleick, Ken Conca, Nils Petter Gleditsch and others.

Insofar as it relates to the Palestinian–Israeli water conflict, the term 'cooperation' is similarly misunderstood. The water-related treaties that Israel has signed with its neighbours – specific sections of the 1994 Peace Treaty with Jordan, and the 1995 'Oslo II' Agreement with Palestine – are regularly held up as examples of cooperation (e.g. Amery and Wolf (2000), Feitelson and Haddad (2000), Haddadin (2001), Zaslavsky (2002)). The evidence explored throughout this book asserts that in the case of Palestine, relations are much more coercive than they are cooperative – what Jan Selby refers to as Israeli domination is dressed up as cooperation (Selby 2003b). Not only is the spirit of the treaty regularly violated, but the treaty itself was asymmetrically structured to limit Palestinian participation.

One must consider positionality whilst reading accounts of the exemplary cooperation over Palestinian–Israeli water issues. Consider the perspective of the Palestinian smallholder eeking out a living from a rain-fed plot of land right beside an Israeli settlement industrial farm, supplied with water taken from beneath the farmer's feet. This is the case of Madama, a Palestinian village in the West Bank, which serves as a microcosm of all that is wrong with water in Palestine (see Box at end of this chapter). Strikingly similar situations at the interstate level exist along the Nile and the Tigris and Euphrates rivers. The most powerful riparian state in each of these cases manages to maintain the lion's share of the water at the same time as they maintain an image of goodwill and cooperation.

Those who water their gardens in Cairo or Tel Aviv may not be aware of the hidden politics that lie behind the water they use. The Palestinian and Ethiopian farmer, though, can provide a detailed account of it – should they ever be asked. The external analyst intent on improving the quality of cooperation is obliged to consider all perspectives, pursuing with eyes wide open the power plays that underlie the setting.

The Role of Power in Water Conflicts

Water flows towards power and money.
Mark Reisner (1986)

In its most simplistic form, this study's main message is too obvious, for some, to elaborate upon. Power matters. Traditional realists repeat this with monotonous regularity, and few people in fact will debate it. The main exchanges sustained between academics centre around to what degree power matters, and how power may be conceptualised, wielded and measured. The debate is healthy in the fields of political science and international relations, if ultimately unresolved. The debate is essentially dormant in the water world, however.

The realist view of international relations is supported, at least superficially, by considering the dynamics of international relations on three major river basins, as shown in Figure 1.1.

Perceptions of conflict and cooperation within each of these basins differ. The global water community emphasises the co-operation that exists through the Nile Basin Initiative, the Joint Water Committee on the Jordan and the burgeoning academic Euphrates–Tigris Initiative for Cooperation. The 'cooperative' focus is countered by those analysts observing the dynamics from the point of view of the weaker basin states. Perceptions formed in the highlands of Ethiopia about the benefits of the NBI are entirely different from those formed in Cairo. Similarly, one could imagine the different opinions water officials in Ankara and farmers in Basra hold of Turkey's multi-billion dollar and multi-dam GAP project.

A much more theoretical aspiration of this book is to explore how power – in its many shapes and guises – explains not only the inequitable outcome of water conflicts, but the perceptions, ideas and discourse that surround it also. The influence that power has in transboundary water relations is best described by Tony Allan, as shown in Table 1.1. Intuitive notions of upstream/downstream advantage are immediately dispelled. The point to be drawn from shaded rows in the table is that the position of a state along a river (its 'riparian position') is not the sole determinant of the allocation of flows. It is downstream Egypt and mid-stream Israel that dictate how the flows are distributed, not upstream Ethiopia or Lebanon. Allan explains that "economic strength combined more or less with hegemonic advantage explains the privileged outcome" (Allan 2001: 222). In other words, control of the flows is determined to a certain degree by power – measured here in such terms as 'strength', 'hegemonic advantage' and 'access to global support'.

Consider, in slightly greater detail, the case of Egypt on the Nile. Essentially, the entire flow of the Nile originates from rain falling in the nine Nile Basin riparian states upstream of Egypt: Kenya, Tanzania, Uganda, Rwanda, Burundi and the Democratic Republic of Congo on the White Nile; Sudan, Ethiopia and Eritrea on the Blue Nile. Yet the well-known proverb states that 'Egypt is the Nile and the Nile is Egypt.' Ethiopians may well state in reply that while Egypt may be the Nile, the Nile is much more than just Egypt. The Ethiopian state has been frustrated by its bigger, downstream neighbour for years. Kenyans who grow up on the banks of the Nile know they are not allowed to touch it – a host of British colonial and Cairo-driven initiatives led to the 1959 Egyptian–Sudanese Agreement that allocates all the flows between the two states (85 per cent for Egypt, 15 per cent for Sudan) – to the exclusion of the rest.

Figure 1.1   Map of the Nile, Jordan and Tigris and Euphrates river basins.

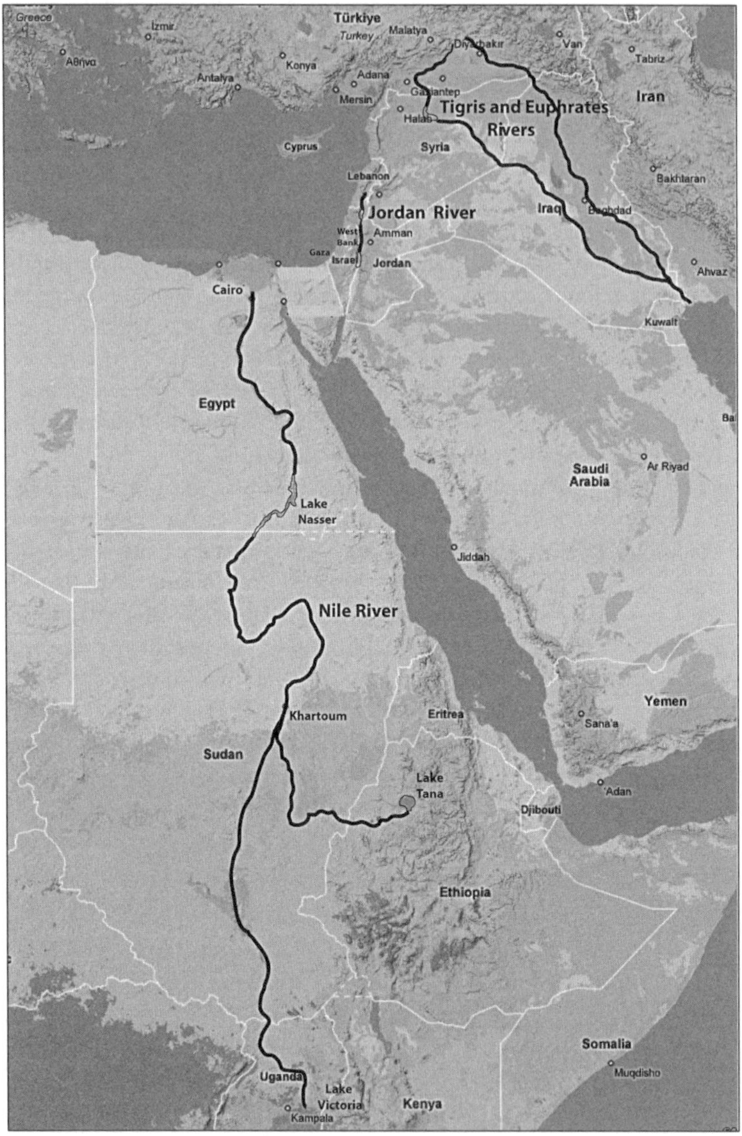

Other indicators of strength might intuitively be added to Table 1.1. Military might, and socio-economic factors (such as the ability to construct dams), may supplement the categories of *economic capacity* and *access to global support*, for example. Each of these factors will come to be seen in Chapter 2 as different forms of power, with 'hegemonic power' revealed as by far the most effective.

To realise how power and hegemony help us to understand and ultimately address water conflicts, one must first consider the nature of power and hegemony. The theory of hegemony was originally developed by António Gramsci in the fascist Italy of the 1930s. Gramsci explained how the ruling classes use a dominant ideology (along with force) to secure the consent of the masses, thereby maintaining a state of 'hegemony' over them. The notion has since broadened extensively, which tends to confuse discussion of the subject. Hegemony is regularly referred to, for instance, when considering the often unchallenged creep of American culture (the most-watched television show globally and in history is Baywatch) and American foreign policy (particularly in the wake of the collapse of Soviet–US bi-polar international system of the late 1980s).[5]

Table 1.1 Factors Affecting Control of Transboundary Flows.

Riparians	Approx. water self-sufficiency (per cent)	Economic Capacity	Hegemonic Power	Access to Global Support
Nile River Basin				
Ethiopia +	100	weak & v. weak	very weak	very little
Sudan	100	very weak	very weak	very little
Egypt *(downstream)*	70	moderate	moderate	significant
Jordan River Basin				
Syria	70	moderate	weak	little
Lebanon	100	moderate	very weak	little
Israel *(mid-stream)*	25	strong & diverse	strong	very significant
Palestine	20	very weak	very weak	very little
Jordan	25	weak	weak	little
Tigris and Euphrates River Basins				
Turkey *(upstream)*	100	strengthening	strong	significant
Syria	90	moderate	moderate	very little
Iraq	100	weak (temporarily)	weak	none

Adapted from Allan (2001: 224). Shaded rows denote the most powerful state in each basin.

Neo-liberal foreign policy-makers, economists and analysts see merit in the efficiencies and stability that may result from the imposition of a dominant set of ideas and method for dealing with international relations and trade. Anti-globalisation activists are joined by millions to decry the destructive effect that a hegemonic pre-determined one-size-fits-all with-us-or-against-us socio-economic template may have when imposed upon on less dominant social and political cultures. Their point is well taken; the 'Washington Consensus' that drove the IMF's imposition upon developing nations in the 1980s and 1990s once appeared unassailable. The paradigm is now regularly called into question and may someday be derided by the very people who preached it.[6]

The concept of hegemony is linked with power theory in a very fundamental way. In his groundbreaking 1974 work *Power: A Radical View,* Steven Lukes has conceived of the third dimension of power operating in the realm of ideas – in much the same fashion as hegemony is active in the subconscious. Lukes quotes Spinoza to demonstrate the breadth of the various forms that power takes:

> One man has another in his power when he holds him in bonds; when he has disarmed him and deprived him of the means of self-defence or escape; when he has inspired him with fear; or when he has bound him so closely by a service that he would rather please his benefactor than himself, and rather be guided by his benefactor's judgment than by his own. (Lukes 2005 [1974]: 86).

There is considerable evidence that the securing of consent, through ideas and the efficacy of ideology, is an essential feature of water conflicts.[7] This analysis, indeed, concludes that the stronger riparian may choose to emphasise existing forms of co-operation, while downplaying the destructive effects of the water conflict, as an element of its hegemonic strategy.

Many other domains are, of course, also influenced by power – scientific research, for instance. Even in cases where the science that drives the research is driven by curiosity, the institutions and funds that make the research possible are not so 'pure'. Government funds drive university-level research in the UK and Europe, as the private sector does in the US. This research is not likely to be directed towards challenging the status quo, just as the researchers themselves may consent to a mild form of self-censorship in order not to 'bite the hand that feeds them.' If the powers-that-be prefer to emphasise cooperation over water resources rather than conflict, data that challenges that view is not likely to be generated, and is much less likely still to shape policy. Such is the power of funded discourse in the purportedly independent academic institutions in the current neo-liberal political economies.

The formation of international water law, like all forms of law really, is within reach of the long arm of power. Power is active and effective during the formation of international law, as it is in its execution also. The solid and mature 1997 UN Convention on the Law of the Non-Navigational Uses of International Watercourses, for instance, specifically guides states towards 'equitable and reasonable utilisation' of transboundary water resources. Yet only a handful of states have endorsed the Convention. We will see in the following chapter how the more powerful states prefer to use the law as guidance for the treaties they sign with their weaker neighbours, rather than as a set of leading to punishment when not adhered to. Weaker states seeking protection, on the other hand, would prefer to see the law implemented.

Power is also evidently effective in water conflicts in its most basic, physical form. Without its military and political clout, Egypt would not have been able to complete the High Aswan dam. Ethiopian, Kenyan, Ugandan and others' claims have been pre-empted, stared-down through diplomacy, or silenced through threat. Turkey, similarly, is less likely to have embarked on its dam-building project had Syria and Iraq posed a substantial security threat at the time.

Yet the influence that power has in transboundary water conflicts has not been systematically conceptualised. Wester and Warner (2002) illustrate this when they boldly ask their readers to question the received wisdom of river basin management, as previously mentioned. The authors argue convincingly how getting stuck in accepted technical paradigms tends to de-fang serious water issues of their political component, and effectively reinforces existing power inequities. The critical view penetrates deep into the internal workings of the water world, and serves as a call for the

> construction of a counterdiscourse that describes instead of prescribes, that focuses on processes and outcomes instead of forms and functions, and that is informed by real-world struggles instead of deformed by donor agendas and élite interests (Wester and Warner 2002: 71).

Though the call is being picked up by the London Water Research Group and others, the counter-discourse is currently in its nascent stages. The processes that allow one side to gain the upper hand in a water conflict have not been catalogued or categorised. The state of hegemony that the most powerful riparian enjoys has scarcely been recognised, much less deconstructed. The extent of the influence of power remains unknown. This study contributes to the counterdiscourse with an intensive examination of the role that power plays in the Palestinian–Israeli water conflict (Chapters 5 to 8), and with an exploration of the process and methods through which the Israeli side has achieved dominance in the sector (Chapter 9).

Why the Palestinian–Israeli Water Conflict?

The Palestinian–Israeli water conflict is a subject many consider to be thoroughly studied already, if not overly so. Seminal hydropolitical works conducted on the subject are offered from such competent authors as Sharif el Musa, Tony Allan, Eran Feitelson, and Aaron Wolf. The role of power in the Palestinian–Israeli water conflict has furthermore been explicitly dealt with in Miriam Lowi's *Water and Power* (Cambridge 1993) and Jan Selby's *Water, Power & Politics in the Middle East* (I.B.Tauris 2004).

Lowi's work focuses on the political dimensions of conflict over surface water, while Selby's work applies a political science perspective to the conflict over groundwater. This study departs from each of the previous works by exploring the conflict over groundwater *and* surface water, and through a more tightly structured analytical framework. The approach of examining the conflict in terms of three forms of power reveals several nuances and sub-texts of the conflict that have not previously been written about. This study also gives considerably more weight to technical aspects, specifically water production and consumption rates.

Lowi's seminal work in fact inspired the title of the present book. Selby's 'domination dressed up as cooperation' thesis is also built upon. By deconstructing the power plays active at all levels in the water conflict, this book serves to lift the veil Selby has identified.

A Case of Extreme Asymmetry

A further reason for which the Palestinian–Israeli water conflict merits a closer look is the severity of the disparity in its outcome. We will see in Chapter 3 that the 2003 allocation or consumption of freshwater resources transboundary to Palestine and Israel was roughly as follows (in terms of millions of cubic metres per year):

Israel – 1,600 Palestine – 275

The 6:1 ratio reflects an even greater asymmetry in power between the two entities. This may be readily grasped by considering that Palestinians are denied all access to the only significant surface water source in the region – the Jordan River. The asymmetry itself is even more severe when considered in terms of per capita consumption. Israel has access to non-transboundary resources (water that lies completely within its political boundaries) and produces 'new' water in the form of re-used wastewater or desalination. Actual water consumption by all sectors in Israel is roughly 2,100 MCM/y, much higher than the figure used for comparison here (1,600 MCM/y), which refers solely to transboundary freshwater. Sources counted as endogenous to Palestine include the springs that rise in the West Bank and empty into the Jordan River. But Palestine has not thus far managed to harness desalination or wastewater re-use technology, and hundreds of thousands of Palestinians are still not served by piped water networks. Total consumption in Palestine is roughly 300 MCM/y, which means a 7:1 ratio weighted towards the Israeli side. While an estimated three-quarters of Palestinians consume between 30 and 100 litres for domestic use per person daily (B'tselem 2000, PHG 2006: 18), Israeli per capita consumption for domestic use is estimated at between 240 and 300 litres per person daily. The big conflict is over agricultural water, however. The politically-organised agricultural sector in Israel consumes about 1,300 MCM/y of water, much of it heavily subsidised by the state. The figures are particularly impressive given that the sector contributed only 1.5 per cent of the Gross National Product in 2001 (IMOA 2001). The contribution of agriculture to the much less technology-based economy of Palestine is known to hover between 20 and 30 per cent of GNP. Yet, the agriculture sector in Palestine is stifled by the Israeli occupation of the West Bank and its resource-consuming settlement project therein. The ratio of Israel–Palestinian agricultural water use is roughly 9:1.

The imbalance is partly explained by a disparity in development and social adaptive capacity between the two states. The more organised and disciplined Israeli state institutions are able to develop its water sector in ways the Palestinians would do well to replicate. The bigger picture should also be borne in mind.

Palestinian institutional weaknesses undeniably contribute to the perpetuation of the asymmetry, but they are not the cause of it in the first instance. This study focuses upon the root causes of the conflict, which are posited as the forces and power plays that lead to *control* of the transboundary flows. With such a mandate, a starkly asymmetric ratio is a compelling reason to dig deeper.

This asymmetrical water distribution is described in several forms in the literature of Palestinian and Israeli NGOs such as the Palestinian Hydrology Group, the Applied Research Institute of Jerusalem and B'tselem. The imbalance is emphatically *not* heard in the official Israeli, donor or – perhaps surprisingly – Palestinian discourse. This latter group also tends to emphasise cooperation in their pursuit of development of the water sector. Consideration of the effects that discourse has on the conflict, and how the more powerful players may be expected to voice it most 'loudly', is key for understanding the role of power in conflict. Prior to proceeding to the chapter relating power and conflict theory to the study, we consider the case of Madama, a village in the West Bank with the dubious distinction of being a microcosm for all that is wrong in the Palestinian water sector (see Box).

Box: Hydrological Apartheid in Madama

Ayad Kamal would very much like to resign from his position as head of Village Council of the village of Madama. As representative to the Palestinian Authority, he is held accountable by his neighbours for much of the drama that befalls the village. This includes arrests and torture by the Israel army (IDF) of the male youth throwing rocks at the cars on the Israeli-settlers-only bypass Highway 60, which runs almost overtop the village; attacks on farmers by settlers from Yitshar, internal conflict between different political factions within the village; and the lack of very basic services – like water. Ayad has a particularly difficult time with the latter issue, as he is unable to offer any good reasons why his constituency in 2006 still has no running water for their homes.

The village of Madama was founded near the beginning of the Islamic Period, on foundations laid by a Roman settlement located at the foot of a hill and a very fresh spring. The Salman al Farsi mosque was built on the hill during the period of Omar Ibn al Khatib (~630 AD). The village's significance derived from being a stopping point for traders using the Tirzah valley up from the Jordan river and eventually across to the Mediterranean. Today Madama is primarily a farming community, growing wheat, lentils and tending olive orchards. For centuries the village women would climb halfway up the hill to collect water from the spring, and take it back down the twenty-minute walk to the village. British authorities in the 1920s protected the spring with basic brickworks, and canalised the water through a pipe to a ground-level reservoir at the heart of the village. While the big cities, settlements and Israeli villages around the village have all benefited from surges in water infrastructure development, Madama's situation has worsened steadily over the last century.

Neither the Jordanian, nor Israeli, nor indeed Palestinian, authorities that have since claimed responsibility for the West Bank have provided basic water services. Changes in climate, or over-pumping from the nearby deep Israeli wells, mean that the spring that used to sustain the villagers year-round now dries up every summer. And when the spring *is* running well, it is routinely contaminated by the nearby settlers of Yitshar.

Figure 1.2　Map of Palestinian village of Madama and Israeli settlement of Yitshar, showing Israeli water and transportation infrastructure.

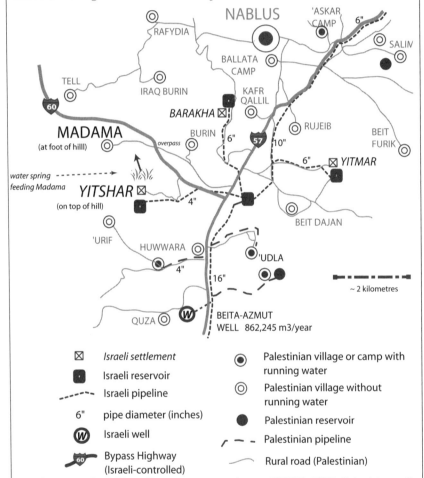

Based on West Bank Water Department network map (WBWD 2003). Palestinian wells that feed primarily Nablus are not shown.

Yitshar settlement originated as a settler 'outpost' on Salman al Farsi mountain around 1983, and by 1984 was settled by mainly American or European Orthodox Jewish religious Zionists. It occupies about 500 dunums (50 hectares) around the top and sides of the hill – agricultural land confiscated from Madama. Palestinian crops near the settlement are scorched by the settlers as a 'buffer zone' that covers more than 700 dunums in total. The 300 or so settler families are sustained through an Israeli-controlled well called Beita Azmut, about ten kilometres away. As shown in Figure 1.2, the well feeds other Israeli settlements like Barakha and Palestinian villages Quza and Huwwara (thereby legitimising the presence of the settlements by providing water for some Palestinians along the way (see Chapter 3)). As a means of the prioritising and outright restricting of the use of water drawn from Palestine to Israeli settlers occupying the land, the water infrastructure network is considered a form of "hydrological apartheid", in the words of Fred Pearce (2006: 187).

Known throughout the West Bank by Palestinians and Israeli soldiers alike to be the most radical around, Yitshar settlers manifest their wrath primarily on the residents of the nearby villages (ARIJ 2000). Madama's spring falls on the border of the hilltop claimed by the settlers, and through the logic of intolerance is therefore a target.

Village Head Kamal testifies that the pipes leading from the spring were first sabotaged by the settlers shortly after Yitshar was established. The settlers would also dump their solid waste around the spring, chase olive pickers away by shooting their donkeys and carrying away their harvest. Little changed with the handover of responsibility for water supply in part of the West Bank to the Palestinian Authority, and in year 2000 the pipes of the spring were destroyed by axes on three separate occasions. Apparently deliberate attempts to poison the spring were made when a number of soiled diapers were left directly in the water at the spring's outlet. International NGO Oxfam-GB endeavoured to help the residents in 2003 by protecting the spring with concrete, burying the pipes, and raising awareness of the settlers' actions to the local IDF authorities (Oxfam 2003b). Oxfam employees set out for the work following two weeks of coordination with the IDF's Civil Administration, and assurances that they would be protected from the settlers. An American employee of the NGO testifies that four settlers shot at them and the procession of donkeys carrying material up the hill, killing another one of the latter. The sabotage has been repeated on several occasions since (Daily News 2005).

The water concerns of the village of Madama do not end there. Attempts have been in fact made by the Palestinian Water Authority and international donors to bring water to the village. The most serious of these was a USAID plan to drill a well at Rujeib and extend a network to seven surrounding villages, including Madama. As we will see in Chapter 6, the Rujeib well project was caught in a personal power struggle between the local Israeli Civil Administration officer of humanitarian affairs and the PWA. The PWA were refused permission by the Civil Administration to mobilise the drill rig to Rujeib as a response for their not cooperating with a new Israeli well to be drilled in the Palestinian part of the Jordan River Valley. The well was temporarily de-prioritised on the USAID project list, and fell off it completely by the time the US government decided to halt planned development assistance to the Palestinians, in January 2006. PWA sources are currently hopeful that there is potential funding for the well through the French Development Agency or Islamic Development Bank. Whether or not these other donors pick up where USAID left off is of crucial importance to Madama. A similar effort failed when the relatively water-rich city of Nablus offered to supply water to the neighbouring village of Burin in 2004 .

Apparently destined to subsist without a stable water source, the residents seek water where they can. Those who can afford it purchase water from tankers at a prohibitive cost. The private Palestinian tankers fill at Israeli settlements when they are denied access by the IDF to Palestinian-controlled filling points. The residents of Madama are wholly aware of the cruel irony that has them paying for water from settlers occupying their land, who in turn receive it at subsidised cost from an Israeli well in the middle of Palestine. They are, in effect, paying for water from the settlers who have taken it from under their feet. Mr. Kamal notes that the poorer residents seek water in the summer by setting out on donkeys with jerry-cans to ancient Roman wells located near Iraq Burin, beyond the settler bypass highway. Some of these old men have had their water poured out in front of their eyes by Israeli soldiers, as punishment for trespassing on the settlers-only road.

This case of hydrological apartheid may be viewed in a number of ways. Perhaps the residents of Madama are simply the hapless victims of bad luck, or of a personal dispute between individuals in the Israeli or Palestinian authorities. Others may consider them victims of weak development efforts by skittish donors and a corrupt Palestinian Water Authority. Such views, however, skirt the basic question why the residents are prevented from drilling a well within the town. Explicitly considering the role that power plays, one might also question the extraordinarily influential role that a young Israeli officer can play in maintaining a discrepancy in water provision between a thousand year old village of farmers and a brand new settlement of urban Europeans. Analysts might further question how power asymmetry may explain the fact that most readers are unaware of the situation.

At the much broader level – and this will be borne out by the concluding chapters of this book – the residents of Madama are not so much victims of circumstance as they are dis-empowered elements of a deeply-rooted 'hegemonic apparatus'. Israeli state hegemony over Palestinian–Israeli transboundary waters reaches from the Israeli soldiers and settlers to the Palestinian Water Authority and the international donor community. It hides the politics behind the reasons for Madama being without clean water. We will return to Madama in the final chapter. Readers are suggested to keep the reality lived by its residents in mind as they proceed through the rest of this study's analysis.

2

Understanding Power and Water

The good old rule
Sufficeth them, the simple plan,
That they should take, who have the power,
And they should keep who can.

William Wordsworth (1770–1850)

RIVERS are wonderful things to study. They are even better things to paddle a canoe down, but they are also fascinating to study. Groundwater aquifers, lakes and rivers link cultures, nations and states in ways that are not always intuitive. A hydropolitical study of the Nile, for example, obliges the researcher to integrate socio-economic and hydraulic factors from areas as diverse as the mega-city of Cairo, the Ethiopian highlands and the Kenyan highland tea farms. Hindu and Buddhist communities from states in strict competition with each other are drawn together by the Ganges river system that passes through Nepal, India and Bangladesh. The effects of the fall of the Soviet empire may today be partly understood through a hydropolitical analysis of the Amu Darya basin which links Afghanistan with post-Soviet Tajikistan, Turkmenistan and Uzbekistan all the way to the Aral Sea. Tensions between apparently allied states may also be uncovered, as in the race between Saudi Arabia and Jordan to pump the non-renewable fossil water of the Disi Aquifer. The study of hydro-politics is necessarily also a peek into geopolitics, engineering, anthropology and the international political economy.

The socio-economic links are driven by the fluid ones, resulting in a complex hydropolitical matrix of politics, social interaction, negotiation and compromise. Hydropolitics, therefore, has no choice but to be a place where many disciplines flow into one another, and so it is that hydropolitics has attracted a broad range of disciplines from international relations, geography, political science, law and engineering. Nevertheless, while our understanding of the politics of the world shaped by water has advanced considerably as a result of the attentions of the last few decades, there has been little focus on the subject's basic underpinnings. Hydropolitics bounces from being the focus of a select group of political scientists, to being ignored altogether or absorbed by those considering the wider perspective of environmental issues in general. Particularly under Elinor Ostrom, this last group in particular has contributed greatly in understanding how transboundary environmental resources may be understood and managed as a collective good.

This chapter offers a review of hydropolitical theory. It begins with a brief review of established water conflict analysis. Theories of power and hegemony are then delved into in much greater detail, laying the foundation for the analysis to come. The limits and utility of international water law and discourse are also added to the suite.[8]

Water Conflict Analysis

Strict geographers like to point to the role of topography in determining the outcome of water conflicts. The inherently compelling aspects of the upstream/downstream concerns were touched upon in the previous chapter, where the limits of its capacity to explain water conflicts were underlined. This is not to say that geography and topography are not important. The states in possession of mountains or of main sections of river are afforded a 'natural' advantage over their downstream neighbours. One may point as evidence to the strategic location of the US on the Rio Grande, Turkey on the Euphrates, South Africa on the Orange and China on the Mekong, a position which assists them all in maintaining an upper hand over Mexico, Iraq, Namibia and Cambodia respectively. According to Warner, this latter group are 'victims of geography'.

Such geographical determinism, though, is unsustainable. Our explanations need a social dimension: the strong cards dealt to the upstream riparian is regularly trumped by a more powerful downstream neighbour. Egypt on the Nile, like India on the Ganges, California on the Colorado and Uzbekistan on the Amu Darya all overcome their physical disadvantage with their upstream neighbours Ethiopia, Nepal, Arizona and Tajikistan. Warner again puts it succinctly when he says that 'upstreamers use water to get more power, downstreamers use power to get more water'. While the realist assertion of this statement does not hold true in all cases (Ethiopia, arguably, may want to use its water for developmental purposes, not geopolitical ones), it serves to reinforce the limited importance of topography – and obliges us to look deeply into different disciplines to find our explanatory capabilities.

Those who analyse the conflictual or co-operational aspects of transboundary water resources have a somewhat limited body of theory to draw upon. Important contributions to the field include those of Naff and Matson (1984), Frey and Naff (1985), Lowi (1993), Frey (1993), Homer-Dixon (1999), Yoffe (2001), Mason et. al. (2003), Gleick (2004b) and Wolf (1998, 2002, 2004), Falkenmark (2001), Ohlsson and Turton (1999) and Turton (2000). Much of this work has been on the development of theories to predict water conflicts, while others have applied game theory to case studies (e.g. Williams (2001) Kaufman (1997) and Mason et. al. (2003)). While not entirely adequate, these approaches provide elements relevant to our power-based approach.

Frey and Naff's Interest-Position-Power matrix

The intriguingly powerful water conflict prediction theories developed by Frederik Frey, Thomas Naff and Ruth Maston in the 1980s are still with us two decades on from their formation. Frey and Naff (1985) utilised three different approaches in order to predict water conflicts: the typology of conflict, perceptions of conflict, and cognitive mapping. By emphasising the importance of each facet of an issue (through *issue profiling*) as well as the significance of the participants and groups involved, the authors deftly draw out the immeasurable aspects of the conflict – notably perception, ideology and power. The framework they propose to contain it all in is referred to as the *interest-position-power matrix*.

The approach makes it possible to score the relative strength of a state in each of the 'three major factors' that allow water conflict prediction: a) the interest a state has in the contested resource; b) the riparian position the state enjoys (upstream/downstream); and c) the power the state has relative to its co-riparians (Frey and Naff 1985: 78 (see also Naff and Matson 1984: 192)).

The main hypothesis of the authors is that the potential for a water conflict is highest when the ranking of states according to the interest–position–power matrix is near equal, implying that conflict is most likely when interests and power of competing riparians are at similar levels. Lowi (1993) develops the argument, stating: "when the security of a state cannot be threatened, either because the water resources are not vital and indispensable, or because the state is hegemonic in the basin insofar as power and capabilities are concerned, the very same body of water will not be considered a potential source of conflict" (Lowi 1993: 170).

Frey and Naff's theories have stood the test of the two decades since their development. They 'predicted' in hindsight, for instance, a lack of violence along the Jordan River following the events of the 1950s and mid 1960s, during which time Israel found itself in a less favourable riparian position. The military skirmishes did indeed end along with the improvement of Israel's riparian position through the improved hydrological position that came with the occupation of territory in 1967 (as we shall see in detail in Chapter 4). Speaking in 1985, the authors also noted that "as far as the Jordan waters are concerned, Israel dominates the scene, strong on all three factors. Major conflict is precluded" (Frey and Naff 1985: 79). The prediction has held in the decades since and seems likely to hold in the decades to come, if by 'major conflict' is understood to mean 'war'. Frey and Naff's most salient prediction may perhaps be found in their consideration of the political strength of the Zionist ideology and agricultural lobbies in Israel when they assert that "there will have to be some major internal political battles fought if Israel is to take some of the progressive measures [it will need to in order to reduce water consumption]" (Frey and Naff 1985: 81). These battles have indeed taken place, and continue to do so, as we shall see in our discussion of the tensions internal to the Israeli water sector (Chapter 4).

The importance that Frey and Naff place on power has inspired the study at hand. Their work, however, is hobbled by at least two limiting features,. The first shortcoming is their under-emphasis of the importance of the *methods* adopted by a more powerful state to avoid conflict over water, once the situation is perceived to be secured to their advantage. The second is that their work is limited to the prediction of conflicts. As such, it puts aside the importance of non-violent water disputes, and does not deal with the tensions that linger when they remain unresolved.

Water Conflict Classification
The classification of water conflicts serves to distinguish between the confusing ties that bind conflict and water. Conflicts related directly to the acquisition of control over natural resources, for example, have been usefully classified in different manners. Homer-Dixon (1999) proposes a motive-based classification: Simple–Scarcity; Group–Identity; Insurgencies; *Coups d'etats*; Banditry and Gang Violence. Peter Gleick (2004a) takes the classification further, with his Water Conflict Chronology. The role that water *does* play in conflict compels Gleick to classify water-related conflicts according to six bases, as presented in Table 2.1.

Table 2.1 Gleick's Classification of water-related Conflicts.

Base of Conflict	Example
Control of Water Resources where water supplies or access to water is at the root of the tensions.	Egypt-Sudan 1958; Israel-Syria 1958; Brazil-Paraguay 1979.
Water as a Political Tool where water resources or water systems are used by a nation, State or non-State actor for a political goal.	Iraq-Syria 1974; Turkey-Syria-Iraq 1990; Malaysia-Singapore 1997.
Water as a Tool for Terrorism where water resources, or water systems are used by a non-State actor as tools of violence or coercion.	East Timor 1999; Kosovo 1999; Israel, Palestine 2001; Nepal 2002; US-Iraq 2003.
Water as a Military Tool where water resources, or water systems themselves, are used by a nation or State as a weapon during a military action.	Ethiopia-Somalia 1948; Israel-Lebanon 1982; Bosnia 1992; Kosovo 1999; US-Iraq 2003.
Water as a Military Target where water resource systems are targets of military actions by nations or States.	Israel-Syria 1967; Israel-Jordan 1969; South Africa-Angola 1988; US-Afghanistan 2001.
Development Disputes where water resources or water systems are a major source of contention and dispute in the context of economic and social development.	Ethiopia-Somalia 1963; Bangladesh 1999; Pakistan 2001; Turkey-Syria-Iraq 1990.

(Gleick 2004a).

When applied to hundreds of water-related conflicts in Wolf's extensive Transboundary Freshwater Dispute Database (2004), the classification system has made it possible to elucidate some very general observations. Follow-on work has revealed, for instance, that there are far more cases of water 'co-operation' in the world than of 'conflict'. That is, of course, just the beginning of the story, and should not be taken to mean that there is generally not much to worry about.

Wolf's database has also inspired and facilitated further research. This includes the work of Marit Brochmann and Nils Petter Gleditsch at the Peace Research Institute in Oslo, who are running a quantitative analysis of a modified version of the database. The most notable recent contribution is that of Ken Conca (2006), who adds an important qualitative perspective to the analysis, particularly with his discussion of the establishment of transboundary regimes. In addition, a group of researchers associated with the London Water Research Group, namely Elizabeth Kistin, Jeroen Warner, Marwa Daoudy, Naho Mirumachi and David Phillips, are taking an even more critical approach to the analysis of the impact of water treaties, working with the assertion that 'a treaty does not co-operation make.' The water treaty negotiated between Palestinians and Israelis, as we will see in Chapter 6, would certainly have benefited from such a critical perspective before it had been signed.

Securitisation

Warner, Turton, Allouche and others have initiated work on bringing together security theory with transboundary water conflicts. Anthony Turton and researchers in South Africa are currently seeing the work evolve into *Hydropolitical Complex Theory*, which promises to open new windows of insight. International Relations theory appreciates that repeated and predictable responses by one state when faced with the actions of another are a recognised (if unofficial) form of negotiation. These serve to establish the 'rules of the game', by communicating to the other side what is and what is not considered acceptable. One manner through which a state may make such displays is through what is known as 'securitisation'. Barry Buzan, a foundational thinker on Security Theory, defines securitisation as the "speech act" that legitimises a state taking exceptional measures over an issue by propelling it into the realm of security (Buzan, et al. 1998). This is one step beyond the well-known tactic of the 'politicisation' of issues used to derive maximum political capital from some event.

Turton's application of these theories to the world of water conflicts (1999a, 1999b, 2003) has been elaborated upon by several others (see e.g. Warner (2004a), Warner (2004b), Greco (2005) and Phillips et. al. (2006)). These authors point out that promoting a water project or issue to a national-security concern enables a government to equate criticism to treason, thereby silencing critical voices. The securitisation of water (and other environmental) issues may also allow politicians to gain even greater political capital than through politicisation in their pursuit of ulterior political interests. By way of counter-point, securitisation also enables non-state actors (e.g. environmental advocates) to bring pressure for policy reform to bear upon the government in power. This tactic will be discussed in relation to the Palestinian–Israeli water conflict in Chapter 7.

The analytical portion of this book is not intended to assist with the prediction or classification of water conflicts. It is focused instead on building up the 'softer' side of our understanding, as Turton has. By incorporating a somewhat rigid conceptualisation of power into the analysis, the study contributes to the counterdiscourse that challenges the status quo of both academic analysis as well as the actual outcomes of the conflicts. A method for weaving concepts of power into water conflict analysis is provided in the following section.

Power and Compliance

Stephen Biko knew from the South African Liberation Struggle that 'the most potent weapon in the hands of the oppressor is the mind of the oppressed'. Arab Nationalist leader Gamal Abdel Nasser stated that "power is not merely shouting aloud. Power is to act positively with all components of power". Power does indeed have many guises. It dances in the business world from board meetings to the golf course. At government ministries power shuffles somehow from the meeting rooms and the water cooler to the pub. In the underworld it is generated by the ability to protect oneself and others, which is a threat to the monopoly on violence the state otherwise enjoys. In the world of celebrity, power hinges on publicity, whose pawns are scripted to step from Rolls Royce's at gala events. The reach and influence of power is extended in all of the above cases if they are located in the nexus between the 'western' capitals of New York, Tokyo, London and Paris. In that sense, prestige is power. Armies mete it out in terms of firepower, though the most successful also rely on strategy and intelligence. Hannah Arendt suggests that "a never-ending accumulation of property must be based on a never-ending accumulation of power" (Harvey 2005: 34). Foucault has taught us that 'knowledge is power'. Wisdom may therefore be an even greater power. California is an 'economic powerhouse' with an economy greater than the majority of nations. The 'powers-that-be' can be thought of as a complex apparatus of levers and pulleys that shape human experience in society. Powers-that-be also refers to the spiritual leaders we choose, or are pressured to follow.

Politicians are understood to be 'in power'. British historian Lord Acton speaks to the structural effects of systematised power, noting that "power tends to corrupt, and absolute power corrupts absolutely. Great men are almost always bad men … There is no heresy greater than that the office sanctifies the holder of it". Nigerian author Chinua Achebe notes, as a counter-punch, that "the most awful thing about power is not that it corrupts absolutely, but that it makes people so utterly boring, so predictable".

Consider further the many guises of power in the natural world. The tiger – carnivorous king of the Himalayan jungle – strides confidently through the underbrush, unbothered by the even greater dynamic power of the waterfall. The waterfall itself is tiny compared with the massive rock that it carves out over the eons. Ultimately the tiger has no power whatsoever over the massif, though gazelles, monkeys and humans alike scatter before its sabre–sharp fangs; and the tiger trembles in turn before the herd of elephants winding their way through the jungle. It normally chooses to avoid the giant herbivores, showing proper respect for the balance of power that has been established within its domain.

In one of his Jungle Books, Rudyard Kipling depicts the scene of a brave or desperate tiger leaping to attack an elephant. The tiger has his hopes crushed along with his spine as the elephant rolls over to escape. Mass and cunning win over muscle and sabre-teeth this time.

Commonly held conceptualisations of power, we see, range from notions of strength to authority, fame, charisma, intellect and weaponry. There is in fact considerable debate about how power works between humans, institutions, the environment or any combination of these.[9] Power plays between states and nations are equally diverse and disputed. Particularly as they apply to relations between states, conceptions of power are known to be "essentially contested" (Evans and Newnham 1998: 446). There is no consensus between or within academic disciplines on how concepts of power can be integrated into a single analytical framework. This holds true for the world of transboundary water conflicts, despite the previously discussed work of Frey and Naff, Lowi and Selby. Before we can understand the patterned behaviours of states in terms of the attempted exercise of power we must first develop an understanding on the many ways in which the compliance of an adversary may be secured.

Understanding Compliance: the King and the Wise Man

> *When the King says it is midnight at noon, the wise man says 'behold the moon!'*
> Omar Khayam (1050–1122)

The wise man may or may not know better than the King that one is more likely to see the moon at midnight than at noon. But that is completely beside the point. If the wise man is repressing his opinion formed from direct observation, it is for very utilitarian purposes. His expressed allegiance to a force much more powerful than himself meant that he might live to provide for his family another day. A different sort of man – though perhaps no less wise – may accept within himself that the King in all his glory knows better than he. The unquestioned compliance with authority in this case affords this man space within which he is 'free' to live his life.

The unwise King himself is little bothered whether the compliance of his subject is through unconscious reaction or conscious decision. The outcome in both cases is that the compliance of his subjects is assured. Like Hans Christian Andersen's emperor wearing invisible clothes, such rulers would do well to seek the genuine opinion of those under their domain. A wise subject's 'opinion' given to the ruler through a coercive system is not likely to be completely honest. Likewise, the compliance of a subject may be assured through submission or with a spirit of defiance.

The point is that compliance may be achieved through methods that are not always intuitive. Power theorists have spent considerable effort in understanding the methods of compliance. Bachrach and Baratz' (1970) typology of power identifies five features of power related to the method through which compliance is gained: coercion; influence; authority; force; and manipulation. *Coercion* in this respect is defined as an exertion of power where A secures B's compliance through the use of threats. *Influence* is understood to occur when A causes B to change their course of action without threat (whether overtly or tacitly). *Authority* is exercised in power when B complies because they recognise that A's command is reasonable and legitimate (as with the case of the King and the wise man). The use of *force* helps A to achieve their objectives by stripping B of the choice of compliance or non-compliance. Finally, *manipulation* is an aspect of 'force', occurring when B complies without full realisation of the nature of A's command (as with the case of the King and the different sort of man) (Lukes 2005 [1974]: 21). Spinoza's observation from Chapter 1 also captures the variety of forms through which compliance may be assured.

In practical terms, this means that those intent on limiting the impact of democratic forces on decision-making processes have an arsenal of weapons with which to do so. The bludgeon may be lifted to deter dissent. The bludgeon may be used to destroy it. Carrots (in the form of tax breaks or lucrative contracts) can be offered to encourage acquiescence. One of the most effective methods to ensure compliance is to command obedience, for example to authority. This may be achieved through the authority's manipulation of context, and in its most efficient manifestation, obedience may be perceived to be the 'natural order of affairs'.

How the powers-that-be ensure that the 'natural order of affairs' is perceived as such will be returned to shortly. What is important to retain at this stage is that each of these methods of ensuring compliance is more efficient than the previous. The powerful party may rule more effectively by establishing unquestioned authority rather than through continuous repression, in other words. As we shall see in the upcoming discussions, one may achieve war-like spoils without the political, economic and human costs of war.

Three Dimensions of Power

The cocktail of tigers, bludgeons, elephants, carrots and authority serve to demonstrate both power's breadth and the fact that an established approach to employing it in analysis is still wanting. Joseph Nye's (2004) contrast of 'hard' power with 'soft' power vividly captures power's extensive influence – at least insofar as it relates to inter-state relations – in a simple frame. Steven Lukes' 1974 Power – A Radical View provides a slightly less descriptive but similarly elegant frame.[10] Nye's conception and Lukes' systematisation of the three dimensions of power serve as the foundational framework upon which the evidence provided throughout the rest of the book is laid.

First Dimension of Power ('hard' power)

Lukes' definition of the first dimension is power in its most recognizable form – the material capacity of one party to gain the compliance of the other. In terms of describing government or state power, 'hard' power refers to the ability to mobilise national material capacity: the capacity, for example, of military might or economic strength, or to maintain the machinery of the modes of production. This is the brawn of the elephant (not its intellect), or the tooth of the tiger. A state poorly endowed with such capacity may ally itself with one that does, and it is in this sense that established political alliances are alluded to as measures of hard power. Attributes of hard power specific to transboundary water conflicts include the rather enduring qualities of riparian position and relative size and strategic value of a state's lands.

The potential effects of an asymmetry in hard power can be all-determining. An overwhelmingly 'strong' state can avoid, reduce or deflect any pressure to enter into negotiations. Unilateral moves are permitted to the state more endowed with hard power, as it alone establishes the rules of the game. Examples from the history of war abound, such as in cases where the victor first establishes dominance on the battlefield then dictates the terms of surrender to its defeated adversary. Hard power may also be considered the equivalent of the French term 'puissance' (Turton and Meissner 2002: 48), or 'power as might'. In terms of negotiations, and in cases of extreme disparity in hard power, the stronger side doesn't so much set the agenda as determine whether or not there even *is* an agenda.

Second Dimension of Power (or 'Bargaining' Power (soft power))
What Lukes describes as the second dimension of power builds directly upon Bachrach and Baratz' characterisation of the "second face of power". Unlike the more 'concrete' form of hard (material) power, the influence of this other face of power is garnered through authority and legitimacy. It consists essentially of stripping one party of the capacity to choose between compliance or non-compliance when confronted with the other party's demands. Faced with no alternatives, the weaker side is stuck in a relationship within which demands for change may be suffocated before they are even voiced. The authors note further that if the demands are not directly suffocated, they might otherwise be either kept hidden – at the discretion of the more powerful actor, of course.

This second dimension of power also relates to what has elsewhere been conceptualised as *bargaining power* (Daoudy 2005a) or 'relational power', because of its derivation from being a legitimate actor in a relationship. It is imperfectly analogous to the French term 'pouvoir' (Turton and Meissner 2002: 48), which implies further the notion of political authority. A certain measure of bargaining power, then, is derived through *legitimacy*. A state may garner legitimacy through a number of methods, including effective negotiation strategies, official recognition through international treaty, the establishment of the moral high ground, discursive engagement at the global conference level, and the manipulation of time during negotiations (or the 'cost of no agreement'). Joe Dellapenna (2003: 289) points out how a state may use a reference to international law to gain a sense of legitimacy for customary practices. This may be viewed as a measure of bargaining power that would allow, for example, continued extraction from a river even if contested.

The second dimension / bargaining form of power is measured by the impact that one's own options and alternatives may have on the other. In that sense, bargaining power is also the type of power a baby may have over its parents, which is substantial indeed. It is by wielding bargaining power that in some situations so-called weaker parties are not as weak as they may appear or perceive themselves to be (Daoudy 2005b). James Scott (1985) famously describes the 'power of the weak' – those who consciously resist their inferior status through means such as strategic consent. Itay Fischhendler eloquently portrays Mexico's exploitation of its bargaining power, as it maintains its interests on the Rio Grande, despite its accumulated debt to the much more 'powerful' United States (Fischhendler 2005).

Relative equality in bargaining power may thus serve to compensate for a relative imbalance in hard power. Daoudy (2005b) describes the impact of "issue-linkage", which can be seen as a tactical use of bargaining power at the negotiations table. By linking the resolution of issues over which the 'weaker' player has an upper hand with issues it is otherwise unable to avoid subordination to, a second-best outcome for the weaker side is possible. The (temporarily) successful scuttling of Turkey's Illisu dam on the Tigris River serves to exemplify this. The Syrian side harnessed its bargaining power by linking environmental and Kurdish human rights issues with its hydrological interests, and aimed them squarely against British financing of the project (Daoudy 2005b: 119). Similarly, Thailand's use of bargaining power tactics with China along the Mekong River has been discussed by Onishi (2005). Considering the case of Israel–Jordan, Fischhendler reminds us that a reverse dynamic may be active, which he labels the 'weakness of the strong'. The basin hegemon, in some cases, may be obliged by virtue of its greater capacity to shoulder the burden when the weaker side reneges on its obligations.

Third Dimension of Power (or 'Ideational' Power (soft power))

> *I am talking of millions of men who have been skilfully injected with fear, inferiority*
> *complexes, trepidation, servility, despair, abasement.*
> Aimé Césaire, in Fanon (1986 [1952]: 9).

Lukes' 'third dimension' of power is the most abstract and arguably most effective of the three. To expose its features, he asks "how do the powerful secure the compliance of those they dominate – and, more specifically, how do they secure their *willing* compliance?" (Lukes 2005 [1974]: 12, original emphasis). He finds the answer in the realm of ideas, assertively questioning:

> is it not the supreme exercise of power to get another or others to have
> the desires you want them to have – that is, to secure their compliance by
> controlling their thoughts and desires? One does not have to go to the

lengths of talking about Brave New World, or the world of B.F. Skinner to see this: thought-control takes many less total and more mundane forms, through the control of information, through the mass media and through the processes of socialisation (Lukes 2005 [1974]: 27).

More specifically, the third dimension of power refers to the "power to prevent people, to whatever degree, from having grievances by shaping their perceptions, cognitions and preferences in such a way that they accept their role in the *existing order of things*" (Lukes 2005 [1974]: 28, emphasis added).

Susan Strange highlights a similar aspect of power exercised through what she terms the 'knowledge structure': "At this level, the strong implant their ideas, even their self-serving ideology, in the minds of the weak, so that the weak come to sincerely believe that the value-judgments of the strong really are the universally right and true ones"[11] (Strange 1994: 176). In contemplating the same question about how to secure willing compliance, Charles Tilly answers in part that "as a result of mystification, repression or sheer unavailability of alternative ideological frames, subordinates remain *unaware of their true interests*"[12] (Tilly 1991: 594 cited in Lukes 2005 [1974]: 10, emphasis added). The emphasis these scholars place on perception, ideas and ideology may allow us to refer to this third dimension of power as 'ideational' power, acknowledging also that "power has an ideational as well as a materialistic content" (Evans and Newnham 1998: 446: 221). The ability to shape issues even beyond the consciousness of a group in conflict is one that is central to our analysis of the hidden ways in which Palestinian compliance in the Palestinian–Israeli water conflict is assured.

The attempt to classify power into neat categories is strictly a device, a tool for analysis. Nuance in this domain is infinite. Each form of power has traits common to the other categories. Some features transcend all three dimensions in any case. *Ability* is an important element of hard, bargaining and ideational power, as in the capability to mobilise resources into action (Evans and Newnham 1998: 446). The ability to mobilise material capacity may prove to be just as important as possession of that material capacity (the US failure in Vietnam, for instance). The ability to *combine* the forms of power may be the most important feature of all – it is the mix that is important. Nepalese water philosopher and engineer Dipak Gyawali informs us that Hindu Samkhya philosophy understands this well. *Tamasik* power refers to the ability to employ brute force and is associated with the colour black, while red *rajasik* power refers to organised strength. White *sattwick* power is the ability to combine the other two, like the flame of a candle fed from and inter-weaving the *rajasik* wick and *tamasik* wax (Gyawali 2002).

The perhaps less enlightened approach employed in western analytical methods and pursued here is more mechanistic. In this way, it is in some cases helpful to group together the second and third dimensions of power into a single category of 'soft' power. Nye (2004) defines 'soft' power as the "ability to get what you want through attraction rather than coercion or payments".

Hegemony and Compliance-Producing Mechanisms

It is when the *existing* 'order of things' is taken as the *natural* order of things that we know hegemony is active. One cannot go far in understanding power relations between parties that are formally equal yet evidently not equally strong, without referring to the concept of hegemony. As previously mentioned, hegemony was the term used by Antònio Gramsci to describe the ideology used by the (fascist Italian) powers-that-be to conceal the control they have over the masses they rule.[13] Soviet hegemony reigned supreme over Eastern Europe, for example – at least until the 'natural order' of Moscow-based decisions was challenged. The "centralised multilateralism of the so-called Washington Consensus" (Harvey 2005: 68) neo-liberal approach to geopolitics certainly seems to be hegemonic in the minds of rulers of relatively weaker states, not least of all in the Arab world.

Like 'water wars', hegemony is a loosely used term. It is often a convenient epithet to lambast the behaviour of regional great powers, accurately or not. This confusion may stem from the lack of clarity of the terms 'hegemony' and 'empire', which are regularly conflated. As Ferguson asks:

> What is this thing called hegemony? Is it a euphemism for "empire" or does it describe the role of a primus inter pares, a country that leads its allies but does not rule subject peoples? And what are the motives of a hegemon? Does it exert power beyond its borders for its own self-interested purposes? Or is it engaged altruistically in the provision of international public goods? (Ferguson 2003, in Warner (forthcoming)).

The realist view of hegemony as dominative and subjective, can be contrasted with the neo-liberal institutionalist approach, which sees hegemony as an inclusive and positive dynamic[14] (see Burges 2005: 891). Linguistically, in Greek, a 'hegemon' (from *hegeisthai*, 'to lead') is someone who guides the way, say a torchbearer in uncharted territory. As such, hegemony can be considered as *leadership buttressed by authority* (Zeitoun and Warner 2006a). Crucially, a hegemonic 'authority' in this sense has a combination of methods to maintain its position. In Gramsci's original conception, this is a mix of force (coercion) + consent. Bludgeons *and* carrots, in other words; hard *and* 'soft' power. In contrast, dominance is defined as *leadership buttressed by coercion*, or the use of material capacity alone.

Warner informs us that hegemony decisively differs from empire in that there is *formal equality* between the hegemonic power and other players – no side has absolute power (Warner forthcoming: 3). A situation of hegemony occurs, then, when the more powerful competitor of two formal equals maintains its control through a *mix* of coercion and consent. A situation of imperial-type rule, by contrast, could be said to exist when control is maintained by the more powerful of formally *un*equal adversaries, primarily through coercive methods.

Thus French and Belgian colonial exploitation of the Congos is 'empire', while US influence over the voting patterns of weaker – but formally equal – allied nations at the United Nations is a form of hegemony. The distinction must be maintained if our analysis is to be accurate. Just as Germany and Romania do not carry equal weight at the European Commission (despite their equal vote), neither do states entering into international water treaties. The hegemony Egypt enjoys over its fellow Nile co-riparians at the Nile Basin Initiative serves to effectively further its interests (Carles 2006). But Egypt does not have formal dominion over the upstream nations, meaning that they have options available to them to influence the situation (primarily in the form of bargaining power) that colonised countries would not. Counter-hegemonic strategies are considerably broader than revolution and independence movements, as Ana Cascao (2007) explains.

In assessing hegemony, positionality is everything – where you sit is where you stand (Allison 1971). Writing on hegemony and on water conflict analysis in general tends to be the political science of the winners. There may be a tendency of supporters of a hegemonic power to take hegemony for granted and only use the term when they fear losing it. These supporters could be expected to view the hegemony as a 'positive' state of affairs. On the other hand, those unhappy with existing power asymmetries are likely to view undesirable manifestations of power as oppressive and 'negative'.

The issue of 'formal equality' is directly relevant to our analysis of the Palestinian–Israeli water conflict. During the formal occupation of the West Bank and Gaza until 1995, the two sides were struggling from within an imperial-type rule imposed by Israel through very coercive methods. The Oslo process provided Palestine near-formal equality with its former occupier, but did little in terms of addressing the asymmetry of power or control over transboundary flows. Chapters 5 to 8 describe in detail the mix of coercive and consensual methods by which Israeli hegemony over the water conflict has been maintained.

Compliance-Producing Mechanisms

Our discussion of power noted the variety of ways in which the compliance of one party to the will of another party may be achieved. Ian Lustick's theory of Hegemonic Compliance structures that variety in a useful way. Drawing on the work of Ámitai Etzioni and David Held, Lustick (2002) identifies four *compliance-producing mechanisms*. Each is loosely related to the three forms of power, as shown in Table 2.2.

So-called coercive types of compliance-producing mechanism (Type I) rely on force, or the direct threat of force. This use of bludgeons can be effective, but is costly in terms of political or financial capital. The more efficient 'utilitarian' (Type II) category refers to the use of incentives. This is the use of 'carrots', and is typically effective in the short term and usually only until more and larger carrots are demanded by the group whose compliance is sought. These are the peerages, tax breaks and lucrative contracts we have already discussed.

The third form of compliance-producing mechanism (Type III) is referred to as 'Normative agreement'. Etzioni considers that the most efficient method for a state to produce compliance is through normative mechanisms, i.e. *conscious beliefs* that it is 'right', or an obligation or a duty to comply. These beliefs are founded on recognition of *legitimacy*. State laws (taxes) and decrees are examples of norms that citizens regularly abide by. A state or entity perceived as illegitimate, or with dubious legitimacy, would not have this type of mechanism at its disposal (and this is the case with the challenged legitimacy of the Palestinian Water Authority, it is argued in Chapter 4).

Table 2.2 Main features of the three dimensions of power and their related Compliance-Producing Mechanisms, showing the efficiency of each.

Dimension of Power (based on Lukes)	Features	Compliance- Producing Mechanisms (Lustick)	Efficiency
Hard Power (puissance)	Force Capacity Riparian Position	(I) Coercive	LOW
Bargaining Power	Legitimacy	(II) Utilitarian (III) Normative Agreement	↓
Ideational Power	Perceptions	(IV) Ideological Hegemony	HIGH

'Soft' Power (pouvoir) { (spans Bargaining Power and Ideational Power rows)

The final type of mechanism used to produce compliance (Type IV) coincides with the concepts of hegemony and the third dimension/ideational form of power. The 'Ideological hegemony' mechanism holds that *ideological hegemonic beliefs* manufactured by hegemonic groups provide them with the most efficient mechanism for eliciting compliance about the ordering of the world. The beliefs that the subjected must hold for this method of ensuring compliance to function are considered *unconscious* beliefs, to distinguish them from the *conscious* type associated with normative exchanges. Under the influence of such unconscious hegemonic beliefs, compliance with the existing 'order of things' is only common sense, and, even worse – *not* complying is insane or even criminal (Lustick 2002: 24).

As foundational conceptual work for ideational power as we have defined it, and ideological hegemony compliance–producing mechanisms, it is worth quoting Gramsci on how one group may ensure the consent of another through ideas imposed upon it:

> This same [weaker social] group has, for reasons of submission and intellectual subordination, adopted a conception which is not its own but is borrowed from another group; and it affirms this conception verbally and believes itself to be following it, because this is the conception which it follows in 'normal times' – that is when its conduct is not independent

and autonomous, but submissive and subordinate (Gramsci 2003 [1935]: 327, emphasis added).

Martiniquan poet Aimé Césaire understood the process of socialisation well when he describes the servility and abasement of the black colonial servant under imperial rule, in the quote at the beginning of this section. All empires fall, however, particularly those built on a foundation of coercion. Rule can be maintained in much more sustainable ways.

Covenants Without the Sword/The Seduction of Efficiency
Lustick's emphasis on the *increasing efficiency* of the four types of compliance-producing mechanisms: coercion → utilitarian → normative → hegemonic (Table 2.2) is important. In simpler terms, hegemons may prefer creating a situation where the hegemonised readily comply rather than complying because they are forced to through coercive measures. Machiavelli recognized the importance of this when he pointed out that "even a ruthless ruler needs to ensure that the ruled believe his rule is justified" [15] (Wester and Warner 2002: 66). As Nye states, "if you can get others to admire your ideas and what you want, you do not have to spend as much on sticks and carrots to move them in your direction. Seduction is always more effective than coercion" (Nye, in Lukes 2005b: 486).

But seduction may not be possible without a certain ability to coerce in the first place. Here Lustick draws our attention to the *Guttmann scale of relationships* between the four compliance mechanisms. According to the theory, utilitarian mechanisms would only work, for example, if Type I coercive mechanisms are understood to be at hand. Similarly, normative mechanisms would not work in the long run without the hegemonised understanding that it is in *their* best interests to comply (Lustick 2002: 23). Thomas Hobbes effectively links Types (III) and (I) in *Leviathan*:

> *Covenants, without the sword, are but words,*
> *and of no strength to secure a man at all …*
> *The bonds of words are too weak to bridle men's ambition, avarice,*
> *anger and other passions,*
> *without the fear of some coercive power.*
> (Hobbes 1996 [1651]: 91 (see also Turton and Meissner 2002: 48)

The party able to both wield the sword and write the covenant benefits from an additional benefit: deterrence. The truly powerful may manage to pre-empt its competitor's request for discussion or basis for conflict. Such power of deterrence enables the stronger side to determine the 'order of things' with minimal effort – as flying a plane on 'auto-pilot' – and is significantly more efficient than the use of threats (hard power) or even setting the agenda (bargaining power). Effective manipulation of the compliance-producing mechanisms would allow one party, in other words, to create a situation of hegemony. By Chapter 9 we will have seen that this is essentially what Israel has completed.

From the world of water conflict theory, Frey and Naff (1985) capture the dynamic most succinctly with the term "projectable power". They refer to "a nation's ability to threaten its opponents credibly at whatever distance is necessary and thus to shape their behaviour regarding water issues" (Frey and Naff 1985: 78). One is reminded of the scowl and message in an angry cat's eyes that successfully says 'stay away!' Projectable power, then, could be a measure of the combined capacity of hard, bargaining and ideational power that a state possesses and/or its will and ability to wield them.

Resisting Hegemony

> *When the great lord passes, the wise peasant bows deeply, and silently farts.*
> Ethiopian proverb, in Lukes (2005 [1974]: 125).

Unlike Khayam's wise man at the beginning of this section, the compliance of the wise Ethiopian peasant is not complete. His expressed displeasure is heard only by himself, and perhaps sensed by an unlucky few around him. Critically, the tiny act of resistance is not noticed by the great lord himself. The great lord reigns, but his rule is not unquestioned.

So begins our exploration into the theoretical world of resisting hegemony. Resistance to the 'natural order of things' takes as many forms as does the power that establishes the order in the first place. London Water Research Group researchers Ana Cascao and Jeroen Warner are leading efforts to examine active resistance to hegemony in water conflicts. They are identifying counter-hegemonic and anti-hegemonic strategies informed by tactics that are generally associated either with increasing the 'weaker' party's bargaining power or chipping away at the unquestioned assumptions that perpetuate a state of hegemony. This exciting work is producing substantial theoretical and policy implications with particular relevance to the Palestinian–Israeli water conflict, though is not discussed in further detail here.

Power and International Water Law

> *Beneath the rule of men entirely great, the pen is mightier than the sword.*
> Edward Bulwer-Lytton (1803–73), *Richelieu* 1839.

The first and lesser-known part of the famous quote refers to an ideal situation unfortunately rarely seen in river basins globally. Where codified law and order prevail, the laptop may be more influential than the fighter jet, but otherwise it is the law of the jungle that determines the outcome. The implications for Jordan River riparians are significant. A blunt assertion by eminent lawyer B.V.A. Rölling reinforces one of this study's main tenets – that it is power, not riparian position or law, that determines outcomes in water competitions:

> In all positive law is hidden the element of power and the element of interest. Law is not the same as power, nor is it the same as interest, but it gives expression to the former power-relation. Law has the inclination to serve primarily the interests of the powerful (B.V.A. Rölling 1960, cited in Malanczuk 1997: 33).

On the other hand, there is ample evidence throughout the world of states avoiding situations where the law of the jungle reigns. Principles of water sharing between nations *have* been developed, even when the states involved are unequally powerful. The principles have formed customary international water law, and have the potential to help level the playing field between adversaries. The main limiting factor of the utility of international law to deal with those cases where the playing field is not level is that it still lacks the teeth to punish, and hence to deter transgressions. This is true for both primary types of international law associated with water, as discussed in the following two sections.

Customary International Water Law

Dellapenna (2003) describes the development of customary international water law, demonstrating that "in the absence of treaty, international law arises through a process of claim and counter-claim that produces an explicit or implicit agreement" (2003: 289). Stephen McCaffrey (2005) reminds us that, due to this organic growth of customary water law through customary practices, *all* states are bound through its customary principles, whether or not these are codified and ratified.

Customary international water law (IWL) is the set of rules meant to govern relations between riparians when sharing freshwater resources. This set of rules has developed, perhaps most notably, into the concept now generally referred to as the rule of *reasonable and equitable utilisation*. The term infers a concept of restricted sovereignty, and was first codified in 1966 under the Helsinki Rules on the Uses of Water on International Rivers (IWL 1966).[16] The best evidence of the institution of this larger set of customary rules was given when the UN General Assembly adopted the 1997 Convention on the Law of the Non-navigational Uses of International Watercourses (UN ILC 1997) (hereinafter referred to as 'the 1997 UN Convention'), and later again in the 'Berlin Rules'. According to McCaffrey (2005), the 1997 UN Convention defines a state's three most basic obligations:

- *Equitable and reasonable utilisation* of shared freshwater resources (referred to hereafter as the principle of 'equitable and reasonable utilisation').[17]
- *Prevention of the causing of significant harm* to other states through activities related to an international water course ('no significant harm').
- *Provision of timely advance notice* by a state planning new measures that may adversely effect the other states involved ('advance notice')

Such water-sharing principles are indeed active globally. As we saw during our discussion of water conflict theory (Chapter 2), Gleick and Wolf have demonstrated that the overwhelming majority of competing co-riparian states have worked out some form of water-sharing agreement between themselves. These agreements tend to rely much more on the 'restricted sovereignty' principles of the 1997 UN Convention, and much less on the notions of "absolute sovereignty or absolute riverine integrity" (Wolf 2000b: 133).

However, expressions of power are evident in the structuring of these agreements. As we shall see in Chapter 6, principled agreements do not necessarily lead to a level playing field or to equitable and reasonable outcomes. Danilo Zolo, for instance, notes that the agreements tend to apply and adjust the rules of customary water law to suit the purposes of the parties (2005: 2). There is furthermore ample room for power manipulations at each stage of the process of reaching an agreement, from pre negotiations to post-agreement monitoring.[18] The 1995 water agreement signed between Palestinians and Israelis, as we shall see, has in essence prevented what IWL prescribes, and has led instead to a wholly 'inequitable' and 'unreasonable' utilisation of water resources.

International Humanitarian Law

Just as the UN Convention has evolved from international customary law, so has International Humanitarian Law (IHL) evolved from the unwritten 'rules of war'. The set of protocols that form IHL may offer some protection to water systems and resources *during* conflict, even without offering effective means of prosecuting violations or seeking reparations. The rules of war mean to dictate the 'humane' conduct of war. From the miserable outcomes of barbaric wars came a code of conduct, proudly upheld for some time by chivalrous gentlemen-officers. When the enemy raised a white flag, for instance, an army would know this meant surrender and would stop firing. Non-combatants and the infrastructure upon which they rely, it was understood, were to be kept out of harm's way.

Such rules were eventually codified beginning with the end of First World War, in the series of documents that came to be known as the Geneva Conventions. Both the essence of water as a necessity for human well-being, and the vulnerability of water-systems to armed conflict, were referred to specifically in Additional Protocol I, 1997. Article 54 (Paragraph 2) and Article 55 deal with the protection of the "Natural Environment" and of "Objects indispensable to the survival of the civilian population" during wartime (ICRC 1994).

The first attack by the nascent Palestine Liberation Organisation was upon the newly-built Israel National Water Carrier in 1965. Had it been successful, the attack would have violated the basic principles of IHL, as the Carrier is indispensable to the survival of the Israeli civilian population. Israeli breaches of water-related IHL, particularly from 2000 onwards, have been significantly more sustained and destructive. Some of these are discussed in Chapter 5, but are the kinds of violations that are generally not dealt with in any sort of international forum.

The problem with borders – consideration of sovereignty

Many have waxed poetic about the influence that the very nature of water may have on international relations. Indeed, the difficulty that law has in grappling with transboundary waters is due in large part to the fact that water is fluid and not susceptible to rigid human constructs like geographical borders. Water certainly seems to ridicule boundaries, and creates havoc for those who would legislate on water as if it is a static resource. The effects run deep, as Israeli water lawyer Eyal Benvenisti (2002) points out:

> The two basic building blocks of the global political and legal environment - the concept of sovereignty and the allocation of jurisdiction by political borders - have joined forces to preclude an efficient and sustainable use of transboundary resources … Most transboundary resources remained subject to the control of more than one state. As a result, the respective entitlements of states concerning their shares of transboundary resources remained rather vaguely defined ever since the global environmental crisis emerged towards the middle of the twentieth century (Benvenisti 2002: 22).

A response to the difficulties of legislating transboundary water is seen in the discussions surrounding 'flexible' or 'adaptive' law, as with du Bois in Allan and Mallat (1994). Treaties can be written to include, for instance, time or event-triggered re-visiting clauses and/or amendments known as "minutes" that allow adaptation (Fischhendler 2004). For all of the difficulties inherent with attempting to harmonize fundamentally different / incompatible systems, international water law is beset by an even greater challenge: the lack of enforceability due ultimately to international law's subordination to power.

The Influence of Power on International Law
Bulwer-Lytton reminds us that 'the pen is mightier than the sword' only when governance is in order, while Hobbes remarked that 'covenants without the sword' to back them up are of little use to protect anyone. Global governance systems by the end of the first decade of the twenty-first century remain sufficiently mixed up, and international law sufficiently repressed, to ensure that the pen is not mightier than manifestations of power.

Picking up on the sentiment from the Copenhagen School of Security Studies, Barry Buzan asserts that "the balance of power … [is] an intrinsic product of anarchic international systems" (Buzan, et al. 1998: 12). From a perspective of international political economy, Susan Strange goes further still: "the outcomes in an international society that has no legitimate overriding authority are necessarily determined by relationships of power and far less by law, custom, or social convention" (Strange 1987: 123). She thus puts in common language what the respected legal voice Rölling noted in the quotation cited at the start of this section.

Lack of enforceability is the key limiting factor for both International Water Law and the water-related clauses of International Humanitarian Law. Short of fair treaties negotiated in good faith, customary water law in the current weakly structured international legal context is not likely to be able to redress imbalances of power and or the absence of level playing fields between riparians. John Waterbury (2002) describes the inevitable result, at least along the Nile River. Even within the well-structured World Bank-led Nile Basin Initiative, the competing states may be more guided by cut-throat competition than by notions of 'equitable and reasonable' utilisation:

> There will be conflict, manoeuvring, acrimony and nonviolent retribution surrounding water issues. The real battlefields for developing countries are likely to be found inside international institutions … specialised UN agencies, the World Bank, and the regional development banks. Here contesting riparians will jockey for position, line up support, seek to place their people in key positions, and try to mute the voices of their rivals (Waterbury 2002:10).

The point should be clear by now. When the context is set by a weak international legal environment, it is power that determines the rules and outcomes of competition over resources. It does not necessarily follow that chaos and disorder will reign, as Gleick, Wolf and Conca have pointed out. Between the extremes of benevolent inter-state cooperation and the law of the jungle there often *is* evidence of order between competitors. *But this order is structured and maintained by those states which have the power to do so.* This point is central to the arguments made during the analytical portion of this book, and underpins the theory of hydro-hegemony.

On the other hand, it does not follow that just because international water law is currently weak it may be disregarded. Cynicism about the role of law is, however, the attitude commonly adopted by global water establishment institutions, policy-makers, diplomats and academics engaged from either hegemonic or hegemonised viewpoints. At the 2005 SIWI World Water Week, for example, the head of the Global Water Partnership stated publicly that those who think that there is any role for law other than for guidance "are dreaming in technicolor". Such dismissals may be attributed to having fallen prey to hegemonic ideas. The order of things – or 'reality', as those annoyed by other challenging assumptions call it – excludes a more important role for law in the water world. Public assertions by prominent personalities tend to reinforce the hegemony. But discourse itself both is a product of and reproduces power, as we shall see following.

Power and Discourse: Re-writing Reality

The truth is always something that is told, not something that is known. If there were no speaking or writing there would be no truth about anything. There would only be what is.
Susan Sontag (b. 1933).

The final element of theory required to appreciate the pending analysis of the Palestinian–Israeli water conflict is the influence of discourse. Knowledge and the ways through which it is created, disseminated and absorbed are fundamentally socio-political processes. In other words, 'reality' is in the eye of the beholder. Like the concept of hegemony, this is not a new idea. Commenting on the formation of environmental policy, Maarten Hajer notes that "it has become almost a platitude to characterise public problems as socially constructed" (Hajer 1997: 42). This section touches upon the role that discourse plays in such social constructs, starting with a superficial questioning of the nature of knowledge and ending with a question that is one of the keys to understanding the central point of this study: who sanctions the discourse?

Constructed Knowledge

The importance of realising the subjective nature of *truth* was not lost on the liberation psychologist Franz Fanon, who recognised that "truth is that which hurries on the break-up of the colonialist regime; it is that which promotes the emergence of the nation; it is all that protects the natives" (Fanon 1990 [1963]: 39). Yet truth has also been recognised as the first casualty of war, a fact which if accurate is not likely to favour the natives' struggle.

So is revealed one of dozens of contested views about truth – what is truth; where does it lie; how is it determined and – can it be 'manufactured'? If truth can be manufactured, then who produces it? And what might be their motives? Without delving too deeply into the nature of knowledge, beauty and truth, it is worth acknowledging that the way different people deal with it is entirely subjective. A conventional physical resources scientist would argue that an objective and measurable physical reality exists, regardless of what politicians or philosophers might think. An orthodox social scientist argues that reality is based upon how human beings perceive it, and that it is therefore quite transformable by humankind. Politicians, obliged by their survival imperative in a democratically elected system to say different things to different people, are often thankful for this latter, constructionist, view of reality. The existence of altered and alternative viewpoints is what enables people to engage in the construction of knowledge in the first place. Those viewpoints generally held to be the most common, we shall see, generate a powerful force that cannot be ignored.

Evidence of the appeal of the socially constructed nature of knowledge is found in the various expressions of its meaning by numerous disciplines through the ages. An incomplete inventory is offered in Table 2.3.

Space does not permit full discussion on the nuances and similarities between each of the concepts noted in Table 2.3, although the final two points are elaborated upon in the following sections, principally because they assist with our understanding of ideational power. In his study of narrative, William Cronon (1992) offers lucid insight into how knowledge is constructed through narrative, and hints at the power this garners:[19]

> It is a commonplace of modern literary theory that the very authority
> with which narrative presents its vision of reality is achieved by obscuring

large portions of that reality. Narrative succeeds to the extent that it hides
the discontinuities, ellipses and contradictory experiences that would
undermine the intended meaning of the story. Whatever its overt
purpose, it cannot avoid a covert exercise of power; it inevitably sanctions
some voices while silencing others. A powerful narrative reconstructs
common sense to make the contingent seem determined and the artificial
seem natural (Cronon 1992: 1349, emphasis added).

Table 2.3 Concepts relevant to the socially-constructed nature of knowledge.

Term	Origin	Definition
Received Wisdom	(traditional)	A position on an issue accepted generally by most of and the most influential elements of society.
Paradigm	(Greek)	A way of thinking can become normalised when those who employ it see it as having achieved something (Horrocks 1999).
Conventional Wisdom	J.K.Galbraith	"Ideas which are esteemed at any time for their acceptability, and ... predictability" (Dunleavy 2003).
Manufactured Consent	Lippman, Chomsky	A technique of control necessary [to government] because common interests elude the public and must be the domain of a "specialised class" (Chomsky 1992).
Hegemonic Convergence	Gramsci, Hajer	When policy debates reflect special interests and concerns, and concur around a certain issue (Allan 2003: 1).
Discursive Hegemony	Hajer	Whereby actors have secured support "for their definition of reality" (Hajer 1997: 59).
Knowledge Stabilization	Conca	Interaction between epistemic communities (in water) leads to a situation where "A dominant construction of a problem becomes embedded; an officially sanctioned body of universal, technical knowledge begins to emerge ..." (Conca 2006: 53).
Sanctioned Discourse	Tripp, in Allan (2001: 182)	The "delimitation separating the types of discourse perceived to be politically acceptable from those that are deemed politically unacceptable at a specific point in time" (Feitelson 2002: 298).

Cronon's observation appears to be a variation of Hajer's view of 'organisation as a
mobilisation of bias', whereby "some issues are organised into politics while others
are organised out" (1997: 42). One mechanism that assists with the organising is
what he terms 'story lines'. These elements of a viewpoint held by a specific group
voiced in common serve to rationalise the approach of the group towards an issue
– and forcibly excludes the approaches of other groups. In such a contested
context, it is the more powerful group which determines what becomes the
dominant understanding of the 'truth'. Warner captures the meaning succinctly,
noting that 'the ability to define truth and meaning produces and is a product of
power' (in Zeitoun and Warner 2006a: 3).

That politicians and special–interest groups are able to manipulate the truth is not in and of itself a problem. When the resultant constructed reality is used by one group to the detriment of another is when it becomes an issue of general concern (i.e. when it 'sanctions some voices while silencing others', in Cronon's words). As we shall see in our discussion on Palestinian and Israeli water discourses (Chapter 4), both sides are actively engaged in such manipulations of reality, and both indeed take it further, out of the world of words and into the realm of ideas. We turn now for a closer look at the mechanisms that allow such manipulations.

Discursive Hegemony

Hajer defines *discourse* as "a specific ensemble of ideas, concepts, and categorisations that are produced, reproduced and transformed in a particular set of practices and through which meaning is given to physical and social realities" (1997: 44). 'Discourse' is created from the hundreds and thousands of meetings, media reports, policies, conferences and political events that work against and with each other to present or re–present an issue. As the ideas collide and align themselves along common story–lines, according to discourse theory, they combine and co–evolve until a consensus is reached, thereby developing from simple interaction into what Hajer terms a "coalition of discourses". Such an evolution of discourse is conceptualised graphically in Figure 2.1. For Hajer, the story–lines are the cement that binds the coalition, so that when the coalition is united along a common story–line, a form of "discursive hegemony" results (1997: 60). The coalition of discourses may then tend to embrace alternative viewpoints that are more or less aligned with the dominant one, while marginalising or excluding viewpoints which might challenge it

Figure 2.1 also emphasises how the development phase of the discourse coalition may be considered *conscious*, insofar as the debates and the actors' awareness of them are open and public. By contrast, actors new to the field (fresh students or uninitiated policy–makers, for instance) may arrive to find a discourse already established, and therefore tend to accept its ideas and viewpoints *sub–consciously*. [20] These terms recall our discussion of compliance–producing mechanisms (Chapter 2), where we noted that compliance produced through normative means was played out consciously, while compliance produced through ideological hegemonic means was associated with the sub–conscious.

If the creation of discourses may define reality and exclude contending viewpoints, there is ample room for power to play. The influence power wields in this domain lies in its ability to shape consensus, thereby creating a coalition and determining the resultant dominant viewpoint. This form of power is known generally in the literature as *discursive power* or *discursive hegemony*. Because it is active at least partly at the sub–conscious level, discursive power can be considered a form of ideational power.

The concepts have been dealt with extensively in the water world, though water people understand them in different terms: Ken Conca, for instance, speaks of a 'knowledge stabilisation process,' while Tony Allan regularly employs Charles Tripp's expression of 'sanctioned discourse'.

Figure 2.1 The evolution from interaction to coalition of discourses.

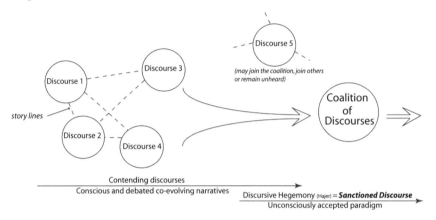

Sanctioned Discourse

The concept of sanctioned discourse evolved within the world of water policy research, with Charles Tripp's emphasis on the constraints imposed upon those who may wish to speak or think *outside* of the discursive hegemony (Allan 2001: 182). A helpful interpretation of sanctioned discourse is offered by Anders Jägerskog who defines it as: "the prevailing dominant opinion and views which have been legitimised by the discursive élite" (Jägerskog 2002: 1).

Feitelson's definition of sanctioned discourse (see Table 2.3) aptly acknowledges the temporal aspect of the term, which he examines through consideration of the evolution of the Israeli sanctioned discourse on water throughout Israel's political history. One of many story lines he identifies as holding the sanctioned discourse together is the widely held belief (amongst the elements of the Israeli water sector) that water–sharing between Israel and Palestinians is a "zero–sum game". If Israel were to concede any water to Palestinians, those who tell the story goes, it would be at Israel's expense (Feitelson 2002: 310). Similarly, Julie Trottier identifies an official Palestinian Water Authority (PWA) discourse as one where all of the woes of the water predicament are blamed on the Israeli occupation and the theft of Palestinian water. She also notes a shift in discourse depending upon who the PWA is addressing, i.e. their citizen clients or the international donor community, which she refers to as "parallel sanctioned discourses" (1999: 165). These discourses are discussed at length in Chapter 4.

We may observe from these examples that discourse varies with context and according to the receiving audience. Nevertheless, it is the dominant 'coalition of discourse' that ultimately drives policy–making on the issue in question. We turn now to a closer look at *who* sanctions the discourse, and *how*.

Who Sanctions the Discourse?

> *If our choice of narrative reflects only our power to impose our preferred version of reality on*
> *a past that cannot resist us, then what is left of history?*
> William Cronon (1992: 25)

The theory has it that contending discourses jockey for position, resulting in the weaker discourse being beaten back and the emergence of a louder, stronger discourse. The debates that are not sanctioned at this stage, the questions that are not allowed to be asked, are determined chiefly by the context within which the discourses are being contested. In other words, it is those groups or institutions that have the most influence on political issues and policy within a particular discourse that set the agenda. The short answer to 'who sanctions the discourse?' is thus the more powerful.

There is no short answer as to exactly *how* a discourse is sanctioned. Just as discourses may exist in parallel, it would appear that there are different weights of discourse. The discourse of the weaker party is expected to have little effect outside of its own intended political domain. In contrast, the stronger, more vocal and eloquently expressed discourse of the powerful coalition will be heard by a much wider audience. Contrast the degree of impact of statements advocating economic reform issued by generations of Marxist activists with the ideas established at Bretton Woods and by subsequent financial institutions. Consider, on the other hand, the effects of ignoring a loudly expressed discourse, as an inward–looking Apartheid regime discovered in the 1980s.

There is in fact ample evidence of the discourse of the weaker of two contending groups not being 'heard' by its more powerful competitor. Herodotus' historic statement that 'Egypt is the Nile and the Nile is Egypt' is a case in point. Ana Cascao (Cascao 2005) points out that while Egypt may be the Nile, the Nile is certainly more than just Egypt. Yet the identification of the two implied by Herodotus' statement certainly captures the guiding principle of the discourse influencing Egyptian water policy. Scholars and practitioners point to the Egyptian government readily securitising transboundary water issues, not only denying upstream states the development possibilities provided by the river passing through their territory, but even closing down the opportunity of discussing the 1959 Egypt–Sudan water sharing agreement that has maintained the status quo for nearly half a century (Mason, et al. 2003). Ethiopian, Tanzanian or Ugandan discourses contesting Egyptian hegemony over the Nile go essentially unheard beyond their respective domains. Rather incredibly, such discourses also go un–noticed by international water professionals actively engaged in water development projects there.

Such features of discourse become particularly significant during negotiations between conflicting parties. Israeli water insider Shaul Arlosoroff, for example, acknowledges that the discourse of his Palestinian counterparts

> must always satisfy their internal pressures, and they thus claim that we are stealing all the water, etc.. We know this – and they know we know this. We know they don't really mean it, and so we move on (Arlosoroff 2004, pers. comm.).

The insight provided by Arlosoroff neatly captures the important aspect of *the ability to ignore the discourse* of the other. This option is open only to those that have sanctioned the discourse, not to the weaker side. It is a primary effect of power asymmetry, and has great consequences for determining the outcome and perceptions of the Palestinian–Israeli water conflict. Having completed our review of foundational theory, we return to explore that imbalance in greater detail.

3

An Asymmetrically Distributed Resource

The meek shall inherent the earth, but not the mineral rights.
John Paul Getty 1892–1976

POLITICS, stated Harold Lasswell in 1936, has as its main concern to describe 'who gets what, when, where and how'. Prior to the analysis of the inherently political Palestinian–Israeli water conflict, it is essential to complete a detailed review of such distributive issues, or just who gets the water, when, where and how. This chapter's review of the physical attributes of the contested resources shows that the bulk of them are directly or indirectly under Israeli control. To a large extent, the assymetry that characterises the conflict must be described in terms of cubic metres and pipelines. Sadly, the more aesthetically pleasing aspects of water are inevitably submerged in the sea of numbers required to establish an objective physical understanding and quantification of control over and distribution of the flows

Overview of the Transboundary Water Flows

The common notion of the land of Palestine and Israel as dry and desertic is worth reconsidering. While the Sinai desert creeps northward from Africa into Gaza and the Negev, the cities of Tel Aviv, Jerusalem and Ramallah, which lie slightly to the north, receive about 600 mm of rain annually. This is more than, say, Paris. Nevertheless, there is an overall physical scarcity of water, and the growing population, driven by encouraging immigration (in Israel) and high birth rates (4 per cent per annum in Gaza) only exacerbates the stress on natural resources. In any case, agricultural consumption far surpasses that of any other sector, such that neither state has had the ability to be self–sufficient in food since the 1970s. As Tony Allan (2001) puts it, 'the area ran out of water a long time ago'.

Transboundary Surface Water Resources
By far the most important transboundary surface water system is that of the Jordan River (Figure 3.1). The Holy River's flows have baptised Christ, and inspired songs by pilgrims for hundreds of centuries. According to the terms of the 1995 Oslo II

Agreement, though, Palestinians are barred from all access to and from any use of it. The Jordan River system is composed of several elements:

- **The Hasbani, Dan and Banias rivers**, which originate in the mountain ranges of Lebanon, Israel and Syria (Golan Heights), respectively.
- **The Upper Jordan River**, which flows from the confluence in northern Israel of the Hasbani, Dan and Banias rivers to the Lake of Tiberias.
- **The Lake of Tiberias**, located at roughly 210 metres below sea level, is roughly 12 kilometres across and has an average depth of only 24 metres. Inflows to the Lake are estimated to range from 500 million cubic metres per year (MCM/y) (Markel 2004b) to 800 MCM/y (Ben–Zvi 1996: 31). The quality of the water is potable with little treatment, although the historic problem of salinization due to saline spring inflows is again becoming a serious quality concern. The lake is also known as the Sea of Galilee or Lake Kinneret.
- **The Lower Jordan River**, which historically flowed from the Lake of Tiberias to the Dead Sea, is today more aptly characterised as a small stream of sewage. With the flow at the head of the LJR dammed since 1964, its primary sources are currently saline springwater diverted away from the Lake of Tiberias, the poorly treated wastewater diverted from Bitunia, and the inflow further downstream from perennial wadis and the Yarmouk River. The water of the LJR is extremely poor, particularly in terms of nitrates and salinity, and has no potential as a source of drinking water.
- **The Yarmouk River**, which originates in Syria and Jordan, flows into the Lower Jordan River roughly 10 kilometres downstream of the Lake of Tiberias. Jordan has built the al Wehda dam and Adassya diversion weir to channel Yarmouk flows for use in the Jordan River valley. Jordan and Syria are in the process of completing the 'Unity' dam. Syria has, furthermore, completed a series of dams on tributaries to the Yarmouk. The already scant flow that does reach the LJR is expected to dwindle to a trickle by 2007.
- **Various wadis** (perennial rivers) that flow into the Lower Jordan River from all sources, including e.g. Wadi al Far'a, which rises in the West Bank behind Nablus. There are a number of other perennial wadis that flow westward towards the Mediterranean Sea, but are hydrologically outside of the Jordan River System. The largest of these is Wadi Gaza, which rises in the West Bank hills south of Hebron and flows through Israel to Gaza.[21]
- **The Dead Sea**, a salty brine roughly 400 metres below sea level. The pre–1964 annual discharge of the Lower Jordan River into the Dead Sea is estimated at roughly 1,300 MCM/y, which is up to 25 times greater than the current inflow (which varies between 50 to 200 MCM/y (Farber, et al. 2004: 1992)). The Dead Sea is shrinking at a rate of one metre of shoreline lost each year, and is the intended recipient of the proposed Red Sea – Dead Sea Canal (see Photograph A5, Appendix A) .

Figure 3.1 Transboundary surface water and groundwater resources of Palestine and Israel: Jordan River System and four aquifers.

Adapted from the Palestinian Academic Society for the Study of International Affairs Center for Economic and Social Rights; United States Geological Survey – Executive Action Team.

Transboundary Groundwater Resources

There is a much greater quantity of Palestine–Israel transboundary groundwater than surface water. Groundwater either comes naturally to the surface in the form of springs or is extracted from hundreds of wells that vary in depth from 20 to 700 metres. Annual abstractions from such wells, according to the aquifer basin[22] they tap into, are shown in Table 3.1. There are four such transboundary aquifer basins:

- **The Western Aquifer Basin (WAB)** is the largest of the four transboundary aquifers in terms of volume. The WAB's estimated sustainable recharge rate is 362 MCM/y. Under the terms of Article 40 of the 1995 Oslo II Interim Agreement, Israel is allocated 340 MCM/y, Palestine 22 MCM/y.
- **The North Eastern Aquifer Basin (NEAB)** has an estimated sustainable recharge rate of 145 MCM/y. Under the terms of the 1995 Oslo II Agreement, Israel is allocated 103 MCM/y, Palestine 42 MCM/y.
- **The Eastern Aquifer Basin (EAB)** has the smallest volume of the transboundary aquifers. The estimated sustainable recharge rate of the EAB is a subject of much controversy. Under the terms of the 1995 Oslo II Agreement, Israel is allocated 40 MCM/y, Palestine 54 MCM/y. Article 40 also refers to 78 MCM/y "remaining quantities" available for development by Palestine, though it is generally accepted a decade onwards that this volume is not feasibly extractable, if the flows exist at all (see Chapter 7).
- **The Coastal Aquifer Basin (CAB)** extends the full width and length of the Gaza Strip and most of the coast of Israel. Its estimated sustainable recharge rate is 485 MCM/y. Unlike the aquifers transboundary to Israel and the West Bank, the allocations for this aquifer were not defined under the terms of the Oslo II Interim Agreement. In 2003, Israel extracted an estimated 429 MCM/y from the CAB, Palestine 135 MCM/y. Roughly 80 MCM/y of the Palestinian extraction is considered beyond the estimated sustainable recharge rate of the aquifer falling within Palestinian political boundaries, which is 55 MCM/y. The water quality is notoriously poor – with nitrate levels exceeding 200 milligrammes per litre (the US Environmental Protection Agency (EPA) standard is 10) and chloride levels exceeding 400 milligrammes per litre (the EPA standard is 250).

Vulnerable Water Supply Infrastructure

Given the considerable levels of military activity in Palestine, the vulnerability of the water infrastructure is well worth consideration. The American Water Works Association measures the robustness of a water system in terms of its ability to withstand or recover from damages, whether man–made or natural. A system where all water sources are physically and militarily protected, for example, and where all of the pipes and accessories are buried out of harm's way, is considered robust. The pumps, transmission lines, booster stations and canals that make up the Israeli water infrastructure are, in this sense, quite robust. Indeed, this is a sophisticated system: Israeli water professionals, by all accounts amongst the best in the world, take pride in locally developed technologies such as water–reducing drip irrigation systems and vertical line shaft pump motors designed for the arid and tough pumping conditions.

The most vulnerable component of the Israeli system is the National Water Carrier, which supplies nearly one third of freshwater consumed in Israel. Considering the alternative sources from hundreds of groundwater wells and the 'new water' produced through desalination or wastewater re–use, however, the system as a whole is robust. Israel has long since completed its 'hydraulic mission' to provide water to the majority of its citizens. The notable exceptions are the Palestinian Bedouin citizens of Israel confined to live in "unrecognized villages" in the Negev, none of which are served by basic services (Adalah 2006).

In contrast to the essentially complete water network coverage in Israel, Palestine is less well provided for: 95 per cent of the population in Gaza and only 70 per cent in the West Bank receive piped water to their home (USAID 2002a). The development agency Oxfam estimates there were an estimated 200,000 to 225,000 residents of the West Bank not served by piped water networks in 2003 (Oxfam 2003). This water is delivered from any of hundreds of wells though transmission lines to local reservoirs. Municipal water crews are then responsible for pumping it through the city networks. In Gaza, the transmission and distribution lines are normally buried in the sand. The rocky, difficult to trench, hillsides of the West Bank explain why the majority of the transmission lines (and many of the distribution networks) there are exposed rather than buried. The distribution systems throughout Palestine, furthermore, are generally inadequately maintained, accounting in part for the estimated average of 36 per cent of water "lost" through leaks in the rusting old pipes (PWA 2004a).

By virtue of its high number of sources and complex network of transmission lines, the Palestinian water system can be characterised as flexible, and – at the national level at least – as having a relatively robust capacity to deal with disturbances. At the local level, though, some villages and many households rely on single sources of water delivered through fragile and ageing infrastructure. Palestinian water infrastructure at the local level is therefore vulnerable to disruption by military activity. The consequences of this will be seen in our review of the events of Jenin in April 2002, in Chapter 5.

Control Over Water Resources in the West Bank

There is an extensive body of literature dealing with the Palestinian–Israeli water conflict. The overwhelming majority of contributions address the conflict either in terms of water allocations or water use. As such, there is a dearth of analysis concerned with which side has *control* of which flows. The fundamentally political part of Lasswell's question about distribution – *who decides* who gets what, when, where and how – becomes impossible to ignore. This question is answered here through a review of the physical characteristics particular to each source of water, which allows for an examination of how they can or cannot be controlled.

The focus of this discussion will be the transboundary water resources located in the West Bank, rather than those found within the political borders of Israel or the Gaza Strip. Control of water in these latter locations is clear – Israeli

Table 3.1 Natural recharge, discharge and well abstraction rates from three of four aquifers transboundary to Palestine and Israel, 2001.

Basin	Recharge		Discharge	Wells					Springs					
	Average estimated Recharge	Range	Wells and springs inside and outside the West Bank	Pal. and Israel wells	Palestinian	Sub-total	Israeli		Pal. and Israeli springs	Palestinian	Sub-total	Israeli		
							Inside	Outside				Inside West Bank (Saline)	Outside West Bank	
							the West Bank						Fresh	Saline
EAB	161	125-197	204.8	62.7	26.4	36.3	34.3	2.0	142.1	45.5	96.6	88.3	0.94	7.36
NEAB	145	132-177	184.1	91	19.1	71.9	12.9	59.1	93.0	17.8	75.2	0	75.2	
WAB	366	317.5-366	621.0	571.6	26.8	544.8	2.8	542	49.4	2.6	46.8	0	46.8	
TOTAL	672	-	1009.9	725.3	72.3	653	50	603.1	284.5	65.9	218.6	88.3	130.3	

All figures in MCM/y. EAB = Eastern Aquifer Basin; NEAB = North Eastern Aquifer Basin; WAB = Western Aquifer Basin. Table does not include the Coastal Aquifer Basin, which is transboundary to Israel and Gaza (SUSMAQ 2001a: Table 2.7) institutions control the abstraction and development of transboundary waters found within its political borders, just as Palestinians – from 2005 onwards and barring repeated Israeli military incursions – do in Gaza. The situation in the West Bank, as we shall see, is infinitely more complex. The discussion is based on the figures of Table 3.1.

Palestinian Control over Water Sources in the West Bank
Flows in the West Bank controlled by Palestinian management structures take on a variety of forms.

- **PWA wells** in the West Bank are owned and operated by the Palestinian Water Authority, and have been developed following the PWA's creation in 1996. There are currently four such wells, each of which are high–capacity (>100 m3/hour), and producing in total roughly 3.5 MCM/y, as shown in Table 3.1.
- **Agricultural wells** in the West Bank were traditionally privately owned and regulated, though they fall under the jurisdiction of the PWA according to the 2002 Water Law. There are over 300 such low–capacity wells in the West Bank producing an estimated 34.5 MCM/y. The majority of the wells were dug prior to the Israeli occupation of 1967.[23] There is resistance to the change from the traditional family based management structures to the central management efforts of the PWA, which poses serious legitimacy constraints on the latter, as we will see in Chapter 4. Unlike in Gaza, nonetheless, the PWA is able to maintain a certain degree of control over these once–private wells.[24]
- **Municipal wells** in the West Bank are regulated and billed for primarily by municipalities, though according to the 2002 Water Law they fall under the jurisdiction of the PWA. Having been detached from any central planning policies during the Israeli occupation period, the service–delivery capabilities of some municipalities is more substantial than that of the PWA (e.g. Nablus, Hebron, or in the case of Ramallah – the Jerusalem Water Undertaking). The exertion of PWA control over municipal wells here, as with the agricultural wells, is not a development welcomed by all.

Israeli Control Over Water Sources in the West Bank
Israeli management structures control a similar variety of flows in the West Bank.

- The so–called **West Bank Water Department Wells** consist of thirteen wells operated and maintained (but not owned) by the West Bank Water Department (WBWD). Originally formed as the Jordan Water Resources Authority in 1962, the WBWD was created in 1967, and run until 1995, by the Israeli Civil Administration (ICA) of the Israel Defence Forces. Several dozen more wells drilled during this period by the ICA in the West Bank, through the WBWD, were designed to serve Israeli settlements as well as Palestinian villages, and continue to do so. Although the WBWD institutionally falls under the legal jurisdiction of the Palestinian Water Authority, decisions about the operation of

WBWD wells (i.e. which clients are prioritised – Israeli settlements, Israeli military camps or Palestinian villages) are taken by the ICA. In 2006, the flow–switching valves continue to be literally turned by Palestinian hands under Israeli command, just as they have been since shortly after the beginning of the 1967 Israeli occupation of the West Bank.

- **Israeli wells inside the West Bank** are owned and managed by the Israeli water–provider Mekoroth. Although data on the production capacity of these wells is not made available to the public, it is known that there are over 25 such wells (WBWD 2003) producing between 44 and 59 MCM/y (see Table 3.1). The bulk of this water is distributed to Israeli settlements, primarily to industrial–scale agricultural land in the Jordan River Valley, and to Israeli military bases. A smaller share is distributed to the lowest–priority client – the Palestinian villages.

- **Water purchased by the PWA from Israel** is delivered through 25 connection points by Mekoroth under administrative systems set up through the WBWD prior to the 1995 Oslo II Agreement. The volume purchased ranges from 22 to 36 MCM/y (World Bank 2004). The seller of water in this case holds power over the buyer. Israel has threatened to cut supplies to its Palestinian clients, even if these are in very bad fiscal shape, as was the case of Bethlehem in 2006 (Ma'an 2006).

- **Water purchased by Palestinians in the West Bank from Israeli settlers** is a further Israeli–controlled source of water. The more than 200,000 Palestinians who are not served by piped networks normally collect rainwater during the winter. When stocks run out during the summer months, they are obliged to buy water from private Palestinian water tankers, which if blocked from their regular filling points will fill up from Israeli settlements.[25]

Apart from partially controlling water resources inside the West Bank, Israel also controls abstractions across the entire Western Aquifer Basin. This is achieved primarily through superior pumping capacity. As demonstrated by Figure 3.2, the analyst examining who controls the water flows must consider not just the number of wells, but their capacity as well.

The Israeli side's relatively superiority of abstraction capacity is one manner through which the skewed distribution of the water in this aquifer is maintained on average 362 MCM/y for Israel and 22 MCM/y for Palestine. Abstraction – and over–abstraction – from the Western Aquifer Basin is thus determined through Israeli pumping policy alone, a point that is returned to in Chapter 8.

Achieving and maintaining hegemony at the aquifer or river–basin level is not possible in this era without a command of technology. Dams must be built to divert flows, and sophisticated high–precision vertical turbine pumps run by powerful motors are required to extract water from deep wells. The Israeli side excels in this technology, and even exports it globally. The Palestinian side attempts the same level through technology transfer from the Israeli side, but remains in comparison a novice. Without the technological advantage and superior pumping capacity, hegemony at the basin level would not be possible. Indeed, it would not be conceivable.

Figure 3.2   Comparison of quantity and capacity of Palestinian and Israeli wells in the Western Aquifer Basin.

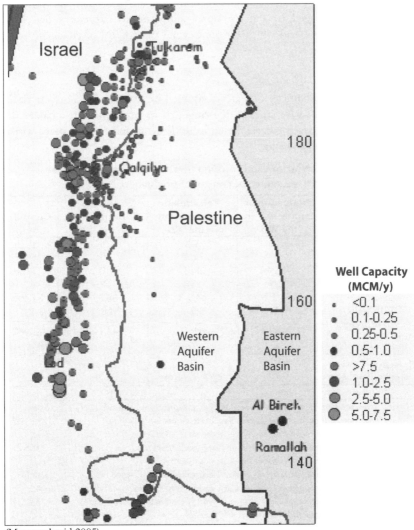

(Messerschmid 2005).

West Bank Water Sources Beyond State Control

- **Rainwater** in the West Bank is captured privately by households, in cisterns. It cannot be billed for and is usually not regulated or treated. While the quantities are not significant at the national level, captured rainwater is of critical importance to the farmers who depend on it as their primary source.

• **Groundwater** which flows naturally from the surface in the form of springs is an important traditional source of water in the West Bank. Though natural springs fall officially under the jurisdiction of the PWA, they are generally metered and managed by the traditional administrative structures that have existed for centuries, and which remain beyond the control of either Israeli or Palestinian authorities.

Summary of Control Over Transboundary Sources

Table 3.2 presents a summary of water consumed by residents of the West Bank, classified according to who controls the origin of its production. It includes the water consumed by Israeli citizens living in settlements and military bases within the political borders of Palestine.

Table 3.2 Water production and consumption from within the West Bank, classified according to the source of control of production, 2003.

Source	Production or Supply in / to the WB	Palestinian Consumption in the WB	Israeli Consumption in the WB	Control by
Rain water	n/a	5 [26]	0	P
PWA Wells	3.5 [27]	3.5 [27]	0	P
Agricultural Wells	34.5 [28]	34.5	0	P
Municipal Wells	15.8 [28]	15.8	0	P
Springs	154.2 [29]	63.8 [28]	88.3 [29]	I / P
WBWD Wells	8.9 [27]–11.9 [28]	5.9 [30]	4.5 [31]	I
Israeli Wells inside WB	44 [32]–59.4 [28]	6.9 [27]	48.1 [33]	I
Jordan River System	n/a	0	0	I
Supply from Israel	38 [34]	22.5 [27]–36 [35]	9 [36]	I

Total Production/Availability of fresh water from sources inside the West Bank	188
Total Palestinian Consumption from groundwater sources inside the West Bank	130
Total Palestinian Consumption from all sources inside the West Bank	135
Total Palestinian Consumption inside the West Bank, from all sources	~ 165
Total Palestinian Consumption inside of Israel, from all sources	0
Total Palestinian Consumption in the West Bank under Palestinian Control	122.6
Total Palestinian Consumption in the West Bank under Israeli Control	~ 42
Total Israeli Consumption inside the WB from Israeli wells in the West Bank	~ 53
Total Israeli Consumption inside the West Bank, from all sources	~ 61
Total Israeli Consumption Under Palestinian Control	0

All figures in MCM/y. **I** = production or supply controlled by Israeli actors; **P** = production or supply controlled by Palestinian actors. The table counts water consumed by Palestinian citizens, Israeli settlers and Israeli military.

There are several features to note from Table 3.2. The first is the inequity in total consumption between Palestinians and Israelis, particularly between Palestinians and Israeli settlers living in settlements inside the West Bank. These roughly 230,000 settlers[37] consume more than one quarter of the water consumed by approximately 2.4 million Palestinians in the West Bank, as shown in Figure 3.3. By contrast, as no citizens of Palestine live there, Palestinian consumption inside Israel is nil. While this fact may be self–evident and hardly worth representing graphically, the point is made to highlight the asymmetry that exists at the base of Palestinian–Israeli relations over water issues.

Figure 3.3 Comparison of Palestinian and Israeli water consumption inside the West Bank and Israel.

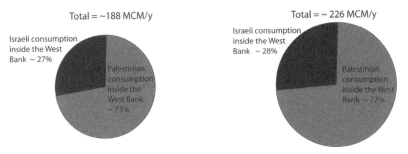

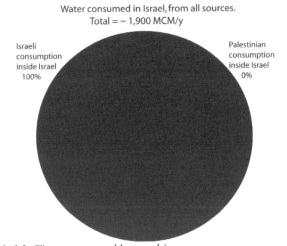

Based on Table 3.2. (Figures very roughly to scale).

The second feature of note from Table 3.2 is the relatively little control that the official Palestinian water provider (the PWA) currently has over any of the water produced or consumed inside the West Bank. In Figure 3.4 this is shown to amount to only about one third of the water consumed in the West Bank (i.e. the combined consumption from PWA, Agricultural and Municipal wells). This small measure of control can be reduced yet further when one considers that the real control of the PWA over once–private agricultural wells and the tightly held municipal wells is challenged, and is tentative at best.

The third feature of note from Table 3.2 is the relatively large degree of control that the Israeli authorities (through Mekoroth) have over water consumed and produced *inside* the West Bank, as shown in Figure 3.5. Through their control over West Bank Water Department wells and the selling of Mekoroth water to the PWA, official Israeli structures control roughly one quarter of the water consumed by *Palestinians* inside of the West Bank.

A final point worthy of note from this analysis is the manner in which the water produced by Mekoroth and distributed by the WBWD is administered. As we have seen, the WBWD is responsible for the operation and maintenance (but, again, not the ownership) of thirteen wells drilled when the Palestinian institution was under the direct command of the Israeli Civil Administration, until 1995. Despite the fact that the PWA now pays most (but not all) of the staff salaries, as well as the fact that several WBWD projects are funded by international donors, we see from the sixth line in Table 3.2 that almost half of the water that the Palestinian institution manages (i.e. 4.5 MCM/y) is still distributed by command of the Israeli state–governed Mekoroth to Israeli settlers living on occupied land inside of the West Bank.

Figure 3.4 Palestinian water consumption in the West Bank, by source of production.

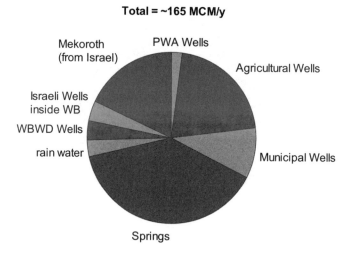

Total = ~165 MCM/y

Mekoroth (from Israel)

PWA Wells

Agricultural Wells

Israeli Wells inside WB

WBWD Wells

rain water

Municipal Wells

Springs

The pie charts of Figures 3.3 to 3.5 reveal many aspects of the Palestinian–Israeli water conflict in its current form. Centred primarily on the water of the West Bank, the conflict pits a nascent Palestinian water institution, weakly presiding over roughly one quarter of the water produced and consumed within its boundaries, against a far more mature and efficient Israeli counterpart which controls the production and distribution of a similar share of water inside the same boundaries. Transboundary water resources located in Israel are excluded from the competition. The outcome in terms of water–distribution, as we shall see in the following section, is even more unbalanced than is this asymmetry in control over production and billing.

Figure 3.5 Palestinian water consumption in the West Bank, by source of control and production.

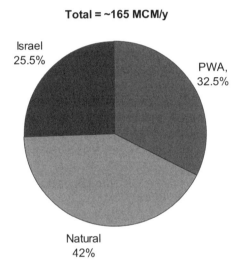

Total = ~165 MCM/y

Israel
25.5%

PWA,
32.5%

Natural
42%

Inequitable Transboundary Water Allocations

We have seen that the guiding principle of International Water Law is 'equitable and reasonable' utilisation. The factors relevant to a judgement about the applicability of the concept (i.e. population, access to alternative sources, economic dependency, etc) may also provide a framework within which to judge the allocations currently in place between Palestine and Israel. In exposing the disparity, the discussion concludes that while the exact quantities for 'equitable and reasonable' distribution remain to be agreed upon, [38] the current distribution is best characterised as inequitable and unreasonable. Table 3.3 is a summary of the transboundary flows allocated to or consumed by each side, taking no account of which party actually controls which resource.

The roughly 6:1 skewed distribution of the transboundary water resources in Israel's favour was posited at the start of this book as a fact compelling explanation. The situation is represented graphically in Figure 3.6, which drives home the point that politics, especially a state's power, determine the outcome of water conflict more than is its riparian position. Despite its midstream position on the transboundary river and aquifers, the Israeli state's ability to control shared waters has ensured that it maintains the lion's share.

The other factors that define equitable and reasonable utilisation must be taken into account, however. The 6:1 skew is reduced, for instance, by consideration of population: Israel's population of 6.5 million is nearly double that of Palestine's roughly 3.5 million. The skew is all the more severe, on the other hand, when one considers that the Israeli side has access to substantially more endogenous water sources (such as the Negev aquifer), as well as the technical and economic capacity to produce the previously discussed 'new' water. Incorporating the value of the water to each state's economy has a similar tilting effect. As we noted in the introductory chapter, the agricultural sector in Israel contributed 1.5 per cent of the Gross National Product in 2001 (IMOA 2001). The contribution of agriculture to the much less technology–based economy of Palestine is known to hover between 20 and 30 per cent of GNP, even though the Israeli settler and military projects in the West Bank stifle farming activity there. The ratio of Israeli to Palestinian agricultural water use is roughly 9:1, while the importance of the activity to each state is around 1:25.

Table 3.3 Allocations or consumption of transboundary water resources between Palestine and Israel, 2003.

Transboundary Water Source	Allocation or consumption (MCM/y)	
	Israel	Palestine
Surface Water		
Jordan River System [39]	660	0
Wadi al Far'a [40]	6	6–12
Wadi Gaza [41]	25	0
sub–total	**691**	**9**
Groundwater		
Eastern Aquifer Basin	40 [42]	68 [43]
North Eastern Aq. Basin [42]	103	42
Western Aquifer Basin [42]	340	22
Coastal Aquifer Basin [44]	429	135
sub–total	**912**	**267**
Total	**1,603**	**276**

The figures do not include endogenous sources of freshwater in Israel or Palestine (i.e. the eastward flowing springs arising from the EAB, or the Negev aquifer), nor does it consider the 'new water' sources such as desalination and wastewater re–use.

It must, furthermore, be borne in mind that the figures of Table 3.3 are for the most part *allocations*, and the figures of Figure 3.6 are of water *use*. Observation of actual abstraction rates shows a further skew in favour of Israel. Palestinian abstraction rates from the Eastern Aquifer Basin, for example, are lower than the 68 MCM/y allocation shown in Table 3.3. The figure is derived from the Oslo II allocation of 132 MCM/y minus the endogenous eastward–flowing springs. The Oslo allocation of 132 MCM/y, however, includes an as–yet undeveloped "extra 78 MCM/y". As we shall see in Chapter 7, most professionals agree this figure is over–rated. Conversely, Israeli abstraction rates from the Western Aquifer Basin regularly *exceed* the Oslo–defined allocations, which we will examine in Chapter 8.

Figure 3.6 Israeli capture of multi–lateral surface water and bi–lateral groundwater flows, 2003.

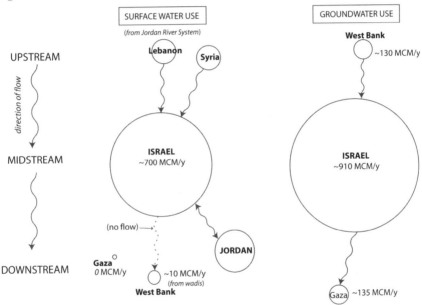

Roughly to scale. The figure of ~130 MCM/y for West Bank groundwater use comes from Table 3.1. The other figures for Palestine and Israel are from Table 3.3. Syrian, Lebanese and Jordanian water use figures derive from Lowi (1993), el Musa (1997) and Phillips et. al. (2005). The Figures shown do not include *consumption* rates, i.e. water purchased by Palestinians from Israeli sources, nor water used by Israelis from sources located within the political borders of the West Bank. Israeli groundwater use often exceeds the allocations shown here (see Chapter 8).

Why all the Fuss?

Accurate calculation of allocations based on the 1997 UN Convention's factors for determining 'equitable and reasonable utilisation' is feasible, if complicated. There is little dispute amongst Israeli and Palestinian water professionals that such calculations will yield a distribution for Israel–Palestine not much different than a roughly 60–40 or 70–30 split in Israel's favour. There is, furthermore, no denying that even if the water conflict were resolved by virtue of an equitable volumetric re–allocation, neither side would become free of exploring other water resource management options.

Apart from the asymmetric distribution of transboundary freshwater flows, the very real physical scarcity of water in Palestine and Israel explains why tempers run so high when discussing it. But the passion the subject arouses does not detract from a basic and oft–ignored truth: the physical scarcity of water can (and is) compensated for through abstract and technological fixes. So what is all the fuss about?

Abstract and Technological Fixes: Virtual Water, Wastewater Re–use and Desalination
Virtual water imported in the form of grain and other foodstuffs serves to mitigate physical scarcity. Consider Israel's dependence on water found in food imports by examining its 'water footprint'.[45] The water footprint of a state gives an indication of its total consumption of water, both fresh and virtual. It is calculated by considering the volume of freshwater consumed by the state annually, subtracting virtual water leaving the state (in the form of agricultural or livestock exports) and adding the virtual water imported by the state (in the form of agricultural or livestock imports). Israel's total water footprint is estimated at 8,600 MCM/y (Chapagain and Hoekstra 2004: Table 4.9). This is more than four times the total renewable amount of freshwater available in Israel (*including* the transboundary water resources shared with Palestine), which is roughly 2,000 MCM/y. Though the report does not provide the water footprint of Palestine all indications from other reports (e.g. Nassar (2002)) reveal an even greater Palestinian dependence on food imports.

By filling the gap between actual available freshwater and the amount demanded, virtual water reduces the tensions between Palestinians and Israel. Its conflict–mitigating qualities are not, as we discussed in the introduction, readily recognised by Israeli or Palestinian political leaders. Unlike the hidden politics going on behind the water conflict, virtual water is not expected to impact upon the water conflict in any loud or visible manner, though will continue to play its very significant role.

The demand for freshwater for drinking purposes will, in any case, continue to rise along with the population, driving the development of alternatives to existing ground and surface freshwater resources. There are several sources of such 'new water', as it is sometimes inappropriately referred to.

Most importantly, there is water that can be 'saved' through demand management techniques. Getting the public to change its water consumption habits is key to reducing the impact on natural resources. Arlosoroff (1998) estimates that up to 20 per cent of the flows consumed by the domestic and agricultural sector

(~120 MCM/y) may be saved this way. Other means of 'saving' water include repairing leaking pipes in old water distribution networks and rainwater catchment, though these methods would simply prevent water from otherwise percolating to the aquifers. The treatment and re–use of urban wastewater is another significant source of 'new' water. In 1994, Israel successfully launched the Dan Regional Wastewater Treatment Facility, which produces roughly 120 MCM/y (IWC 2002b) primarily for agricultural purposes around Tel Aviv and in the Negev desert.

Rejected out–of–hand in Israel since the early 1960s, the *desalination* of seawater is today poised to significantly alter the hydropolitics of the region. The 100 MCM/y Ashqelon Desalination Facility, completed in 2005 on the southern coast of Israel, has effectively put to rest an internal Israeli debate about whether or not to adopt desalination as a policy. The plant produces water – sold by the private operator to the Government of Israel – at 0.57 $/m3 (Talhami 2005: 35) which competes well with the cost of freshwater supply. As the trend continues, we can expect to see what Israeli academic Eran Feitelson refers to as a "new water geography" (Feitelson 2004). Water resources and infrastructure will become increasingly aligned in an east–west direction (from desalination on the coast to demand centres at the interior), departing from the traditional north–south configuration (from the Lake of Tiberias to the Negev desert). The move to desalination has also succeeded in putting to bed – at least temporarily – alternatives that were being developed during the early 2000 period, including shipping in water piped from Turkey's Manavgat River.[46]

Israel's implementation of 'new water' projects is occurring in concert with major improvements in technology, drops in cost, and a shift in its water management discourse, as we shall see later in this chapter. Development on the Palestinian side, by contrast, is certainly not based on the latest technology. The PWA, even with donor support, has been able to do more than complete pilot desalination plants in Gaza; the first wastewater treatment plant destined for wastewater re–use, funded by USAID in Hebron, was frozen mid–project after the election of the Hamas government in January 2006. Palestinian attempts to counter the physical and Israeli–induced scarcity through technological fixes have thus far not succeeded. Virtual water there vitally plugs the gap, though desalination and wastewater re–use remain as potential alternatives the state cannot afford to ignore.

So why all the fuss?
If virtual water is silently mitigating the conflict, and seawater can be treated for the same cost as freshwater, just what is the basis of the Palestinian–Israeli water conflict? The question becomes even more poignant when considering the economic value of the flows being contested. Franklin Fischer of the Massachusetts Institute of Technology has concluded that the volumes being fought over from the Jordan River System (which he estimates at 100 MCM/y, though this is debatable) are worth roughly $20M annually. This is less than the

cost of a single F–16 fighter–jet: a sum not likely to frighten away donors ready to assist with the development of the Palestinian water sector.

Those looking to reason and the rationality of the individuals involved to explain the intensity of the conflict over these relatively minor and cheap transboundary waters will be searching forever. Rather, the explanations are to be found in the realms of ideology and politics; in the symbolic significance attached to these resources. What may be insignificant to an economist, for example, is of utmost importance to people subscribing to religious or nationalist dogmas. Water flows of little importance to the engineer are critically important to people who have long been denied what they perceive as their rights. Control of flows considered relatively minor by local residents takes on a historical pioneering dimension by foreigners claiming title to the land. The hidden politics keep scientific and economic rationales well at bay. We begin to explore the intriguing competition for control of transboundary flows in the following chaper, noting that the conflict varies in form from the violent to the discursive, and seems bound to be perpetuated.

4

Highly Politicised Hydropolitics

THERE was, at the turn of the century, considerable debate as to whether or not the Oslo political process was dead. While pundits still debate the exact date of its demise, there were few one decade on who claimed that the process had any life left in it. The poor analysis and understanding of the process' demise concerns students of the water conflict, precisely because it cannot be separated from the broader political context within which it plays out.

Like the dispossession and suffering of the Palestinians who fled the fighting in 1948, the Palestinian–Israeli water conflict cannot be understood – or resolved – in the absence of any appreciation of the historic roots of the wider conflict. That conflict is rooted in the Zionist conquest of land which became Israel in 1948, in the subsequent Israeli acquisition of further land, and in the Palestinian reactions to such conquests over the last 60 years. Analysts focused on the minutiae of the water conflict alone continue to take mis–steps that contribute little to the analysis. As we shall see, claims that the 1967 war was mainly for control of water, or that the notion of Palestinian water rights is a just a 'dream', are as frequent as they are out of touch with the historical record and agreements signed by the parties themselve.

This chapter offers a summary of the broader political context prior to delving deeper into an extensive review of the region's hydropolitical history. The effect of 'high' politics (Lowi 1993) is evident in the way the broader conflict continues to shape, distort, enable or disable the water conflict. While the water conflict is at times very violent and destructive, it is also fought through discursive processes, particularly since 1967. The tone and content of the discourse also varies considerably, from belligerent declarations of 'water intifada' and threats of cutting off supplies, to apparently altruistic declarations of 'cooperation'. The dominant 'cooperation' narrative tends to treat each side as equal while ignoring the power imbalance between them. The final section of the chapter shows how the discourses compete to become hegemonic, with an unusual coalition forming between the Palestinian and Israeli water officials around the dominant 'cooperation' discourse, and sanctioned by the international donor community.

The Broader Political Context post–Oslo

The 1993 signing of the Declaration of Principles between the PLO and the State of Israel ('Oslo I') and the 1995 signing of the 'Oslo II' Interim Agreement were the first steps in a process that, if nothing else, served to clarify five issues upon which the Palestinian and Israeli officials could not agree. These were termed 'permanent status issues' in the Oslo II, and include the right of return of Palestinian refugees; the status of Jerusalem; territorial borders; the future of Jewish settlements in the West Bank; and water. Each issue is highly politicised on both sides, and is driven by varied but determined interests. By the turn of the century, these included on the Israeli side, national security, Zionism, demographics, and religion. Driving forces on the Palestinian side included nationalism, redress of injustices, material compensation, national security and viability, and religion.

The Agreement was in tatters by 2000 following the failure in Maryland of the 'Camp David II' negotiations. Shortly thereafter, Ariel Sharon's visit to the al Aqsa Mosque in Jerusalem and the second Palestinian intifada led to a brutal Israeli re–occupation of the West Bank and Gaza, dozens of suicide bombers and thousands of deaths. Two years later, the Bush administration in the US attempted to revive the Oslo process with the 'Road Map to Peace'. Israeli policy vis-à-vis the Palestinians, meanwhile, changed from dialogue to blame to unilateral action. The shift in policy was perhaps most visibly marked by the construction of the Separation Wall inside the West Bank, which began in 2002.

Despite the death of the Oslo process and the shift to unilateralism, however, some clauses of the Oslo II Agreement were still active in 2005. These included the geographical designation of Areas A, B and C (with supposed Palestinian jurisdiction over only the urban areas 'A') and – of greatest significance to the present study – the functioning of the Joint Water Committee (JWC). Pulling together the Palestinian Water Authority and the Israel Water Commission, the JWC is the main discursive 'battleground' of the water conflict. That contact between water officials occurred at the JWC throughout the most violent and intense moments of the broader conflict is impressive – and is explained in terms of power asymmetries clothed in dubious cloaks of legitimacy, in Chapter 6.

These local events have not occurred in an international vacuum. The United States, since the early 1990s, has been the main external force at work in shaping Palestinian–Israeli talks. It has tenaciously backed the Oslo and Road Map processes and, in June 24 2002, President Bush declared a "viable Palestinian state" as its official policy. However, its official political support for its key regional ally, Israel, makes it something less than a purely objective mediator. Financially also, Israel receives the largest share of official US overseas assistance – over US$150 billion since 1962 (USAID 2006). Various US administrations have, though, also shown particular interest in the Palestinian water sector. Their US$300M investment between 1995 and 2004 makes the Palestinian Water Authority one of the main Palestinian clients of the US Agency for International Development (USAID 2005),[47] and the US by far Palestine's largest donor in the sector (PWA

2003b). The interests behind these investments will be discussed in further detail in upcoming sections. At this stage, it is sufficient for to maintain that the role and influence of the US over the nature of the conflict cannot rationally be ignored.

A Brief History of the Water Conflict: 1904–2004

The hydropolitical history of the Jordan River valley has been done justice by several authors, including Lowi (1993), el Musa (1997), Wolf (2000a), Feitelson and Haddad (2000), Trottier (1999), Allan (2001), Haddadin (2001) and Frederiksen (Frederiksen 2003). Apart from a wide variety of academic perspectives (realist, structuralist, post–structuralist, liberal, Marxist), the subject has been viewed from every political angle imaginable. The purpose here is to not to repeat what has gone before, but to focus on the power–related aspects of the conflict and the methods of control that have been used within it. Four eras are distinguished: Pre–1948 'Zionist Aspirations'; the 'Ideological Era' from 1948 until the June 1967 war; the 'Israeli Domination Era' from July 1967 until the 1995 Oslo II Agreement; and the 'Israeli Hegemony Era' from 1995 until the final days of the Oslo political process sometime between 2000 and 2005.

Pre–1948: Zionist Aspirations

The history reads as one of engineering feats, development, violence and ideology. As one pours over the engineering plans that have marked the development, one can almost hear the heated arguments, gun shots and quiet side–discussions that accompanied them. As a whole, of course, the history is overlain by a heavy layer of politics. In the words of World Bank economist Ariel Dinar,

> The issue of water in the Palestinian–Israeli conflict is an issue intertwined in asymmetries and power relationships, history and ideological beliefs. Not only did the early Zionists view water ideologically but they were also able to demonstrate their power over the Arab inhabitants through several schemes. The issue of water, security and scarcity also played a large role in how the Zionists viewed and how Israel views water and the necessity to control it and reluctance to share it. There is a kind of psychological scarcity, a scarcity of resource in the eye of the beholder (Dinar 2003: 190).

Interest in Palestinian water resources by the Zionist founders of Israel pre–dates the 1917 Balfour Declaration, which paved the way for Jewish immigration to British Mandate Palestine. Trottier notes how Theodor Herzl suggested a canal from the Nile to the Sinai, stating that "the real founders of the new–old country were the hydraulic engineers" (1999: 41). Plans to couple irrigation to hydropower first materialised under the British in 1922 with the Mavrommatis Plan, which proposed irrigation along the eastern and western *ghors* (floodplains) of the Jordan River. The UK National Archives record in detail World Zionist Organisation efforts to persuade colonial France and Britain to expand the borders of Palestine to include the Upper Jordan River headwaters, and the Lebanese territory that would go along with it (FO 608/274 1920, Rook 2000). Future Israeli president Chaim Weizmann, for example, made his views explicit in 1919 to the then British Prime Minister David Lloyd George:

> The whole economic future of Palestine is dependent on its water supply for irrigation and electric power, and the water supply must be from the slopes of Mount Hermon, from the headwaters of the Jordan and the Litani River ... [We] consider it essential that the northern frontier of Palestine should include the Litani, for a distance of about 25 miles above the bend, and the western and southern slopes of Mount Hermon[48] (Frederiksen 2003: 71).

Their requests eventually denied by the colonial authorities, Zionist leaders followed their hydrological and state–building ambitions by commissioning the Lowdermilk Plan of 1943–1944 and the 1948 Hays Plan (Hays 1948). Such plans may have represented a convergence of interests of the Political and Labour Zionist movements, with the view of land and agriculture of this latter characterised by Sharif el Musa as "essentially romantic, if not mystical" (1997: 277). The Labour Zionist movement's attachment to agriculture was deep indeed, being "viewed as a means for 'redemption' of the land from the 'desolate' state they perceived it to be in, as a means to make the desert bloom, as a source of spiritual renewal for Jewish immigrants and as a means to help them strike roots in Palestine" (el Musa 1997: 276).

The Hays Plan is credited with making the first proposal for the "Palestine Water Carrier" – a project rejected outright by co–riparians Syria and Jordan for its aspirations to divert part of the Upper Jordan River and pump it out of the basin into the Negev desert. The plan was to be later implemented as the Israel National Water Carrier (NWC), under radically altered political circumstances. The year 1948 marks both the Palestinian *nakba* ('tragedy') and the foundation of the state of Israel; most of British Mandate Palestine became Israel, while the West Bank was henceforth administered by Jordan, and Gaza by Egypt.

1948–67: The Ideological Era
The hydropolitical period from 1948 to 1967 is one of the most tumultuous in the history of the Palestinian–Israeli water conflict. The period is characterised by rapid development on the Israeli side, minimal development of the Palestinian side, and clashing Arab and Israeli strategies to secure shares of the Jordan River system.

Water extraction rates in the West Bank and Gaza increased only minimally under Jordanian rule in the West Bank and Egyptian rule in Gaza, the period up until 1967. Such change as there was may have been due more to the development of cheap pumps than any efforts at systematic development. In stark contrast, the newly formed state of Israel embarked upon what may be considered a hydraulic–

driven nation–building exercise, referred to in academic literature as the 'hydraulic mission'. [49] Eran Feitelson speaks of this period as the Israeli "resource expropriation era" (2000: 345), during which Zionist "ideology *dictated* water development. No plan for a new agricultural settlement was ever abandoned only because the cost of supplying water was too high" (Galnoor 1978: 345, original emphasis).

Key driving forces on the Israeli side during this period have been identified as the ideology of redemption (el Musa 1997) and the territoriality (Schnell 2001) of Labour Zionism. Political Zionism was driven concurrently by a quest for national development and practical concerns of national and food security (Dalin in Soffer 2002: 18). Israeli water professionals focused their development efforts on the water resources that were most accessible, that is to say the groundwater found in the aquifers well within the borders with neighbouring enemies Lebanon, Syria and Jordan (Arlosoroff 2005, pers. comm.). The result was a tripling of groundwater production rates from roughly 300 MCM/y in 1948 to nearly 1,000 MCM/y by 1966 (PCIIWS 2002: 40). These efforts coalesced in phase of impressive well–drilling whereby Israel achieved the hydraulic supremacy that has endured ever since (particularly in the Western Aquifer Basin).

Following the realisation by Israeli hydrologists that the state was already pumping near to the sustainable limit of the aquifers, particularly in the Coastal Aquifer Basin, developing the surface water in the Jordan River System took on a more immediate priority (PCIIWS 2002: 41). The first Israeli attempts to divert the Upper Jordan River, by building the input for the National Water Carrier at the B'nei Yacov (Jacob's Daughter) Bridge, were resisted politically by Syria. Their motion to stop the Israeli diversion was blocked by a Russian veto at the UN Security Council, but the work was eventually halted when the US threatened Israel with sanctions. Israel eventually managed to complete the National Water Carrier in 1964, albeit with the intake located at a much lower point – on the northwest shore of the Lake of Tiberias.

Syrian and Jordanian intentions to develop similarly ambitious water projects during the same period were driven by wholly different ideological visions, and they suffered quite different fates. The principal ideological driving force on the Arab side found expression in proud proclamations of Arab nationalism, particularly in the wake of the 1948 *nakba*. There were also very practical hydraulic concerns: the imperative to respond to the needs of over 700,000 Palestinian refugees, particularly those that fled to Jordan. Proposals to develop the Jordan River System were advanced by The Arab League and the Jordanian and Syrian governments, who commissioned the 1953 Baker–Harza Plan; UNRWA, with its 1954 agricultural study and the 1954 'Arab Plan'.[50] Jordan also established the West Bank Water Department in 1965 to manage water resources there.

The hydropolitical tensions that occurred during this decade eventually led to the well–documented mediation efforts of US envoy Eric Johnston, known as the 'the Johnston Plan,' [51] and – notably – to the Plan's eventual demise. Former South

African intelligence officer Anthony Turton comments on the effects of the break–down of the Plan from a security perspective, noting that it left

> Syria and Lebanon with almost total control over the major sources of supply to the Jordan River basin, which gave rise to the intense feelings of insecurity in Israel. This insecurity was based on a threat perception that had been formed in a broader political setting and subsequently became part of the Israeli security doctrine (Turton 2003: 43).

The flurry of large–scale development plans on either side of the Jordan River may be considered a form of low–intensity conflict – a variation of what Gramsci calls a 'war of position'. Co–evolving with these planning and construction activities, however, were events amounting to the closest thing to a real war that the Jordan River has seen.

Israel's completion of the National Water Carrier in 1964 was regarded as outright theft of water by its Arab neighbours. The Palestine Liberation Organisation's (PLO) first ever attack was directed against the NWC on 1 January 1965 (JVL 2006). Nasser–led Syrian attempts to divert Hasbani flows away from the Upper Jordan River that same year were thwarted by Israeli Air Force attacks. Ensuing skirmishes persisted to within one year of the June 1967 war, despite US promises of arms for Israel in exchange for ceasing the attacks (US Embassy 1965). Although it was not primarily motivated by hydraulic concerns (el Musa 1997), the 1967 capture of land gave Israel control of the entire territory on both shores of the Upper Jordan River, the headwaters of the Banias River, the west shore of the Lower Jordan River and the Western, North Eastern and Eastern Aquifer Basins.[52]

1967–1995: The Israeli Domination Era

The outcome of the 1967 war radically altered the region's hydropolitical map: it brought an end to the skirmishing of previous years; reduced "feelings of insecurity" in Israel; and marked the beginning of what Feitelson calls the "Israeli Hegemony Era" (Feitelson 2000: 350). Given the fact that relations during this period were between an occupier and an occupied (and no equality was pretended), what Feitelson may be implying is more accurately described as 'empire' or 'domination'. He accentuates the importance of power relations between the two entities from the outset of this period:

> The outcome of the six–day war changed both the hydrostrategic relationship of Israel and her neighbours, and the power balance between them. …This change in Israeli hydrostrategic situation and its evident military superiority effectively prevented the Arab side from challenging Israel's water plans or use (Feitelson 2000: 350).

Feitelson's quote also testifies to the ever–growing 'projectable' deterrent power that Israel had accumulated relative to its neighbouring Arab states. From a hydropolitical point of view, the significance of the 1967 Israeli conquest of Palestinian land, and of the resources that came with it, cannot be underemphasised. In contrast to the previously tumultuous era, Israeli public interest in water issues after the war all but evaporated. Most Israelis were not even aware of the discrepancies between Palestinian and Israeli water consumption. "As a result of the [June 1967] war", states Feitelson, "Israel gained control over most of the contested water sources, and hence the perceived external threat to Israel's water supply faded. Subsequently, water virtually disappeared from the public agenda"[53] (Feitelson 2002: 302).

This post–1967 period also marked the beginning of the widening discrepancy between Israeli agricultural water consumption and its contribution to the Israeli economy. While the net product of the agricultural sector continued to grow rapidly, other sectors of the Israeli economy vastly overtook it, so that by 2005 it represented about 1.5 per cent of total Israeli GNP (IMOA 2001). The gap was to become the basis of an intense internal debate that was to develop in the 1990s.

One of the main reasons given for continued Israeli water consumption throughout this period – Israeli responsibility to provide water for the Palestinians suddenly under its control (Soffer 1994, cited in Feitelson 2000: n14) – may conceal a second factor that was to become key to the future shape of the water conflict: the intensification of the occupation itself. Hydraulic development of the West Bank and Gaza, from 1967 onwards, was driven by the contending forces of Israeli political–military interests and Israeli responsibility towards the inhabitants of the land the state occupied. An additional driving force behind Israeli policy relations was the hydraulic needs of the Jewish settler movement, which was beginning to colonise the West Bank in ever–increasing numbers (Segal 2003, Feitelson 2005, pers. comm.). The Israeli approach to its humanitarian responsibilities, as we will see in Chapter 9, was to pursue strategies of ever–greater resource capture, and to contain Palestinian challenges to them, with the effect of consolidating the control it had gained over the transboundary resources.

A series of Israeli military orders, put into place immediately following the 1967 war, were the first successfully imposed controls ever to be placed on Palestinian water production.[54] As Sharif el Musa notes, "with such legal tools, Israel did not need to declare formally that the water resources of the Palestinian territories were state property, and it thus could avoid formally annexing them" (1997: 267). The Civil Administration of the Israel Defence Forces took over operation of the Jordanian founded and Palestinian–staffed West Bank Water Department. .

This era was also witness to several key political events: increased immigration of Jews to Israel; the 1979 peace between Egypt and Israel; and the effective abandonment of the Palestinian cause by other Arab States. The impact of the resulting Israeli dominance on Palestinian development was severe, particularly in the agricultural sector in the West Bank and the 'de–development' of Gaza (Roy 1995). Israel had established the political conditions in the region it needed in order to be able to complete its 'hydraulic mission' by the early 1970s. By this time is was exploiting the resource to its maximum sustainable limits, with the design per capita consumption used by Israeli hydraulic engineers rising from 80 to 100 cubic metres per year. Actual consumption in the occupied Palestinian territories hovered around 35 m3/y during this period[55] (el Musa 1997: 269).

In contrast to their declining symbolic significance in the founding ideologies of Labour and Political Zionism, the importance of water issues among Palestinians became increasingly central to a heightened sense of national identity vis–à–vis Israel. El Musa (1997) notes that transgressions against such identity may have run deep:

> Israel's stringent curbs on Palestinian access to water … made the denial of water, like land confiscation, seem like an integral part of its endeavour to dispossess them … Symbolically, water has become for the Palestinians another sphere of Israeli injustice toward them (el Musa 1997: 287).

Individual and collective Palestinian resentment to the 'order of things' established by the occupying Israeli forces was fuelled by the extension of Israeli dominance of Palestinian water affairs to pricing and institutional control. Jan Selby, for instance, points out how Israeli settlers were paying one third the cost for domestic water charged to Palestinians, and receiving even larger subsidies for agricultural water (2003a: 80). A sense of injustice grew with awareness that the Palestinian–operated West Bank Water Department served the purposes of the Israeli Civil Administration more than those of the Palestinian West Bank inhabitants. Palestinian claims that Israeli intentions were to maintain a weak Palestinian institutional capacity are supported by considerations of the crippling measures imposed by Ariel Sharon. As Minister of Agriculture until 1981, Sharon implemented a policy of not hiring Palestinian hydrogeologists (el Musa 1997: 272) and dismantling the Palestinian well–drilling department (Nassereddin 2005, pers. comm.).

The stark contrast between the impressive hydraulic development for Israel and Israeli settlers with the stifling and stalled development of the Palestinian water sector continued throughout the decades of military occupation. By 1991, however, the special status enjoyed by the Agricultural sector in Israel since 1948 was being questioned openly by the Israeli public (Ben–Zvi, et al. 1998), particularly in the wake of the 1989–1991 drought [56] and the beginning of political negotiations with Palestinians and Jordan (Wolf 2000a: 102).

The outcome of the negotiations with the Palestinians proved to be a historic turning point, though perhaps not one as significant in re–shaping the hydropolitical atmosphere as the capture of the Jordan headwaters in 1967: "Palestinian water rights" were recognised (1995 Oslo II Agreement, Article 40, Paragraph 1). The Oslo II Agreement also spawned two institutions that were to shape Palestinian–Israeli water activity over the following decade – the Palestinian Water Authority and the Joint Water Committee. By creating a Palestinian counterpart with formal equality, Israel's control of transboundary flows shifted in form – both in definition and practice – from 'domination' to 'hegemony'.

1995–2005: The Israeli Hegemony Era

Having briefly increased after the dry period of 1989–1991, Israeli public interest in water issues, was on the retreat again by 2000.[57] Reflecting the internal tensions that generated them, Israeli water policy in 2003 was still sending out mixed signals. These include, on the one hand, the 2002 threats made against Lebanon's small–scale plans to draw on its Wazzani Springs for drinking water, (see Chapter 7) and against the previously mentioned proposals for mega–projects to import water from Turkey in 2003. On the other hand there were a number of scientifically rational achievements such as increased wastewater re–use, the squeezing out of yet more 'dollars per drop' in agriculture, and the long-anticipated dawn of the desalination era, with the Ashqelon desalination plant in 2005. The confusion created in the sector by these polarised tendencies may be what led to the characterisation of the current water discourse in Israel as "fragmented" and "muddled" (Feitelson 2002: 306).

The trend identified within this murky context does not bode well for the future of water security in the region – a renewed commitment by most elements of the Israeli water sector to a supply–side water management paradigm through freshwater imports and the manufacturing of 'new' water. In other words, creative technological fixes devised to fuel the ever–increasing demand (which we shall see is driven primarily by the Agricultural sector) gain more currency in the Israeli Parliament (the Knesset) than do attempts to curb it. Water demand management may be promoted throughout the Middle East, but is rarely practised. Itay Fischhendler (forthcoming–a) identifies continued over–abstraction during this period as a response to political pressure coming primarily from the agricultural lobby. The reason most often invoked for reducing the allocation cuts to the agricultural sector by the Israeli water commissioner, the epistemic community, members of parliament and farmers is "state security" (Fischhendler forthcoming–a: Table 3). Despite the state's heavy dependence on virtual water imports, the ideal of food self–sufficiency and notions of threats from neighbouring riparian countries continue to shape Israeli water policy. This is reflected in the most commonly heard discourses, as we shall soon see.

Developments in water issues on the Palestinian side during this period, once again differ significantly. The first significant Palestinian attempts at 'national' development of the water sector throughout the West Bank and Gaza were made in 1995 by the Palestinian Water Authority (PWA). The newly-formed PWA inherited the triple burden of a responsibility to meet the water needs of over three million Palestinian citizens, an under-developed water sector, and an inequitable distribution of the resource with its Israeli counterparts. Its response was an attempt to embark upon a Palestinian 'hydraulic mission' intended to develop the resource in accord with the principles of Integrated Water Resources Management and to provide water for all citizens. Approximately US$830 million of donor assistance was invested in the water sector between 1996 and 2002 (PWA 2003b). PWA reports claim that its accomplishments include: a) the founding and development of the PWA as an institution; b) a 30 per cent increase in total water production; c) a 5–20 per cent reduction of losses in networks; and d) a general increase in water-network coverage (PWA 2003a). The PWA may further point to the public acclaim it has received for what many regard as exemplary cooperation amongst ex-enemies through the Joint Water Committee (IMFA 1999, JWC 2001, Shamir 2004) and participation in many donor-funded joint water initiatives.

Actual accomplishments in the Palestinian water sector are somewhat less rosy than their portrayal in reports. Though total water production might have increased (and there is debate about this), average per capita consumption during the same period has dropped (Attili and Phillips 2004); 200,000–225,000 people in over 100 communities remain unconnected to networks (B'tselem 2001), and the quality of water continues to decrease, particularly in Gaza (al Farra 2005, Madhoun 2005). Also, the prestige of water institutions has suffered from the fact that the Oslo II Agreement never matured to the intended Permanent Status negotiations. Originally scheduled for 2000, the failure to progress in this area has fuelled popular Palestinian resentment about the lack of any redress for the asymmetrical distribution of the shared resources. The population was, in any case, quite aware that the "Palestinian water rights" recognised by Israel in the 1995 Oslo II Agreement were never quantified, not to mention implemented. Palestinian water professionals attempting to implement Integrated Water Resource Management methods over a geography still very much controlled by Israel have been routinely frustrated by the skewed licensing procedure of the Joint Water Committee (as we shall see in Chapter 6). While they may have dropped off the Israeli public's radar, hydropolitical tensions in Palestine during this period continued to simmer in a low-intensity and unresolved conflict.

We recall that the Palestinian–Israeli water conflict does not take place in a vacuum, but in a highly politicised environment determined by both international and domestic forces. It is to the internal forces active on both sides that we now turn.

Internal Israeli Tensions – The Agricultural Lobby

The very complex and intricate decision-making process of the Israeli water sector has been well documented in the literature. The institutional structure includes the 1959 Israel Water Law as well as the roles and responsibilities of the office of the Water Commissioner, the Ministry of National Infrastructures, the Israel Water Commission and the over 30 members of the Water Board. Academic Arnon Soffer (2002) lists some of the major players (which he refers to as "pressure groups"): Mekoroth, Tahal, the moshavim and kibbutzim, Arab agricultural organisations, environmental organisations, the Israeli Defence Forces, universities, etc.

Several conflicts and debates occur between the groups. Each is involved, to some degree, in jockeying for influence over internal Israeli water allocation policy. The traditional lines of this internal Israeli water conflict are drawn between the agricultural lobby and those groups advocating economical or scientific rational use of water. The 2002 Israeli Parliamentary Committee Inquiry found, for example, that Water Commissioners are frequently chosen on the grounds of their being either pro or anti the agricultural lobby, depending on the outlook of the government in power (PCIIWS 2002). More recently, environmental organisations have entered the fray to lobby for ecological allocations. The Ministry of Finance is philosophically at odds with the agricultural lobby, yet it maintains a very distinct position from those water scientists promoting desalination. Schnell points to one of the effects of these conflicting pressures: "Israeli decision-makers have persistently refused to reduce consumption to levels compatible with existing renewable resources. Instead they insist on increasing water supply by expensive means like desalination, while allowing over-pumping and deterioration in the quality of the natural reservoirs" (2001: 215).

The criticism is rather poignantly exemplified by the findings of the Parliamentary Committee. The candid and introspective review of Israeli water policy is telling, not least of all for one of the conclusions it emphatically draws:

> The Committee rejects the claim, as if "a spendthrift agriculture" is the cause of the crisis in the Israeli water sector, and that the crisis may be resolved by means of drastic cuts to agriculture, or its liquidation. In the eyes of the Committee, agriculture has a Zionist-strategic-political value, which goes beyond its economic contribution (PCIIWS 2002: 12).

Ideology, it seems, continues to trump rational scientific or economic policy at the Israeli Parliamentary level, forty years after the 'Ideological Era' was supposed to have come to an end. Fischhendler documents the effects of these internal Israeli tensions: he discloses the consistent gap between the freshwater allocation cuts to the agricultural sector proposed by the Israel Water Commission, and the much smaller cuts actually implemented in the wake of pressure from the agricultural lobby (forthcoming–a: Figure 3). He convincingly demonstrates that the institutional structure of the Israeli water sector[58] allows the politicisation of the allocation process and encourages widespread manipulation of the notion of state security (Fischhendler forthcoming–a: 24). Competition between roughly equally legitimate and powerful actors creates conditions which are ripe indeed for the politicisation of their respective objectives. So, while internal tensions generate debate and a healthy reflexive discourse within the Israeli community, sustainable resource regulation remains a distant goal.

Internal Palestinian Tensions – Challenged Legitimacy
Like its Israeli counterpart, the Palestinian water sector is composed of numerous active and contending social groups. Tensions between them stem, in part, from

the administrative legacy left by the many governments which have over ruled the land and its resources. There was a lack of central authority control under the Ottoman empire until 1919, weak central control during the British Mandate period until 1948, minimal control or development under Jordanian and Egyptian rule until 1967, and full control during the Israeli occupation until 1995. The competing groups include private well-owners, municipalities, the West Bank Water Department, agricultural co-operatives, environmental NGOs, and – most recently – the Palestinian Ministry of Agriculture, the Ministry of Planning and the PWA.

The complexity of the Palestinian water sector increases when one considers other factors, such as the significant tensions created when the PWA 'outsiders' inherited the considerable challenge of managing the water system[59] (el Musa 1997). An illustrative case is the national Water Law, signed by the Palestinian Authority (PA) in 2002. Palestinian water NGOs were excluded from the development of the law, to such an extent that they were entirely unaware of its being drafted.[60] A poor separation of powers also hampers governance in the Palestinian water sector: There are important differences between the theoretical structure envisaged by the 2002 Water Law, and the confused reality of the situation three years later (see Figure 4.1).

Figure 4.1   Theory and reality of governance structures of the Palestinian water sector.

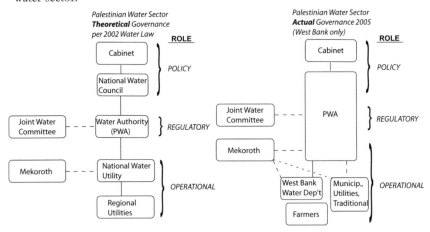

(After Eng. Fadel Kawash and PA Water Law, March 2002).

The 2002 Water Law was passed despite mildly-voiced resistance from the larger municipalities and expressions of concern from then PA chairman Yasser Arafat about the utility of passing a law upon a resource over which Palestinians did not have full control (Bossier 2005). Such procedures contribute to an increasing questioning of the legitimacy of the PA, as well as the PWA. Legitimacy, we recall, was identified as a key feature of bargaining power (Chapter 3).

The legitimacy of the PWA is further called into question by individual well-owners and those families that administer traditional water-sharing arrangements (Trottier 1999: 164), particularly in Gaza. Its shaky political standing is all the more poignant considering that its authority is not based on technical competence, viewed as weak by many of the more experienced engineers of the WBWD. Jan Selby (2003b) offers a more blunt perspective: "In many respects … the PWA is little more than a donor construct, its main responsibility being to coordinate donor projects, and the vast majority of its personnel being employed on a project basis" (Selby 2003b: 134).

Unlike the relatively healthy and reflexive in-fighting over water allocations characteristic of the strong, centrally governed Israeli water sector, debates in the Palestinian water sector reflect the weaknesses of centralised governance under the PA and the questioned legitimacy of the PWA. Palestinian municipalities and families in fact still retain some of the power that the PWA continues to attempt to wrest away from them through new legislation.

Contending Hydropolitical Discourses

The internal Palestinian struggles take place within a context in which they have to contend with even stronger discourses voiced by the Israeli and international communities. There are, in fact, several distinct Palestinian and Israeli water narratives active in the conflict: Some are diametrically opposed, and clash outright, but otherwise rarely cross paths; others align themselves in coalitions to exclude more independent ones. Each, in fact, is an expression of ideational power – a bid to ensure the compliance of the other through the force of ideas. The dominant discourse in the latest period of the water conflict is generated by the Israeli side, and is termed *Needs, not Rights* for its advocacy of basic Palestinian water needs, and against Palestinian water rights. It finds support amongst international donors interested in 'developing' the sector, and it became 'sanctioned' by the powers-that-be. As we shall see, the sanctioned discourse eventually also holds sway over the official Palestinian discourse, muting the voices of the more strident proponents of Palestinian water rights. The once predominant, and belligerent, narrative of Israelis opposed to cooperation with Palestinians also faded somewhat, but does appear to be making something of a comeback.

Israeli Hydrostrategic Discourse

Trottier (2003: 8) points out how different groups can benefit from discourses of either 'water peace' or 'water war'. In the case being reviewed here, dramatic discourses of the latter variety have been voiced by many, primarily by proponents of Israeli expansion opposed to negotiations with or concessions to Palestinians. This group puts forward hydrostrategic arguments to support their political views, arguing that giving up all or parts of the West Bank threatens Israeli control over water – and by extension, Israeli state security. Wolf (1995: 73) has defined 'hydrostrategy' as the influence of the location of water resources on strategic thinking. He gives the example of the map prepared by ex-Israeli Water Commissioner Menachem Cantor for the first Camp David negotiations (Figure 4.2). The map indicates which territory Israel should retain in order to keep its control over critical water resources. In the West Bank, this includes the prime water-rich areas of the Western Aquifer, which Palestinians have been prevented from developing since 1967, and over which the Separation Wall runs today (as we will discuss further in Chapter 5).

Hydrostrategic views are held by a range of authors approaching the conflict from various perspectives, including Sherman (1999), Kiser (2000), Zaslavski (2002), Sitton (2001), Frisch (2002), Alpher (1994, in Wolf 2000a) and others. The use of evidence-based argument by some of these authors is known to be in short supply.[61] A well-documented example of extreme views is the case of the 1990 Israeli Ministry of Agriculture advertisement in the Jerusalem Post, promoting what Minister Rafael Eitan called a "reasonable survival instinct" to justify his position against negotiations with the Palestinians (Sherman 1999: 29). More recently, Eitan has accused the PA of threatening a "water intifada" (Harel 2002). An anti-negotiations stance was taken by academic Hillel Frisch in 2002, who concluded his paper given at the Begin–Sadat Centre for Strategic Studies as follows:

> Burdening Israel with further obligations [to relinquish more control over water resources] stemming from another round of "peace" agreements would place solving the augmented deficit completely within the realm of science fiction. As [Israeli water academic Martin] Sherman rightly points out, demand for water in Israel is not only inelastic, but high water consumption is necessary to provide the lifestyle that justifies the sacrifice citizens make to Israel's security (Frisch 2002: 20).

Such security-based calls for increased consumption are not common in Israel, though the use of constructed knowledge to further political gains may be.[62] Twelve years after Eitan staked out his position, a remarkably similar stance was adopted by Jossef Dreizin, Director of Water Planning at the Israel Water Commission. Dreizin warned, in 2004, against the consequences of following through with the Likud government's 'Disengagement' Plan from Gaza and four settlements from the West Bank: he stated that withdrawal from the settlements in the North Eastern Aquifer Basin "will be a final blow to Israel's water economy in the Gilboa, Harod and Beit She'an areas"; and that a substantial financial investment will be required "in developing alternative water sources and transporting water to the area" (Yitzhak 2004). Considering the hydrogeology of this aquifer and the well-established effective Israeli control over the NEAB (Chapter 3), such pronouncements by a technical decision-maker are clear testimony of ulterior political agendas. Though evidence of hydrostrategic discourse abounds, a less provocative discourse held greater sway over Israeli water policy vis-à-vis Palestinians in the first years after Oslo.

Figure 4.2   'Hydrostrategic' territory for Israel in the West Bank.

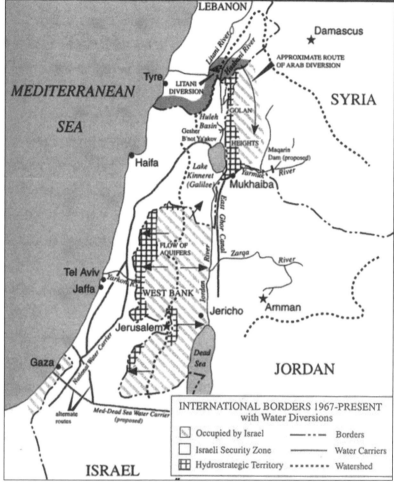

(Adapted from Cantor, in Wolf 2000a: 99).

Israeli Needs, not Rights Discourse

The hydrostrategic discourse advocating increased control over water resources has been countered during the Oslo period by many Israeli actors who advocate cooperation with Palestinians. This ensemble of groups has generated a *Needs, not Rights* discourse, so called due to its two main features: a) an acceptance that there are legitimate Palestinian domestic needs and, b) a refusal to countenance Palestinian water rights.

While this latter group opposes the proponents of the hydrostrategic narrative on issues of internal Israeli water allocations and in the approach taken to Palestinians, there is considerable common ground between the two. Arnon Soffer

(2002), for instance, points to a clear Israeli consensus on the issue of water cooperation with its neighbours, stating that there is "no debate [amongst the various elements of the Israeli water sector] about the need to share the water with our neighbours based on agreements made" (2002: 34). Likewise, Feitelson remarks that members of the Israeli Knesset who "differ on Israeli–Palestinian issues can still form a coalition on water issues" (Feitelson 2005a: 418). Such views and ideas recall those of the period of cautious optimism that came at the height of the political processes in the early 1990's, expressed in such works as Lonergan and Brooks (1994) or Amery and Wolf (2000). The consensus is clearly centred around Palestinian *domestic* water needs, however, and not developmental or agricultural ones.

The consensus extends to the rejection of Palestinian water rights. Prior to the water resource control Israel enjoyed after the 1967 capture of land, the concept of water rights was frequently drawn upon by Israeli individuals and organisations. From Pinhas Rutenberg's attempts to maintain water-use concessions for hydro-electric projects on the Jordan and Yarmouk for his Palestine Electric Corporation (FO 371/104953 1953) to Israeli state large-scale development plans (see e.g. Tahal 1959, US Embassy 1965, Stork 1983: 24, Arlosoroff 2000: 60, Medzini 2001: 62), the 'right' to water was in one way or another usually acquired.

Israeli aversion to the term 'water rights' seems to have developed following the 1967 war, and appears to be based on practical utility, rather than principle. So strong is the sentiment against using the term that the 1994 Jordan–Israel Peace Treaty was finalised with compromise wording specifying "rightful allocations" instead of 'rights'[63] (Schwarz 2004). Given the reticence, it is somewhat surprising to find in the Israel–Palestine Oslo II Agreement the explicit statement "*Israel recognises the Palestinian water rights in the West Bank*" in the first sentence of Paragraph 1 of Article 40. The contradiction requires explanation.

One view amongst Israelis who negotiated the Agreement is that their acceptance of an agreement recognising Palestinian water rights was a "mistake", and occurred because of a mix-up in strategies between different Israeli negotiators active on the multi- and bi-lateral tracks[64] (Fischhendler forthcoming–a: 18). A more radical view has it that "by the explicit recognition of Palestinian water rights Israel has opened …a Pandora's box and created the most dangerous precedent in her history" (Starr, in Sherman 1999: 100). Either way, ten years after Israeli recognition of Palestinian water rights, and despite claims to the contrary (e.g. IMFA 1999), they remain unquantified, unfulfilled and, in effect, denied. Apart from being considered a mistake, Palestinian water rights are also characterised as a "dream" (Soffer 2005, pers. comm.) and a "joke" (Arlosoroff 2005, pers. comm.), even by those otherwise pre-disposed to cooperation with Palestinians. In the same light, attempts to raise the subject at international fora are openly and routinely side-stepped or otherwise dismissed as 'unhelpful'; and this despite numerous and repeated attempts by Palestinians and the international academic community to put the discussion on the agenda.

Enjoying the support of groups otherwise opposed to each other, the *Needs, not Rights* narrative has become the discourse dominating the sector. It is advanced as the official policy of the Israel Water Commission, with the full support of the Palestinians' largest donor, as we shall see. As such, it is the discourse that is brought to bear most forcefully on the Palestinian side, which has its own variety of paradigms.

Palestinian Cooperation Discourse

Trottier notes how the PWA uses "parallel sanctioned discourses", showing that different discourses are promoted according to the receiving audience. She identifies one dialogue, revolving around nation-building development projects, with the international donor community, and another, centred on the exploitation of political capital and emphasising the unfairness of the Israeli occupation policies, with the local community. Allouche borrows a term from Wolf to denote a different active narrative – what he calls "water nationalism". Allouche states that Palestinian proponents of this discourse insist upon absolute sovereignty over all water within the borders of Palestine, resulting in them taking a position that "despite their legitimate concerns, is certainly a main deadlock in reaching a solution" (Allouche 2004: 295).

Evidence of resentment of Israeli policy towards Palestinians in the water sector is readily found in unofficial PWA declarations and interviews with PWA staff. There is scant evidence of it, however, in the official literature or in practice. The analytical attention paid to the informal discourse has tended to miss the fact that the PWA is in fact following a third distinct and clearly elucidated discourse – one of cooperation with their Israeli counterparts. Evidence of the commitment of the official Palestinian side to cooperation is the continued PWA presence at the Joint Water Committee, as well as the endorsing of the 2001 'Joint Declaration of Protection' for protecting water infrastructure from armed combat (JWC 2001). This cooperation was maintained throughout periods of extensive destruction to the Palestinian water sector, and otherwise undignified circumstances, as we will see in Chapters 5 and 6. Further evidence of an official Palestinian discourse of cooperation is offered by the PWA's tacit agreement not to go public with any of the coercive behaviour active at JWC meetings (see Chapter 6). Support for the PWA *Cooperation* discourse does not come from those elements of Palestinian civil society that question the legitimacy of the PWA, but certainly does come from their Israeli counterparts and the international donor community.

If the Palestinian *Cooperation* discourse has been be overlooked or under-emphasised, it may be for reasons relating to the nature of power, as discussed in Chapter 2. It may be due to an unquestioned acquiescence to the 'existing order of things' amongst those examining it. Any implications that the main obstacles to political settlement are Palestinian demands in the face of Israeli domination, rather than the domination itself, speak of a tacit consent to the established order of things. In any case, there is a much louder discourse voiced within Palestinian civil society, one that directly contradicts the Israeli *Needs, not Rights* discourse.

Palestinian Rights First Discourse

It was, perhaps, wholly predictable from a realist perspective that Palestinian claims for water rights increased after the 1967 land conquest while Israeli claims for rights fell away (see previous section). The most vocal calls for attaining Palestinian water rights comes from groups within Palestinian, Israeli and international civil society. These include the Palestinian NGOs Palestinian Hydrology Group, the Applied Research Institute of Jerusalem, the Water and Environment Organisation, the Palestinian Academic Society for the Study of International Affairs, and the Palestinian Environmental NGO Network; and Israeli NGOs B'tselem, the Galilee Society and Physicians for Human Rights and international organisations like the New York-based Centre for Economic and Social Rights.

The call is echoed in the founding development plans of various bureaux that form the Palestinian Authority, which may be considered the equivalent to the ambitious Israeli hydraulic plans of the 1950s. No less than eight master plans for development of the sector based on the acquisition of the water along with the rights are found in publications from the Palestinian Ministry of Planning, the Palestinian Council for Reconstruction and Development and the Palestinian Water Authority. Each plan either proposes or refers to a Palestinian national water strategy that may be summarised thus: *the attainment of water rights followed by or along with the development of new sources.* This strategy is most explicitly spelled out in documents prepared by the European-funded Negotiations Support Unit of the Palestine Liberation Organisation, and has been presented on numerous occasions at international fora.

In what may be a classic case of discourses colliding, the informal Palestinian *Rights First* narrative is at odds with the official Palestinian *Cooperation* narrative. The contradicting messages may be explained by considering a) that the PWA is maintaining parallel discourses aimed at different audiences, and b) the PWA has shifted its discourse during the Israeli Hegemony Era towards *Cooperation*, in face of the pressures deriving from the Israeli *Needs, not Rights* discourse. On this latter point, it may be noted that PWA collisions with the relatively inconsequential *Rights First* discourse promoted by Palestinian civil society affect the institution much less than would a clash with the rather more influential Israeli *Needs, not Rights* discourse. And a large part of the influence of the Israeli discourse is gained from the support it derives from abroad, as discussed following.

Donors' Cooperation, not Rights Discourse

There is reason to believe that the PWA *Cooperation* narrative listened to by the international community is at least partly driven by that community itself. Donors' use of development funds to advance their own political goals is well documented in the literature of development studies and international development agencies, and donor-driven agendas are particularly evident in the politically charged world of donor assistance for Palestinians.[65] Given the 'high' politics going on beyond the water conflict, the inclination of donors to use official development assistance to pursue foreign policy goals is not surprising. The US, in particular, is well known to pursue such "chequebook diplomacy" (Lasensky 2005). Official declarations from the United States Agency for International Development (USAID) repeatedly and proudly claim, for instance, that they "have remained steadfast in implementing a multi-year program" of water and wastewater infrastructure development in Palestine[66] (USAID 2005). Yet, American financial investment cannot reasonably be divorced from US interests, especially considering their key mediation role as coordinator of the trilateral Tripartite (water) Committee. Belgian analyst Wilfrid Bossier notes, for example, that it may be

> no coincidence that the water sector is singled out by the World Bank and USAID "as an ideal sector for peace-making" … The fact that cooperation with the [Palestinian Authority] has not been halted [throughout the violence of 2001–2004] … and that the JWC remains active on the ground are telling the same story about keeping the flame of peace and cooperation alight, so that one day it may be rekindled (Bossier 2005: 22).

USAID efforts at ensuring continued cooperation in the water sector during the decade following the Oslo II Agreement may thus be linked with the stated policy of the US administration of promotion of political cooperation at all levels. This promotion of cooperation has manifested itself in ways not always seen as cooperative, however. There is no debate amongst international or Palestinian officials and technicians active in the Palestinian water sector that the US Embassy or USAID see little value in the Palestinian *Rights First* discourse, even when this was the official discourse of their client, the Palestinian Water Authority.

US intentions became most obvious during the water-related negotiations of the Camp David II summit in Maryland, mid-2000. Several of the negotiators present have detailed the US 'facilitation' of the discussions on water-related issues, which were actually held remotely from the other talks on topics of central relevance to the Permanent Status Agreement (in Emmetsburg). This arrangement was pre-ordained without Palestinian agreement, possibly because US officials believed that the water-related matters could 'poison' the attainment of an eventual Permanent Status Agreement, though there was a certain degree of water-trading under discussion (Lautze, et al. 2005). The primary US intervention arose while the late head of the PWA Nabil el Sharif was presenting the Palestinian view on the attainment of water rights, at a period well into the negotiations as a whole. Anonymous sources who were present testify that one of the US facilitators interrupted him, stating that the parties were debating irrelevant topics, and following this by writing the statement "US = $" on the whiteboard in the room. "This is what you should be discussing", she is claimed to have said, following up the admonishment with a warning that the parties should reach consensus rapidly because the main Agreement was within reach, noting further that the Palestinian negotiators on water were not permitted to speak to the main negotiators located in Camp David. The implication was clear to all: negotiating on principle is not pragmatic, as there is not enough water for everyone. The conflict can be resolved because water can be manufactured (through desalination), and the US will pay for this.

One may gather from the anecdote a close alignment of the American side with the Israeli *Needs, not Rights* narrative, and to a lesser degree the official Palestinian *Cooperation* narrative. We may label the hybrid discourse *Cooperation, not Rights*. The relatively marginal Palestinian *Rights First* and Israeli *Hydrostrategic* discourses do not currently match US interests, and could be expected to hold much less sway over American institutions and policy during this period.

A certain degree of 'co-evolution' between stated US foreign policy and the official discourses of Israelis and Palestinians may furthermore be expected. Promoters of the sanctioned discourse stand to make important gains by aligning interests and approaches. The consequences may be seen in the fading influence of the Palestinian *Rights First* discourse during the Israeli Hegemony Era and in the exclusion of dissenting opinions expressed at various Palestinian–Israeli fora otherwise designed for debate.

The influence of the *Needs, not Rights* extends beyond America, aligning other international donors into its coalition of support through a process of pragmatic attrition. Essentially every donor active in the water sector in Palestine has dealt with the issue of access being denied to their staff by the Israeli military authorities. Criticism is led by the World Bank, which has widely and repeatedly documented the effects of such Israeli policies on donor projects in a series of reports (e.g. the World Bank's *Two Years of Intifada, Closures and Palestinian Economic Crisis* was updated and re-published as *Twenty-seven Months of Intifada*, and later as *Thirty Six Months of Intifada*). The issue highlighted by these reports is that of 'donor fatigue', which follows from the daily struggle to implement projects and to progress from emergency programming to medium-term development projects. After repeated setbacks, and under sustained pressure from head offices to 'deliver', the locally-based foreign donor agencies end up acquiescing to the status quo. The donors eventually abandon their principled stances in support of plans originally promoted by the PWA or Palestinian water NGOs under a *Rights First* discourse, and instead prioritise those projects that are feasible under the current Israeli occupation. The former plans have in fact been rendered impracticable by the mechanics of the military occupation, which hinges on the use of hundreds of checkpoints and roadblocks to restrict the movement of Palestinian civilians and goods, including those required for the implementation of water projects. The result of donors' practical acquiescence, to the operational environment determined by the Israeli military, is that they become effective supporters of the *Cooperation, not Rights* discourse upheld by USAID. At some point, the evolving coalition of discourses becomes 'sanctioned' by most major players, exercising an indirect but important bearing on maintaining the asymmetric character of the water conflict.

Accumulation Through Dispossession or a Broader Strategy of Asymmetry?

The pragmatic attitude of proponents of the *Needs, not Rights* discourse can be encapsulated as follows: 'there is not enough water for all of us, so let's not talk about water rights. Let's cooperate to make the best of the situation'. This appeal has considerable sway. It effectively precludes any discussion of inequitable distribution, thereby perpetuating it, all the while presenting the approach as progressive and conciliatory. The status quo is the default position preferred by the more powerful.

We have seen that Israeli control over transboundary water resources has evolved from pre-1967 high intensity conflict, through domination during the occupation years, and hegemony from the 1995 Oslo II Agreement onwards. The situation may be compared to the ever-hungry and predatory nature of the capitalist system, what David Harvey (2005: Ch. 4) calls "accumulation through dispossession". New opportunities to make profits must constantly be made available, through continually opening up access to wider markets (especially where demand may be fabricated) and/or to reserves of cheaper labour.

Certainly, the gathering of Israeli control over water resources has come at the direct cost of a loss to the Palestinian side, both individuals and the collective. In that sense, the win–lose situation that has endured up to the present is a fitting example of 'accumulation through dispossession'. The limitations of Harvey's theory in relation to the Palestinian–Israeli water case are revealed with the realisation that ever-increasing control is *not* really possible. Apart from the springs that rise and flow solely within the West Bank, the Israeli side has controlled – directly or indirectly – essentially all of the transboundary resources from Lebanon to Jordan. There are real limits to which extensive control can be acquired.[67] There are now only qualitative ways to accumulate further control, i.e. fine tuning to make control more stable or more efficient. Efficiency may be increased, for example, through the release of more flows to the West Bank for the production of cheaper agricultural goods, thereby harnessing the competitive edge to be gained by paying cheaper Palestinian wages. Such 'accumulation through exploitation' is a research area worth examining in greater detail, but there is little evidence of the practice shaping Israeli policy in the sector.

British academic Mushtaq Khan provides compelling evidence of a general Israeli strategy of maintaining disparity with the Palestinian side at the broader political and economic level. Khan states that the "primary objective [of the Palestinian Authority under the Oslo process] was to negotiate the territorial and constitutional limits of a Palestinian quasi-state in the context of an extreme asymmetry of power and resources vis-à-vis Israel" (Khan 2004a: 43). Specific research will be required to prove that asymmetric containment of the Palestinian State as a general Israeli strategy applies also to the water sector. As we have seen, water has always held a high ideological value in Zionist ideology – from its earliest aspirations for the Litani River in Lebanon to the 'no-drilling' orders placed by the Israeli occupying authorities in 1967 and the current refusal by those who promote cooperation to consider re-allocation of transboundary flows with Palestinians. El Musa predicted the link between larger land concerns and the unintended effects on water: "all in all, when it comes to Israel's territorial aims in the West Bank, one cannot help think that after the rabbis feel redeemed, after the generals feel secure and the hydrologists' thirst is slaked, Palestinians will be left with a tattered West Bank fragment, insecure and dry" (1996: 77).

There is, furthermore, reason to believe that the whole settler project itself was directed by hydraulic concerns, indeed, its architect – Ariel Sharon – has essentially admitted as much. Asked in an in-depth 2001 interview whether a withdrawal of settlers from the West Bank would ever be a possibility, Sharon replied "Is it possible today to concede control of the Mountain [Western, Eastern and Northeastern] Aquifer[s], which suppl[y] a third of our water? Is it possible to cede the buffer zone in the Jordan Rift Valley? You know, it's not by accident that the settlements are located where they are." (Ari 2001). Consider the location of the two largest Israeli settlements in the West Bank – Ariel and Qadumim: each is located directly above the Eastern (upper) edge of the Western Aquifer Basin, as shown in Figure 3.1. Israeli wells drilled in these locations could effectively prevent some of the water from flowing westwards through Palestine. In that sense, the location of the settlements may be seen as an attempt to reverse Israel's 'downstream' and vulnerable position on the aquifer, by placing Israeli settlers 'upstream', directly over the top of the hydraulic divide.

The possibility of an intended strategy of contained asymmetry in the water sector is further supported by other considerations. Take, firstly, the hypothetical situation in which the roles are reversed – where the asymmetry of power still greatly favours Israel, but Palestinians control 90 per cent of the flows and sell whatever is beyond their needs to Israel. One would expect to hear hydrostrategic arguments being raised by Israeli side. These would be likely to prevail, as dependency on Palestinians would not be tolerated for long. Secondly, the technological advances in seawater desalination and wastewater re-use have not, to date, reduced the intensity of the water conflict. Despite the reduced pressure on freshwater resources due to the 'new' water flows, Israel has shown no interest in the possibility of re-allocating flows to the Palestinians. As Israeli groups take Israeli water policy in new directions, old, repeated and apparently intractable Palestinian claims for equitable distribution will continue to be seen as obstructive.

Were the current asymmetric distribution of transboundary waters not contained, Israeli policy-makers of all political persuasions would face the need to make compromises to achieve their visions in the sector. This, though, is only likely to occur if the discursive identification of water with security is shattered. It simply does not follow that asymmetrical containment in the water sector is a necessary condition for Israeli state security, or even progress in other sectors. Neither is inequitable distribution the inevitable result of the wider Israeli strategy of asymmetrically containing the Palestinian population. The point being made here is that the general strategy enables the particular policy – not the other way round. An imbalance in overall power (including an asymmetrically contained economy) enables a preferred mode of operation in the water sector for the powers-that-be. The following chapters present hard evidence that this preferred mode of operation is a 'fundamentally careful policy' towards Palestinians,[68] one that is maintained through multiple expressions of ideational, bargaining and hard power.

5

Hard Power – Coercing the Outcome

TWO very physical and concrete cases serve to exemplify expressions of hard power in the Palestinian–Israeli water conflict. We may recall from Chapter 2 that hard power refers to the brawn of the elephant, not its intellect, and is measured in terms of military might, economic strength, political support and riparian position. The case of the water infrastructure damaged during the Israeli military incursions into Jenin in 2002 serves to demonstrate how asymmetry in hard power can have disastrous effects for the elements of Palestinian civil society, while causing much less grief at the official Palestinian or international level. The second case, that of the Separation Wall built primarily inside of the West Bank, serves to demonstrate how power enables facts to be established, quite literally, 'on the ground'. It is not suggested that in either case that control over water resources was the motive for these expressions of hard power – we have seen how this control is already firmly established by Israel through other means such as territorial conquests and legislation. Each case serves to demonstrate instead the real effects of disparity in hard power – one side bears the brunt of the violence. Both cases also serve to demonstrate the failure of water officials on both sides to carry through the Joint Water Committee's 'Declaration of Protection,' made in 2000.

The JWC's Joint Declaration of Protection
Fourteen months prior to the most intense period of fighting throughout the West Bank and Gaza, representatives from both sides of the Israel–Palestine Joint Water Committee (JWC) made a highly publicised *Joint Declaration for Keeping the Water Infrastructure out of the Cycle of Violence*. Orchestrated by the United States Agency for International Development, Israeli and Palestinian water officials met on the border of Gaza to issue a declaration that reads in part:

> We call on the general public not to damage in any way the water infrastructure, including pipelines, pumping stations, drilling equipment, electricity systems and any other related infrastructure. The two sides also call on all those involved in the current crisis not to harm in any way the

professional teams that conduct regular maintenance or repair damages and malfunctions to the water and wastewater infrastructure (JWC 2001).

The 'Joint Declaration' is regularly upheld by many analysts as evidence that no matter what the politicians and the combatants may do to each other, the water officials carry on in a spirit of cooperation to keep water outside of the 'cycle of violence'. The message has been so often asserted in academic and policy fora that it has become almost a mantra, uncritically repeated by Israeli and Palestinian officials and 'joint' NGOs, such as the Israel–Palestine Centre for Research and Information. In direct violation of the spirit of the declaration, however, the months following its endorsement were characterised by extensive damage being inflicted upon Palestinian drinking water infrastructure and by the regular obstruction of Palestinian water repair crews throughout the West Bank and Gaza. The Separation Wall has also had significant effects by denying access of Palestinian farmers to their wells. In a classic example of a 'covenant without a sword' (see Chapter 2), the declaration did very little to secure the Palestinian crews or infrastructure, and it certainly failed to keep water out of harm's way. The declaration may have served more to veil the effects of the violent conflict rather than to reduce or mitigate it, a story we will return to in Chapter 6.

Damaged Water Infrastructure, Jenin April 2002 [69]

This section will explore the hard power of each riparian through an examination of the case of drinking water infrastructure damaged by the military activity that occurred primarily between the Israeli Defence Forces (IDF) and Palestinian factions from 2001 to 2003. Damage occurred throughout each city and many villages in Palestine, from Tulkarem to Rafah.[70] Our analysis focuses on the case of Jenin during the peak of destruction, in April 2002.

Description of Events and Damages

Drinking water systems in Jenin

Home to roughly 43,000 people, the Municipality of Jenin is situated on the northernmost hills of the West Bank, which form the foot with the Plains of Galilee, and the border with Israel. Jenin inhabitants are currently supplied with drinking-water from four main sources, as shown in Figure 5.1. In April 2002 the residents relied primarily upon the PWA Well (operated by the Water Department of the Municipality of Jenin) and private agricultural wells. Most of the private wells are located on the outskirts of the city, in the zone of less intense military activity. Many of these are 'illegal,' insofar as they were not licensed according to the procedure established by the Joint Water Committee under the terms of the Oslo II Agreement, and they are not operated by the Jenin Water Department. Residents of Jenin also depend on a water supply-line controlled by Mekoroth, fed by the three West Bank Water Department wells shown. Lying outside the zone of high intensity conflict, the priority for these three wells is to supply to the nearby Israeli settlements of Sa'nur, Qadim and Janim as well as some nearby Israeli military camps.[71] To a lesser degree, the Jenin Water Department also supplies water through the shallow 'Municipal Well', located in the city centre. The 'Jalame Filling Point' is a Mekoroth-controlled filling-point that enables water tankers to transport water to Jenin. It became operational a year after the events of 2002.

Figure 5.1   Schematic of Jenin Municipality drinking water system, 2003.

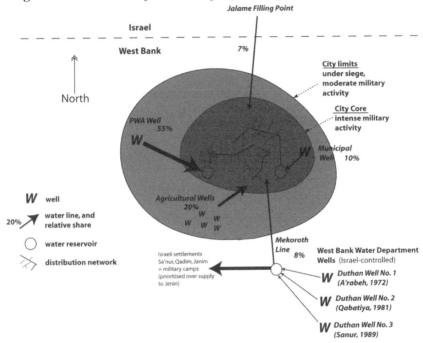

Events of April 2002

The Municipality of Jenin was invaded and occupied by the Israel Defence Forces (IDF) on three separate occasions in 2001 and 2002: from 8–15 September 2001; from 28 February–7 March 2002, and from 2–19 April 2002. Destined to become the subject of extensive international media interest, and to enter the annals of Palestinian history, the April 2002 'invasion of Jenin' resulted in the death of dozens of combatants from both sides and at least twenty-two Palestinian civilians (Amnesty International 2002). The incursion is also remembered for the magnitude and extent of physical destruction it inflicted – the demolition and bulldozing of 140 blocks of flats and the partial destruction of 200 more in the refugee camp, which left up to 4,000 people homeless (Amnesty International 2002). The dozens of tanks and bulldozers driven through narrow streets throughout the camp and city were also responsible for considerable damage to the water and wastewater

networks, depriving thousands of people of running water for up to two weeks, as
shown in Figure 5.2.

Figure 5.2 Number of people with water services disrupted, Jenin, April 2002.

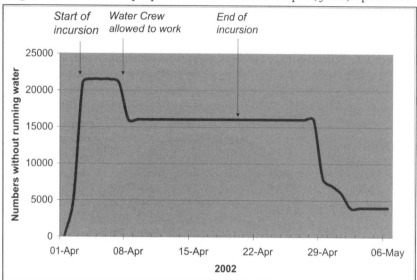

Description of damages

The April 2002 IDF campaign in Jenin was carried out by ground forces supported
by the Israel Air Force (IAF). Vehicles used included armoured personnel carriers
(APCs), Merkava–3 tanks and armoured Caterpillar D–9 bulldozers as well as
Apache and Cobra helicopters. The D–9 bulldozers were able to disrupt vehicle
traffic by digging trenches across main roads with their rear rippers or by piling
earth mounds across them. The D–9s also demolished the dozens of blocks of flats
and, along with the tanks, were the main cause of the destruction of the drinking-
water system.

Logs taken by Water Department emergency repair crews detailed the extent of the
damage to the municipality's infrastructure. An incomplete list includes:

• The 14-inch transmission line from the PWA well was dug up and damaged over
  a length of 60 metres.

• The 10-inch transmission line near the Telecom Centre (Haifa St.) was dug up
  and damaged over a length of 60 metres.

• The 6-inch mainline at the bottom of the Refugee Camp was dug up in at least
  one location.

• The 6-inch mainline near Dahliya Square was dug up and damaged over a length
  of 60 metres.

• The 3-inch mainline on the eastern edge of the Camp was dug up in several
  locations.

- The 4-inch mainline near al Sharkye and the Abu Snan chamber was damaged over a length of 180 metres.
- 2-inch lines were dug up in several locations (Haifa St., Al Sharqiya, Al Orme) over a total length of 3,000 metres in the City and 7,400 metres in the Refugee Camp.
- inch, ¾-inch and ½-inch distribution lines and house connections were damaged at numerous locations over a total estimated length of 3,600 metres in the City and 8,000 metres in the Camp.

Adapted from EWOC (2002).

The estimated cost of damage to the water infrastructure from the April 2002 incursion alone is US$ 2.1 million (World Bank 2002). The total estimated cost to water and wastewater systems during this and other incursions into Jenin between 2000 and 2003 is estimated to be US$7.6 million (IMG 2004).

IDF disruption of the attempts by the Jenin Water Department to repair the damage is also documented. The Palestinian operator of the PWA Well, for instance, was dismissed by the IDF tank crews, who occupied the well site to use it as a staging post for their troops and vehicles. Following repeated requests from the Jenin Water Department and the Palestinian Water Authority, the operator was allowed by the IDF to return three days later. Once able to operate the well, he was kept under guard on-site for weeks, until the end of the campaign. Upon withdrawal of Israeli troops from the well site, the Water Department found minor damage to the water testing equipment, and defecation in all rooms but the toilet.

The log, furthermore, details how the repair crews were regularly obstructed by IDF forces occupying the city. As a full curfew had been imposed upon the residents of the town, repair work by the Water Department was carried out only following close coordination with the commanding Israeli military authorities. In some cases, the repair work was carried out in the presence of certain squadron leaders, only to be destroyed again the same night by the same soldiers. This occurred on three separate occasions with an important valve junction in the al-Sharkiya neighbourhood, as seen in Photograph B4, Appendix B.

It is important to note that the only transmission line *not* to be damaged was the Mekoroth line. Despite requests by the Jenin Water Department, made through the PWA, to the Israeli water authorities to compensate for the water lost through the damaged pipes, no increase in supply through the Mekoroth line was made. Mekoroth continued to prioritise water delivery to the nearby settlements and military camps, despite the thousands of people in Jenin without any source of water at all.

Analysis of the Destruction

Indiscriminate and Deliberate Damages

The damage suffered by the water system due to military activity is not restricted to physical harm. It may be classified into the following categories: a) indiscriminate destruction of infrastructure, b) deliberate destruction of infrastructure, c) economic and d) political. Table B1 of Appendix B defines each classification, and offers evidence of the first two types.

Much of the damage suffered by the water infrastructure is evidently due to indiscriminate military activity. A certain amount of destruction is inevitable when dozens of 70 tonne tanks and armoured bulldozers career through crowded city streets. This kind of damages was substantial, given the vulnerability of Jenin's water supply system: many of its pipes are not buried (as we saw in Chapter 3). Most of the water lines that were buried were only deep enough to protect them from normal vehicular traffic, not military traffic, leading to hundreds of hard-to-detect pin-hole leaks. The countless water mains ripped up along with the road may also be classified as indiscriminate. The water mains that were damaged for longer stretches point to less indiscriminate intent. The obstruction of repair crews carrying out emergency work, as well as the repeated destruction of the emergency repair work, and even the destruction of repair equipment itself, can all also be considered deliberate disruption of water services.

Whether the deliberate acts of destruction were the actions of individual soldiers acting against orders, or a policy determined by the local commanding officer, remains to be clarified. Judging from the lack of destruction to the wells and reservoirs, it can be at least concluded that there was no clear IDF policy to systematically destroy the drinking-water system of Jenin. On the other hand, the reduced pressure in the water main arriving to the besieged city from the Israeli-controlled Mekoroth line, as well as the number of deliberate acts of destruction obliges one to consider whether or not the destruction was carried out intentionally. In all cases, the consequences of the armed conflict for the water system were severe.

Such destruction may be symptomatic of post-modern urban warfare. It is at the same time an axiomatic violation of International Humanitarian Law (IHL), which calls for the protection of "objects indispensable to the survival of the civilian population" during wartime (Chapter 2). Discussing the effects on water systems of other urban conflicts, field-worn humanitarian-aid water practitioners with the International Committee of the Red Cross (ICRC) regretfully conclude that it is "difficult to determine whether the shelling of water installations was deliberate or indiscriminate … The military advantage of any action depended on the kind of war that was being waged. It had been thought that the practice of cutting off water supplies, prevalent in the Middle Ages, had been rendered obsolete by the moralization of war. Unfortunately, it was becoming clear that any such hope was illusory" (Nembrini 1995: 50).

The nature of the damage suffered by the water infrastructure in Jenin contrasts considerably with the extensive destruction to exposed water towers in southern Lebanon in 2006. IDF forces there destroyed or damaged at least fifty such reservoirs (Unicef 2006), provoking considerable speculation that this was part of a campaign aimed at either getting the civilian population to leave, or at least to not return. The Israel Air Force destruction of Gaza's sole electrical plant in June 2006 appears just as deliberate, and proved even more disruptive to water supply. Such violations of IHL are well documented, but the keepers of the Geneva Conventions (the ICRC), like the victims themselves, have had little success in countering the power of fighter jets, tanks and bulldozers.

Heightened Internal Tensions

The destruction suffered in Jenin is even more revealing when considered at the political level. The damage inflicted upon the water infrastructure may have heightened existing internal Palestinian divisions (Chapter 4) between the local service-provider (the Municipality of Jenin) and the national water authority (the PWA). The damage suffered by the municipality exposed the inability of the PWA to effectively mitigate (let alone to counter) the destruction, despite the spirit of the very public JWC 'Joint Declaration'. From their offices in Ramallah and Gaza, the heads of the PWA were not able to use the offices of the JWC to have more water released to Jenin via the Israeli-controlled, undamaged, Mekoroth line. The PWA, moreover, neglected to publicise the Israeli violations of the JWC declaration or the break-down in cooperation with its Israeli counterpart. Such behaviour can be explained, in part, by the Palestinian water authorities' concern not to jeopardise the delicate relationship they enjoyed with the Israelis through the JWC.

The Results of Asymmetry of Hard Power

The fate of Jenin can also be seen as a direct result of the extreme asymmetry in hard power between the Palestinian and the Israeli sides. The repeated military incursions were, in the first instance, an expression of Israeli military superiority. The Israeli military forces used their machinery to impose a tight siege upon the city which, in many cases, prevented municipal crews and humanitarian-aid agencies from reaching the theatre of operations. Furthermore, as this theatre was a civilian sector of Palestine, it is noteworthy (if self-evident) that damage to the water infrastructure occurred solely on the Palestinian side, and not at all within the political borders of Israel. The nature and outcome of the conflict is likely to have been considerably different given a reversal of the situation, i.e. if Palestinian forces had been destroying parts of the water network of the nearby Israeli city of Afula. The asymmetry in hard power extends to relations between Palestinian and Israeli water authorities, practitioners and academics. Neither of these held any influence during the height of the military activity, despite the good intentions stated in the JWC Joint Declaration. The failure of water officials from both sides to provide additional water through the Mekoroth line further reveals the extent to which water issues were subordinated to military interests during this time

The Wall

The second example of an expression of hard power in relation to the Palestinian–Israeli water conflict is the case of the 'Separation Wall'. The Wall – as it is most commonly referred to, though it is also known as the 'separation fence', 'the fence', or 'the Apartheid wall' – is built from eight metre high pre-cast concrete panels in some sections, barbed wire and electrified fence in others. Both wall and fence sections are accompanied by trenches, IDF patrol roads, watchtowers and electronic surveillance zones, in an expensive and elaborate effort to physically separate Palestinians from Israelis (Gregory 2004), and is shown in Figure 5.3.

Figure 5.3   Israel's Separation Wall in the West Bank, May 2006.

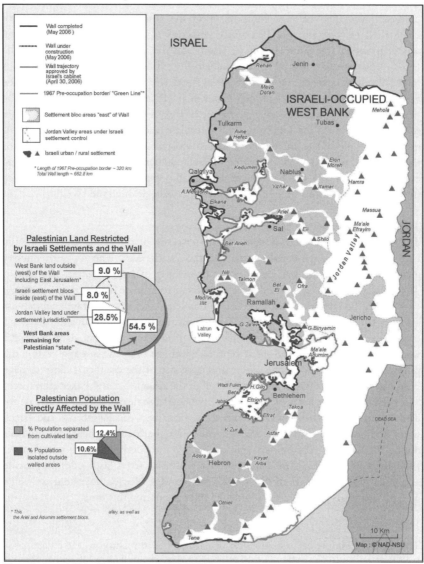

Negotiations Affairs Department (NSU 2005a).

The wall, initiated in 2002 by the Labour government, by mid 2005 was over 200 kilometres long, 80 per cent of which is located inside the West Bank. Over 5,300 Palestinians are caught living between the Wall and the border of Israel, and it is estimated that 280,000 Palestinians will be separated from their land by the time the intended 680 kilometre route is complete (NSU 2005a).

Figure 5.4 Israel's Separation Wall around Qalqilya, November 2003.

Palestinian Hydrology Group

Arguments for and against the wall are heated. Many Palestinians and Israelis claim the wall is a 'land grab', as it had informally annexed 6.1 per cent of the West Bank's most fertile lands by 2004. The Israeli government claims it is to protect Israeli citizens living in Israel, or Israeli settlers living inside the West Bank. Many others, though, claim it is a 'water grab'. As it is located along the most productive parts of the rich Western Aquifer, there seems some basis to this latter view, particularly given the hydrostrategic maps and interests of the 1970s (Figure 4.2).

A closer look from a hydraulic perspective at the effect of the Wall around Qalqilya is revealing. Figure 5.4 offers a close-up view of the wells seen in Figure 3.2, with the Wall winding through them. The first feature to note is that there is no evident relation between the route of the wall and the location of the Palestinian wells. Nineteen wells belonging to residents of Qalqilya have been put out of access by the Wall, while many others remain on the 'Palestinian' side. Recalling also the 'hydraulic supremacy' of Israel in tapping into the shared aquifer beneath both sides of the border (Figure 3.2), doubt must be cast on what purely hydraulic motives would exist for the Israeli side to capture those sections of the resource. The only way to prevent Palestinians from tapping into the Western Aquifer at all would be to confiscate all the Palestinian wells, as any that are left in Palestinian possession can – in theory – be drilled deeper to compete with the wells on the Israeli side. This is not, therefore, a classic case of 'accumulation through dispossession', to return to Harvey's phrase. The argument that plans for course of the wall are motivated by any desire for a greater accumulation of water has been rendered void. What is more, the terms of the Oslo II Agreement prevent Palestinians from developing or improving any wells at all in the Western Aquifer, and the terms are strictly enforced. Considering further the superior Israeli pumping capacity which can and, on occasion, has put the water level out of reach of the shallower, older Palestinian wells, one can conclude that there is little hydraulic imperative for the effective confiscation of the land. The Israeli side, through technology and decree, already has complete control over Palestinian abstractions of the Western Aquifer.

This line of reasoning, however, does not, preclude the possibility that water interests had no influence whatsoever over the idea or route of the Wall. Having seen the importance of water in notions of Israeli state security, there is the possibility that those elements of the Israeli nation responsible for the Wall's inception have been influenced in part by the promoters of the anti-negotiations hydrostrategic arguments. As an ominous manifestation of Israeli hard power, the Wall in any case has significant impact on shared water resources.

The Wall and Water Resources

Just as it was in the case of whether the damage to the water infrastructure in Jenin was deliberate or indiscriminate, it makes little difference to the farmers or the Palestinian state whether the Wall was intended to obstruct Palestinian access to the water resources of the Western Aquifer or not. The Wall has both a local and national impact on the transboundary flows. Locally, the impact of the Wall is felt first and foremost by farmers. Though provisional arrangements have been made by the Israel Civil Administration to allow farmers to access their fields and wells located on the 'other side' of the Wall, soldiers manning the gates randomly clamp down on passage, disallowing at their own discretion permit-holders to pass

(PENGON 2003). Deprived of routine operation and maintenance, the old wells are more likely to fall into a state of disrepair, with disastrous consequences for the farmers' families and neighbours, whose primary source of income is the harvest. The other (non water-related) effects of the Wall on civilians, such as having restricted access to health services or neighbours, or being unable to engage in a viable economy, are just as crippling, and have been well documented elsewhere.[72]

Nationally, the impact of the Wall on water resources is felt in terms of dispossession. By the end of the first phase of construction in 2003, 25 to 50 wells were put out of service by the Wall. The combined production of these wells amounted to roughly 6.7 MCM/y (PHG 2004a, PWA 2004b), and the figure could rise as high as 15 MCM/y if lessons from Gaza are drawn (Messerschmid 2007). As the Oslo Agreement cemented pre-1995 levels of Palestinian water production at 22 MCM/y, the result is that roughly 30 per cent (up to a possible 75 per cent) of the Palestinian allotment from the productive Western Aquifer is 'lost'. The loss of 30 per cent of this coveted Western Aquifer water is not insignificant for state-building efforts, though it does pale in comparison with the Israeli allotment of 340 MCM/y from the same aquifer.

The high value of the water-rich lands means that the Wall imposes further hidden costs in terms of water resources. The Palestinian state development plans rely on an 'equitable and reasonable' allotment of all shared resources, including the Western Aquifer. Future Palestinian development along the Western edge of the West Bank relies on the readily exploitable aquifer. The effect of putting land off-access to Palestinians is to severely restrict national development plans, as water will have to be supplied at a much higher cost from deeper sources much further away (Messerschmid 2007). There are even more severe implications arising from potential 'land swaps' between Israel and Palestine, as were suggested at the Camp David II talks. The allusion to a swap of a certain acreage located above the Western Aquifer (for Israel) with the same size of land taken from southeast of the West Bank (for Palestine) fails to acknowledge the extreme difference in the values of the land. One dunum of verdant land near Qalqilya is of exponentially higher value than a dunum in the dry, stony hills of the southern West Bank, not least of all because of the richness of the water resources.

Analysis of the Impact of the Wall

Heightened Internal Tensions

According to the 2002 Water Law, all water resources and infrastructure is the domain of the Palestinian Water Authority. As we have discussed, however, the PWA does not have effective control over many of the smaller, agricultural wells. Many of these – such as those around Qalqilya – are still effectively owned and controlled by the families who owned them before 2002. Unlike the four high capacity PWA wells, the PWA has little effective sense of ownership over these agricultural wells. This may help to explain the PWA's silence in regard to the construction of the Wall and the 'loss' of the wells. The PWA is known to have made little official protest over the Wall, and in fact did little more than issue an unpublished report (PWA 2004b). Certainly there have been no public declarations about the national impact of the Wall, let alone about its impact on farmers. There also appears to have been little, if any, unofficial discussion of it at the Joint Water Committee (Nassereddin 2005, pers. comm.). The silence of the PWA, in the face of their cities being choked off and their farmers being separated from their fields, has not been lost on the Municipalities of Qalqilya, Tulkarem and surrounding villages. It would be understandable if the legitimacy of the PWA in the eyes of these residents takes a substantial drop, particularly when it was already challenged by virtue of being so far from the centre of Palestinian power in the West Bank (Ramallah)[73]. With their domestic position on shaky ground, the PWA as an institution is obliged to seek support where it can find it. Once again, it is found with its Israeli counterparts, despite the asymmetry in power relations between the two.

The Results of Asymmetry of Hard Power

Israel's unilateral decision to build the Wall primarily on Palestinian territory (rather than along the border) was made possible by the larger state's much greater capacity of hard power. Lacking the political allies, ideology or tanks to counter the Wall's construction, the Palestinian Authority could do little other than protest. It is not simply speculation to consider that were the power asymmetry between the two sides was less extreme, the Israeli side would have considered building the Wall on the border if at all, just as it is not currently likely to build one inside southern Lebanon following the Summer 2006 war there.

Israel's construction of the Wall inside the West Bank also serves to highlight two other outcomes made possible by power disparity. Once again the futility of the Joint Water Committee's 'Joint Declaration' to keep water out of the 'cycle of violence' is exposed. As with the damages suffered by the water infrastructure throughout the West Bank, the letter of the declaration has been violated by the winding of the Wall around Palestinian wells and its effective annexation of the fertile land on the Palestinian side of the precious Western Aquifer. The second outcome is the failure of the Joint Water Committee as a joint decision-making body. Were it structured to resolve or mitigate events that claim up to 30 per cent of one side's allotment of resources, the JWC might prove inherently relevant and resilient to both sides. Unable to deal with the effects of the Wall, however, the utility of the JWC in dealing with conflictual as well as cooperative water issues is called into question, whether or not the JWC is actually intended to prevent unilateral actions. The asymmetry in hard power allows unilateral actions by the Israeli side, which closes down all options for discussion or negotiation. It is testament to the sword being mightier than the covenant. But the covenant – particularly if it is well crafted – can also serve the powerful, as we will see in the following chapter.

6

Bargaining Power – The Joint Water Committee

THE internal workings of the Joint Water Committee serve in this chapter as the stage on which Palestinian and Israeli expressions of the second dimension of power may be examined. A fascinating array of jockeying, discourse and conflict takes place at the JWC, most of it going on behind the scenes. These power plays will be classified according to the three compliance-producing mechanisms Lustick has offered us: coercive, utilitarian and normative (Chapter 2).

The Joint Water Committee is formally composed of the Israel Water Commission (IWC) and the Palestinian Water Authority (PWA). True to its intent as a court for a certain level of collaboration over a portion of the transboundary aquifers located within Palestinian political borders, the JWC has continued to meet throughout the worst of the last years of violence. The JWC has thus been lauded as a model of transboundary water cooperation worthy of replication in other basins, particularly by USAID and some NGOs such as the Israel/Palestine Centre for Research and Information. A growing list of critics, however, note the limited effectiveness of efforts to steer the JWC towards joint management (e.g. Dinar 1999, Kliot 2000, Daibes 2004). As Jöchen Renger concludes in his study of the obstacles preventing cooperation between the two sides, "despite the fact that Israel and the Palestinian Authority are working together in some areas of water management, this does not mean that they are cooperating" (1998: 49). By calling into question the difference between 'working together' and 'cooperation', he usefully draws our attention to the ubiquitous misuse of the latter term. This chapter's critical view of the JWC encompasses exertions of hard and bargaining power, disclosing its reality as much more of an arrangement that perpetuates the asymmetric status quo than a forum for joint management.

Power Assymetry Structured into the JWC

The Joint Water Committee is the administrative structure set up under the terms of Article 40 of the 1995 Oslo II Agreement for 'joint' Palestinian and Israeli management of the water resources located within the political borders of the West

Bank. Crucially, the jurisdiction does not extend to transboundary resources located with the political border of Israel, while Gaza seems to be left unconsidered. The most operational feature of the JWC is its licensing procedure, as shown in Figure 6.1. Unlike perhaps any other transboundary resource management regime, the procedure is active not just at the technical level, but at the political and military levels as well. At the technical level, decision-making powers within the JWC are divided between the Israeli and Palestinian sides, though we will see how hidden power plays distort the apparent equality. The Inequities structured into the JWC at the political and military levels are much more evident.

Figure 6.1   The Joint Water Committee – Project Licensing Procedure.

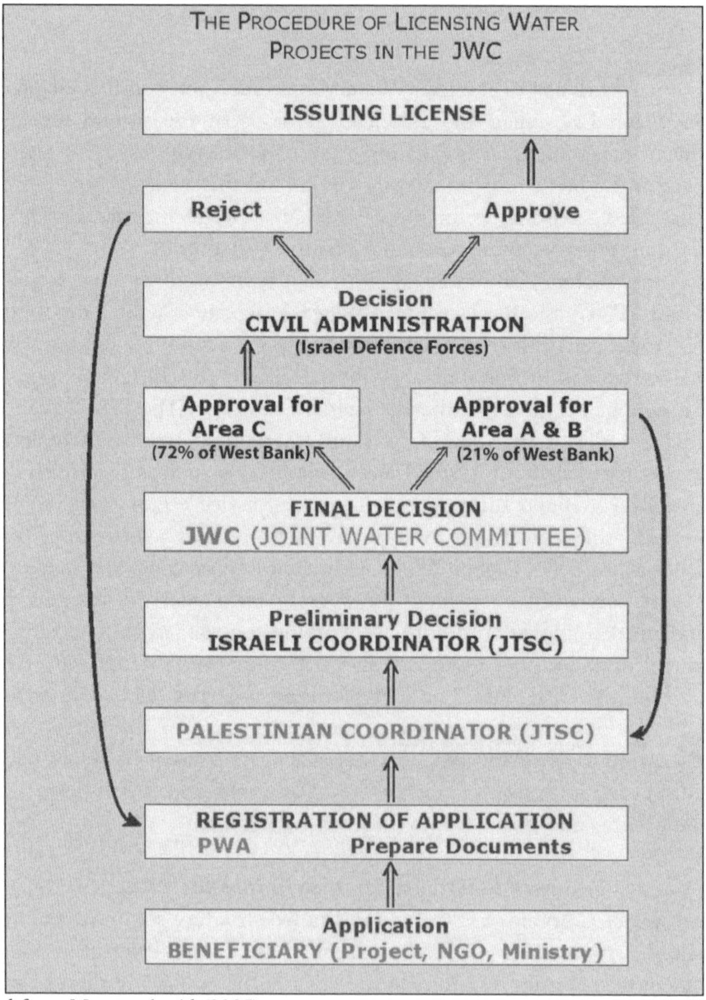

Adapted from Messerschmid (2005).

According to the JWC licensing procedure, for example, the Civil Administration of the Israel Defence Forces (IDF) makes the ultimate decision in the licensing procedure for all permits requested in Areas 'C' of the West Bank. Under the terms of Oslo II, Areas 'C' are areas outside the urban centres designated to remain under full Israeli control for an interim period, and comprise roughly 72 per cent of West Bank territory (NSU 2004). An estimated 6.8 per cent of the West Bank confiscated by illegal Israeli settlements also falls outside of the jurisdiction of the JWC (PASSIA 2004: 281). This leaves roughly 21 per cent of the land within the Palestinian political boundary of the West Bank subject to formally symmetrical JWC authority.

Over more than three-quarters of the West Bank, then, this licensing procedure establishes a set of norms which ensure that Israeli military interests take precedence over both Palestinian developmental and joint Palestinian–Israeli water management interests. Dozens of water development projects, particularly those in areas outside urban centres (which are typically the preferred locations for new wells or wastewater treatment plants), are thus either forced to relocate considerable distances away from the preferred location[74] or to remain subject to Israeli strategic militarily interests.[75] One predictable outcome of the licensing procedure – as British academic Jan Selby notes – is that a procedure intended for proper joint water management becomes a "license for environmental destruction" (2005: 12). Furthermore, as the strategic interests of Israeli water and military authorities are themselves subject to larger political interests, the entire process is, by default, subject to the imbalance of power between the two sides. Such an overtly structured mix of political, military and technical interests is as rare as any public acknowledgement of it.

An Effective Israeli Veto
Structured inequity favouring the existing (im)balance of power is further revealed by considering the limited extent of the JWC's jurisdiction. In accordance with the terms of Oslo II, the JWC quite explicitly does *not* have jurisdiction over the transboundary water resources located within the political borders of Israel. There is also an implicit restriction on the extension of its jurisdiction to those transboundary resources located within the borders of the Gaza Strip. As Gaza is located 'downstream' on the underground flows of the Coastal Aquifer Basin, abstraction and contamination levels within Gaza have no impact on the quality or quantity of the resources on the Israeli side.[76] It is entirely consistent with the realist view that the Israeli negotiators of Oslo II were not concerned with joint management (or control) of transboundary resources downstream from its position, as in Gaza. Efforts were evidently focused on the shared resources located upstream of the Israeli position, where pollution and abstraction can become concerns for Israel.

The effect of the circumscribed jurisdiction structured into the licensing procedure of the JWC is considerable. Data-sharing, joint monitoring, licensing activities and other normal resource management activities do not apply to the transboundary resources located within the political borders of Israel. The one-sided 'sharing' of activities extends even to the Israeli settlements located inside the West Bank, whose freshwater consumption or wastewater generation rates must be guessed at by the Palestinian side.

From a water management perspective, partial data-sharing of a resource precludes meaningful use of the data even when it *is* available. Attempts at rational water management over a series of urban islands on one half of the resource is as impossible and nonsensical as managing a few small strands of trees within half a forest. Environmental destruction is the very predictable result. The hard facts frustrate the international donors attempting to implement nation-wide Palestinian master plans as much as it does the Palestinian Water Authority.

The JWC's restricted domain, furthermore, gives Israel an effective 'veto' over decisions.[77] If any of the technical, political or military interests of the Israeli side may be compromised by a Palestinian project tabled at the JWC, the water project will be blocked. Because Israeli water projects inside Israel (or in Israeli settlements inside the West Bank) are not tabled at the JWC, there is no equivalent Palestinian veto. In this way the 'one person – one vote' symmetry of the JWC is belied by its asymmetrical licensing procedure. The disproportionate degree of control thus afforded the Israeli side reaches further - from setting meeting agendas, through recording their minutes, to even coercing their outcomes, as we shall now see.

Coerced Compliance

The use of coercion at the Joint Water Committee is routine. In theoretical terms, it may be considered the 'sword' which backs up the 'covenant' of the more efficient forms of bargaining power. Evidence of Israeli coercion during the 'Israeli Domination Era' (1967–1995) abounds, particularly for the period when the West Bank Water Department (WBWD) was under direct Israeli control. As far back as 1982, for instance, the Israeli Minister of Agriculture (then Ariel Sharon) implemented a series of restrictive measures to 'de-develop' the institution. No Palestinian hydrogeologists were hired and the increasing competence of the Palestinian well-drilling department was cut short by the replacement of its crews by solely Israeli ones (Nassereddin 2005, pers. comm.). Only a kind of autistic development was possible under these conditions, condemning the Palestinian institution to remain enfeebled. Some hopes for genuine maturity arose when it came partially under the wing of the PWA in 1995.

Despite decades of close association with their Israeli colleagues at Mekoroth, the Palestinians running the WBWD retained little leverage with them beyond 1995. The long-time director of the WBWD recounts the refusal in 2000, for instance, of the request made through the JWC to deliver water to the village of Burqa, northwest of Nablus (see Figure 3.1). The Palestinian proposal was for five cubic metres per day – enough to provide water for roughly 40 people with the standard 130 litres per person per day. The suggested source was a Mekoroth-controlled line linking the Israeli settlements of Sheve Shamron and Homesh. The request was refused by the Israeli side at the JWC for technical reasons, stated as "there is not enough water" (Nassereddin 2005, pers. comm.). The Palestinian side had no choice but to accept the outcome of the effective Israeli veto at the JWC, and the inhabitants of Burqa remain without water services to this day, unable to tap into the Israeli water main that crosses the gates of their village.

The Israeli side also has the option of forcing a favourable outcome through its economic and administrative capabilities, as exemplified by Mekoroth's billing procedures. As we saw in Chapter 3, Mekoroth controls the flows for those water transmission lines inside of the West Bank that supply both Palestinian villages and Israeli settlements. The senior WBWD engineer responsible for verifying the flows billed to the Palestinian villages by Mekoroth describes the process in the following terms. The PWA (through the WBWD) is charged for the bulk meter readings taken at the well, minus the quantity billed to the settlements. Water losses along the transmission lines, which can reach as high as 30 per cent in the leakier pipes or in regions where water is illegally siphoned off, are thus counted on the Palestinian bill. The weaker side footing the bill serves as an example of an exertion of hard power enabled by the inequity structured into the JWC.

Such violations of the spirit (but not the letter) of the 'joint' cooperation are assisted by the JWC's lack of transparency. The Israeli side's response to the PWA Deputy Director's reported remarks in the Palestinian press in 2001 demonstrate this opacity. Having given his opinion of the heavy-handed Israeli attitudes and dealings at the JWC, the Deputy Director was countered by his Israeli counterpart, according to a senior PWA official present in the room at the time, that 'if you think that the media will give you more water, then get it from them' (Barghouti 2004, pers. comm.). Few further remarks have been reported in the Palestinian press, despite the decreasing level of cooperation and increasing violence since then. The Palestinian water officials appear to be caught up in a coercive *modus operandi* that is very sensitive to such Israeli threats of reduced cooperation. The 'wriggle room' available to the Palestinian side is all the more compromised by more 'utilitarian' type methods by which their consent is assured, as discussed in the next section.

'Utilitarian' Compliance

Methods that use *incentives* to gain compliance were classified as 'Utilitarian Type II' compliance-producing mechanisms in Chapter 2, where they were also associated with bargaining form of power. Both the Israeli and the Palestinian sides have such incentives at their disposal, and regularly employ them at the Joint Water Committee.

Effective Israeli Use of Utilitarian Compliance-Producing Mechanisms
Many of the compliance-inducing carrots available to the Israeli side stem from the JWC's skewed licensing procedure. Through it, the Israeli side is effectively offered

a range of choices when faced with a Palestinian proposal for a water project. They may either a) accept it, and have its progress terminated by their colleagues in the Civil Administration at the licensing stage or the IDF at the implementation stage[78]; b) reject it, using the effective veto; or c) bargain for it. This last option involves extracting a 'price' from the Palestinian side, typically a favour in the form of Palestinian approval of an Israeli project that would otherwise not be accepted. As Selby states, "in cases where the Israeli authorities cannot achieve their projects through the legal-institutional mechanism of the JWC, they can always resort to their far superior coercive capabilities to ensure that their pipelines get constructed as and when they require" (Selby 2003b: 135). The mode of operation for the Palestinian water authorities, it follows, becomes more one of constant bargaining and deals; the coercive *modus operandi* of the Israelis actually becomes the *modus vivendi* of the two parties locked into a perpetual pragmatic compromise.

Israeli pressure on Palestinians to agree to wastewater treatment plants serving both Palestinian cities and Israeli settlements is an example. A German hydrogeologist, working for more than a decade in the sector, testifies that approval of Palestinian requests to provide wastewater treatment plants solely for Palestinian needs is regularly made conditional on the extension of those services to neighbouring Israeli settlements (Messerschmid 2003: 3). The 'choice' facing the Palestinians is limited: they may either reject the project, thereby risking the continued contamination of the aquifer (and being accused of doing so deliberately), or agree to the project, becoming complicit in Israeli efforts to legitimise the settlements.

A similar dynamic, though one with a different outcome, is found in the 2002 case of the 'Jericho 7' well. According to a Palestinian representative present at the meeting, the Palestinian side refused the Israeli request tabled at the JWC to drill the well, on the grounds that it was to be located in the Eastern Aquifer Basin (EAB). Though Israel had long been extensively pumping the EAB from within the borders of the West Bank, it had been agreed under the terms of Oslo II that all future development of the EAB would be for Palestinians (Oslo II 1995: Article 40, Para. 7(6)). For reasons bluntly stated as retaliatory "punishment",[79] the Israeli Civil Administration subsequently refused permission to a Palestinian constructor contracted by the PWA to move a rig through the West Bank to drill the well near Rujeib (Barghouti 2005, pers. comm.). Though it was also intended to serve the residents of Madama, the Rujeib well project was subsequently removed from the list of projects considered for funding by USAID, and was never completed. Head of Madama Village Council Kamal Ayad (see Box, Chapter 1) remains unimpressed when informed of the latest reason he is denied water to his village.

The result of this horse-trading between Palestinian water authorities and a representative of the Israel Civil Administration is, at first glance, at least equal in its destructive effect – both sides lost the opportunity to drill a well. Given the disparity in control over water resources and the relatively greater need for new wells in Palestine, however, the outcome was significantly more damaging to

Palestinian development efforts than to Israeli economic ones. Such are the limits of Palestinian bargaining power when faced with Israeli hard power.

Ineffective Palestinian Use of Utilitarian Compliance-Producing Mechanisms
Bargaining power is theorised as deriving from the influence one of the parties has as a legitimate actor in their relationship with others. As the official counterpart to the Israeli water community, the PWA is thus invested with a certain measure of such power. Their attempts to secure the compliance of the Israeli side, indeed, have relied on bargaining power, though they have proven essentially ineffective.

A somewhat counter-intuitive example is the PWA's exploitation of the partial alignment of Palestinian development needs and the foreign policy of the right-wing Israeli Likud government shortly after the Oslo II Agreement. A high-ranking manager of the PWA explains how Israel–Palestinian cooperation at the JWC became smoother with the ascent of the Likud government led by Netanyahu in 1996. The Likud policy of the of promoting greater Palestinian dependence on Israeli structures resulted in more Palestinian villages being connected to water lines feeding Israeli settlements. The Palestinian side at the JWC was aware of this partial alignment of interests, and able to capitalise on the interests of the Israeli government for greater inter-connectivity, thereby ensuring at least that more Palestinian villages were provided with water (if not independence). The manipulative tactic may have legitimised the PWA in the eyes of the villagers as much as it legitimised the continued presence of the Israeli settlements. When the Labour government of Ehud Barak came to power, and the newly appointed Israeli Water Commissioner halted the projects that had been initiated by his predecessor in order to "study" them, the exploitation of this possibility came to a temporary end (Barghouti 2005, pers. comm.).

Like their Israeli counterparts, the PWA is able to employ a range of incentives in the horse-trading nature of JWC meetings. One such carrot is the PWA's choice about whether or not to raise the issues of Palestinian water rights and the need for new Palestinian wells. Faced with the prospect of returning to their political leaders with such requests, the Israeli members of the JWC have been known to "beg" the Palestinian side to avoid bringing up the issues.[80] In theory, the PWA is thus offered an opportunity to leverage its own interests, perhaps demanding in return the granting of a permit for a contested well. In practice, however, there is scant evidence of any significant advance by the PWA through this method. In the spirit of pragmatism and camaraderie that has built up between the members on both sides of the JWC, the PWA representatives willingly or begrudgingly comply with their Israeli counterparts' requests to avoid bringing up such 'thorny' issues.

As a national institution in a near state, a good measure of the PWA's legitimacy stems from its relationship with its Israeli counterpart. Considering the PWA's relatively minor authority in terms of actual control over water resources (Chapter 3) and poor esteem in the eyes of the Palestinian public (Chapter 4), it can be understood how its remaining official legitimacy is something the institution would very much like to preserve. The challenged legitimacy may further translate the PWA's desire to remain relevant into an existential institutional need. Its self-preserving obligation to remain legitimate reinforces the PWA in a pragmatic *modus vivendi* at the JWC. The PWA remains securely settled in a position of subordination vis-à-vis the more powerful Israeli side. There is considerable evidence that the subordination is not just a result of a lost battle of bargaining power, however.

Normative Compliance

The consequences of the tenuous legitimacy granted to the PWA by their Israeli counterpart are also manifest in the negotiations which led to the straightjacket it finds itself in. Lustick's normative 'Type III' compliance-producing methods are able to ensure that the weaker side sees it as right to comply, perhaps even as a duty – such as the citizen paying her taxes. A Palestinian water academic active throughout the 1990 Madrid and 1994 Oslo negotiations explains how the Palestinians did not always see their obligations in such a light, even during the period of Israeli occupation. Marwan Haddad's public testimony on the scenes behind the negotiations reveals the start of a slide towards a subordinate relationship, and also the frustrations that continue to stem from it:

> Negotiation on the interim transfer of authority of water … continued for four months with a tough Palestinian position, and ended with an order to the head of the negotiations team to sign a long and humiliating transfer agreement of over forty pages written by the Israelis. This is essentially serving the Israeli occupation with Palestinian hands (Haddad 2004).

The eventual endorsement of the Oslo II Agreement by the Palestinian leadership on the one hand legitimised the creation of the PA and the PWA. The act also, however, obliged the PWA to accept three conditions that were to shape the water conflict for the foreseeable future: a) the level of control that the Israeli side had achieved by 1995 over water in the West Bank; b) the management of water resources through the asymmetrically-structured JWC; and, c) a relationship that appears to have been one of subordination from the outset. All this was as a result of the hydropolitical history and of its being compounded by an agreement drafted solely by the Israeli side.

Each Israeli application of coercive and utilitarian methods to gain Palestinian compliance that we have reviewed props up the situation of subordination. Regardless of the mechanics that generated it,[81] the act of endorsing an agreement that overwhelmingly favours the more powerful is in effect a sanctioning of the stronger side's use of bargaining power. Having established the effective use of its 'sword', the Israeli side has the ability to craft the covenant. It may be that it has been crafted for the collective or unilateral good, though the evidence we will continue to present suggests that it is consistent with the 'fundamentally careful policy' vis-à-vis Palestinians in the sector.

Lessons may be drawn from a consideration of the motivations of those who willingly participated in the process. Those Palestinians benefiting directly from the Oslo process by filling the seats created at the PWA may be quite willing to play the part in the process that many claim had always been intended for them (e.g. Said (1996), Khan (2004b)). Framed as an unstoppable process leading eventually to a Palestinian state, the 'new' Palestinian water negotiators may have seen it as their duty not to obstruct Oslo, though this is pure conjecture. In such an atmosphere, any insistence that the jurisdiction of the JWC should also extend to water resources inside Israel, for instance, would be seen as either obstructive or impractical. Partially subordinate from the outset, Palestinian participation in the JWC ensures that ever-increasing power is transferred to the Israeli side through their compliance with the norms of cooperation.

With a Palestinian Water Authority obliged and ready to attempt to fulfil the terms of Article 40 of the Oslo II Agreement, the Israeli side had only to recall the norms to ensure that its interests are met. What was once confirmed only through coercive or bargaining means could now be enforced through the terms of an international treaty. Palestinian compliance to the institutional order has become an obligation. Though Israeli interests have changed since the agreement was signed, the methods of normative compliance gained through the functioning of the JWC are still regularly employed.

Israeli 'Agenda Setting'

Our discussion of the influence of discourses on outcomes noted how "some issues are organised into politics while others are organised out" (Hajer 1997: 42). Anyone who has convened or chaired a meeting knows that setting the agenda is a very efficient means of 'organising' exactly which issues will or will not be discussed. There is ample evidence of such agenda-setting dynamics at work in Joint Water Committee meetings, in various forms: gentle coercion to keep some issues off the agenda; breach of procedure; delays in calling for and holding of meetings; control over attendance at meetings; stifling of discussion; and control over the minutes of the meetings.

Firstly, we have seen the Israeli aversion to any discussion of Palestinian requests to develop new wells or water rights. Through Palestinian acquiescence to the friendly appeals from the Israeli side the issues are rarely tabled for discussion. Secondly, there is evidence of Israeli breaches of JWC procedure in not bringing all proposals for Israeli water projects inside the West Bank to the table. The construction of the 1,000 cubic metre reservoir for the Israeli settlement of Beit Horon in 2001 and the laying of the 6" line along the Nablus–Ramallah road to feed the Israeli settlement of Shilo are examples of Israeli projects inside the Palestinian West Bank that were not submitted to the JWC for approval, even at the technical level.[82] Palestinian protests about such breaches of procedure for these and other such projects are typically countered with apologies, un-kept promises not to repeat the practice or accusations of similar breaches.[83] Such bypassing of the licensing procedure established at the JWC is a partially effective means of maintaining as a non-issue something that might otherwise develop into a genuine Palestinian grievance.

Thirdly, Palestinian requests for meetings to discuss such issues are regularly denied or delayed by the Israeli side, even during periods of reduced violence and good relations. The opposite is true for JWC meetings called for by the Israeli side, which are frequently demanded for the very next week, leaving little time for the Palestinian side to prepare (Barghouti 2004, pers. comm.). The fourth form of Israeli control over the outcome of JWC meetings is by establishing *who* may attend them. Palestinian requests, for instance, to bring American and Norwegian employees of their engineering project partners to discuss technical issues at the JWC have been refused outright by the Israeli side. Likewise, attendance at the loosely-formed US–Israel–Palestinian tripartite committee water meetings is structured to exclude other groups, and little room for discussion outside of this venue is permitted.

Fifth, issues raised at the JWC by the Israeli side are sometimes not really opened for discussion, with the 'power reputation' of the Israeli side fulfilling its deterring capacity. The JWC meeting held in Tel Aviv in early September 2005, following on the heels of the Israeli 'disengagement' from the Gaza Strip and four settlements in the northern West Bank serves as a case in point. According to a Palestinian delegate, two appendices were fixed to the minutes of the meeting, both of which were written by the Israeli side (Anon. 2005, pers. comm.). The first appendix details the handover of ownership, infrastructure and data surrounding the dozens of wells that Mekoroth operated for the Israeli settlers in the Gaza Strip. The second appendix is a similar technical document relating to the three wells that supplied the Israeli settlements that were evacuated from the West Bank. The main difference between the two appendices is that the second does not transfer the ownership of the wells to the PWA.[84] Reservations expressed by the Palestinian side about signing the appendices were met by an Israeli threat to withhold the data regarding the operation and assets of these wells. The compliance of the Palestinian side was thus assured, and the issue was 'settled' according to the desired outcome of the Israeli side.

A final example of Israeli agenda-setting concerns the keeping of records. A regular Palestinian participant in JWC meetings characterises minutes of previous meetings as 'reflecting only the outcome of the meeting, not the conflict' that occurred during it. In the case of the September 2005 meeting discussed above, *two* sets of minutes were issued. The first was distributed to Palestinian participants as they were leaving the meeting, evidently having been prepared ahead of time (JWC 2005a). The second set of minutes, transmitted to the Palestinians the day after the meeting, contained minor updates to the outcome of the meeting as well as a corrected list of participants.[85] Israeli confidence in Palestinian acquiescence on this occasion was so assured that it was recorded ahead of the event. At this meeting in particular, Palestinian compliance was momentarily uncertain until the Israeli threats of withholding data successfully coerced the intended result. Such a case of the victor writing history – even before it happens – could only occur from within a situation of deep hegemony.

Thus is the agenda derived, determined, set and recorded by the Israeli side. We may note that the asymmetry in bargaining and hard coercive power is enabled by an inequitably structured treaty and coordination body. Our analysis of power and hegemony active at the JWC concludes with an allegory.

Conclusion – The Elephant and the Fly

> To speak of Israeli–Palestinian 'co-operation' in the water sector is to use no less than a misnomer. This is not, however, simply because 'the outcome of co-operation between an elephant and a fly is not hard to predict,' as Chomsky so pithily writes, … but because under Oslo, 'co-operation' has often been only minimally different from the occupation and domination that went before it (Selby 2003b: 118).

The evidence provided in this chapter has supported Selby's assertion that the Joint Water Committee is quite actively 'dressing up domination as cooperation'. What so many practitioners and analysts would see as a model regime between adversaries is also an instrument of control. Analysts emphasising the cooperative aspects of Palestinian–Israeli hydro-relations miss the point that the *quality* of that cooperation is more significant than simply its existence. Though the disparity of bargaining power between the sides is not as extreme as in the case of hard power, the Palestinian ability to wield the former is still limited. Israeli use of bargaining power through the Joint Water Committee, has proven considerably more effective. The resultant degree of control over projects, proposals, and water management decisions enables it to continue to call the shots.

It is impossible to prove that the poor quality of cooperation (the terms 'coordination' or 'collaboration' may be more appropriate) is an intended consequence of a broader strategy of asymmetry (see discussion in Chapter 4). But the very effective grip the Israeli side has over transboundary waters certainly follows those lines, as we have seen in this chapter. The arrangements that determine interaction over transboundary waters between the two sides are so thorough they appear impossible to tamper with – like some form of 'hegemonic apparatus'. In fact, and as we shall see in the following chapter, the hegemonic state of affairs is maintained through the use of methods even more efficient than those we have seen thus far.

7

Ideational Power – Imposing Ideas

Nowadays ... [the] elites of power make history.
C. Wright Mills, in Lukes (2005 [1974]: 57).

THIS chapter examines the Palestinian–Israeli water conflict through the third and most efficient face of power: ideational power. The Wazzani Springs incident in 2002 is the first case used to highlight the power of ideas, couched as it is in a narrative of security. Israeli *master planning* of the Palestinian water sector is given as a second example of the force of ideas. It is elaborated through an examination of the contests over the capacity of the Eastern Aquifer Basin and the proposed 'Hadera–Tulkarem' desalination project. Each case reveals the influence of an elevated form of sanctioned discourse. The influence of the pragmatic Israeli *Needs, not Rights* discourse on donors and academics serves as the third illustration of how ideas take root and a set of dominant ideas is sanctioned. The implications of these expressions of power on the water conflict are substantial: the narrative of Palestinian civil society is discredited by the international community as obstructionist, while the prevailing Israeli discourse is viewed as well-intentioned cooperation.

One must be fully aware of the difficulties inherent with assessments of such an abstract phenomenon. Analysts interested in cataloguing power's third dimension, Lukes suggests, can follow three lines of action: a) to search for observable mechanisms of its existence; b) to find ways of falsifying it; and c) to identify relations, characteristics and phenomena of power for which the first and second dimensions cannot account. This chapter's analysis follows the first and third of these lines by providing evidence of exertions of ideational power and ideological hegemonic compliance-producing mechanisms.

Securitisation and the Hasbani River

The Lebanese–Israeli water conflict warrants a separate study, and the subject is certainly not given due consideration here. Lebanon's Litani River figured in the aspirations of the early Zionists like Chaim Weizman, who requested the British Mandate authorities to include it within Palestine's borders (Chapter 4). Israel's occupation of southern Lebanon from 1982 to 2000 fulfilled these ambitions, albeit temporarily, and led to rumours that persist today that Israel is taking – or intends to take – Litani flows.

While there is evidence of early Zionist designs on the Litani, there is no evidence that Israel has actually extracted any significant portion of its water. Regardless of the intent, there are at least three factors preventing Israel from such exploitation. The first constraint is geography. Cutting through pine-covered limestone mountains, the Litani sits deep in gorges where it flows nearest to the Israeli border (Figure 3.1). At this point, where the famous Crusader castle of Beaufort (*Schi'if* in Arabic) sits several hundred metres above, the river bends sharply westward toward the Mediterranean rather than continuing southwards into Israel. Because it sits so deep in its valley, any exploitation of the river for use in Israel would necessitate large pumping stations to get the water up over the mountains and down into the Hulah canals. Alternatively, the pipes could be laid in a tunnel bore through the mountain range. If a project of either type existed, it would be impossible to hide the waterworks – and there is no evidence to be seen. Secondly, the flows of the Litani at this point Israel are not substantial. The river picks up considerably from the many wadis downstream, but near Beaufort the river resembles a large stream. Back-of-the-envelope calculations suggest that the infrastructure and electrical power required to exploit the resource would be economically unfeasible, in terms of dollars per cubic meter. There is, thirdly, no motive for Israel to exploit the Litani. With the great hydrological gains from Israel's territorial conquest in 1967, Israeli authorities had already secured all of the surface water the state was to need. The recent drop in the cost in desalination removes any last shreds of a motive, as the Israeli side can produce water within its borders at a lower cost than taking it can take it from Lebanon. The Hasbani River is another story altogether.

The Hasbani River and the Wazzani Springs [86]

The short-lived but very vocal near-war between Israel and Lebanon in autumn 2002 provides an example of the ideational at work through the discursive process of securitisation. As we saw in Chapter 2, Turton has shown how the promotion of a water issue to a national security concern enables a government to equate criticism with treason, thereby silencing critical voices and allowing it more 'space' to pursue ulterior interests.

The sabre-rattling started over a water-development project on the Wazzani tributary of the Hasbani River (Figure 3.1). Having recently gained access to the land which had been occupied by Israel for nearly two decades, the Government of Lebanon, with the backing of European donors, invested in a small-scale drinking water project for the previously unserved farmers of the area. As it turns out, the design capacity of the project (less than 10 MCM/y) was much smaller than the furore it created. Jeremy Allouche captures the essence of the short-lived pique of intensity of the conflict:

The interest of [the Wazzani conflict] … was not so much the nature of this incident but rather the importance given by the Israeli press to this event and even more so the reaction of the Israeli officials. The then Israeli Minister for Infrastructure, Mr. Avigdor Liberman, declared that: "Israel cannot let this pass without a reaction. For Israel, water is a matter of to be or not to be, to live or to die" (Allouche 2004: 16).

Minister Liberman's take on the issue was repeated in hundreds of Israeli media pieces and official statements. In discussions with his Russian counterpart, the then Foreign Minister Shimon Peres, for instance, described the Lebanese drinking-water project as a "dangerous provocation" (IMFA 2002a). The Deputy minister of Defence was quoted as saying "the Americans can send an envoy, they can do all the surveys they want, but we know what we have to do" (Sobelman 2002).

It is no longer debated that the volume of water in question posed no threat of physical scarcity to Israel. Nor is it debated that Lebanon has a legitimate claim to some of these transboundary flows, having been 'allocated' roughly 30 MCM/y in 1955 by the Johnston Plan, but having been prevented by Israel from exploiting any of that until 2000. The intensity of the dispute was managed in Lebanon's favour by the US, UN and European Union, though it was ultimately left unresolved.[87] Lebanese water withdrawals in the years following the dispute have not achieved even the design capacity, with 2005 extractions said to be significantly less than 7 MCM/y (Maternowzki 2006). This is attributed as much to low pumping capacity as to the desire of the Lebanese Government to avoid future diplomatic or military confrontation with Israel – a nod to Israel's 'projectable power' of deterrence.

Much Ado about Nothing
The vocal Israeli reactions to Lebanon's small development project may have had much more to do with the highly-charged political atmosphere that exists on the water issue between these states, than any potential conflict over scarce resources (Luft 2002). It is the ideational environment that makes water issues ripe for politicisation and securitisation tactics. Further nuanced analysis comes from various Israeli analysts, including Zisser (2002), who proposes that it is Israeli sensitivity to "unilateral" Lebanese actions that engender the threat of mobilising sufficient resources to attack Lebanon. Academic David Newman (2002) explains the Israeli government reaction as an attempt to conceal the more serious internal water issues that the state faces, such as water use inefficiency. It may, in the end, be impossible to uncover the entire set of motives that drove the over-reaction as a whole. Rather, what makes this case noteworthy is the effectiveness of the use of securitisation, as well as the influence of current Israeli hydrostrategic thinking.

The effect that the securitisation of the water-related dispute had on Israeli public opinion was immediate and deep. The risk projected by Israeli officials (see e.g. Israeli Ministry of Foreign Affairs Statements IMFA (2002b) and IMFA

(2002c) and promulgated in the media (see e.g. Sobelman and Ash (2002); Luft (2002) and Sengupta (2002)) resulted in a discourse that engaged Israeli society in a way that perhaps only a (perceived) threat to security can. Israeli public engagement with this issue certainly stands in stark contrast to its lack of interest in the much more directly relevant Israeli domestic water issues (Chapter 4).

Focusing on the smoke instead of the fire, or creating an issue where one does not exist, may simply be cases of politicking. In openly portraying the Lebanese development project as a threat to Israeli water security (and in some cases to the security of Israel itself), however, these voices are also building upon the ideological Zionist view of water that was so prevalent during the State's founding period, the 'Ideological Era' of 1948–67. The general response of the public to the strong Israeli governmental stance on the issue reveals a) that the hydrostrategic, ideological view of water still holds currency, and, b) that officials and media can quite readily manipulate this fact. The same kinds of justification were used by those academics opposed to negotiations over water with Palestinians, and similar 'hydrostrategic' reasons were given by officials opposed to the 'Disengagement' Plan's proposals to withdraw from the Gaza Strip and four settlements in the northern West Bank. In any case, the hype contributed to successfully deterring Lebanon from developing any further projects, thereby perpetuating effective Israeli control over the headwaters of the Jordan River.

While the case shows the *Hydrostrategic* narrative to be alive and well, it also reveals the limits of that discourse. Those Israeli officials dramatising the 2002 Wazzani Springs dispute (like those opposed to the 2005 'Disengagement' Plan), saw their views over-ruled with the quiet shelving of the unresolved Wazzani dispute, (and the eventual implementation of the Plan to withdraw Israeli settlers from Gaza). The power that was sought through the *Hydrostrategic* discourse was ultimately less influential than the power of the forces at work in the broader political context. In other words, the Israeli Ministry of Foreign Affairs and the Prime Minister's Office pursued specific political goals of their own, and were ultimately not dissuaded by the ideas of those promoting the hydrostrategic discourse. By the end of the Oslo era, the *Hydrostrategic* discourse appeared to be confined to the shadows of the mainstream, sanctioned discourse of *Needs, not Rights*, to which we now turn.

Master-Planning for Palestine

For the present, the sanctioned discourse of *Needs, not Rights* has become dominant and firmly entrenched in Israeli political life. Advocates of contending discourses will, of course, seek to have their own discourse and ideas stated strongly and clearly. The more powerful side in any discursive competition will be the one with an edge over its competitor in terms of intellectual capacity, eloquence, access to media, etc., and it can expect some success in embedding its ideas in the minds of those who matter. The narrative of the weaker side, if promulgated at all, may only be maintained by elements pushed to the fringes of society – at least until those elements gain enough power to pose a challenge. In cases of extreme power asymmetry, we would expect to find evidence of the stronger side going beyond simply shutting-down the discourse of its competitor. Where one side is dominant in all contending sectors, it may even attempt to determine the discourse *of its competitor* – through hegemonic 'Type IV' compliance-producing mechanisms that operate in the unconscious, and exercise its capacity to shape others' perceptions of their situation and their interests.

Such is the case with competing Palestinian and Israeli narratives over transboundary water issues. Through well-timed, well-placed and eloquent projections of its discourse, certain elements of the Israeli water sector can choose not only to not be concerned with the threats directly posed to it by Palestinian actions,[88] but to anticipate and prevent any perceived *future* threats to Israeli interests in the water sector. Such elements of pre-emption and anticipation are evidence of an Israeli move from reactive to pro-active water management on the Palestinian side of the border, in the way a public health sector might progress from curative to preventative treatment of illness. As the Palestinian water sector faces ever narrower alternatives, it finds itself obliged to choose between compliance with the Israeli side or outright rejection. This paradigm of 'you're either with us or against us' effectively divides the Palestinian side, preventing the emergence of a common approach. With the bulk of their legitimacy derived from following the rules established by the Israeli side, non-cooperation with the sanctioned discourse is not an option for Palestinian officials. This, in turn, puts them at odds with the Palestinian water NGOs and other critics less bound by treaty or to uphold appearances.

The following cases provide evidence of Israeli water authorities seeking 'solutions' for Palestine under the *Needs, not Rights* discourse. By implanting the ideas of the 'solutions' in the minds of the international donor and Palestinian water communities, Israel – in the words of the head of a Palestinian environmental NGO – 'has appointed itself regional water commissioner' (Ishaq 2005). Because of its relation to Palestinian development issues, this pro-active form of discourse is referred to as *master planning* for the Palestinian water sector.

The case of the 'Extra 78' and the Eastern Basin

The Eastern Aquifer Basin (EAB) underlying the entire Palestinian portion of the Jordan River Valley is the driest, with the least accessible of all the Palestinian–Israeli transboundary water resources (Figure 3.1). Though all analysts may agree on this fact, there is no similar consensus on the actual sustainable yield of the aquifer. The ambiguity generated by the lack of data has been exploited in a negotiating context structured by extremely asymmetrical power relations, much to the detriment of the Palestinian side.

Article 40 of Annex III of Oslo II identified the "estimated potential" of the aquifer as 172 MCM/y. Apart from the water sources already developed by Israelis and Palestinians within the borders of the West Bank (40 MCM/y[89] and 54

MCM/y, respectively), Schedule 10 of Annex III refers specifically to "78 mcm remaining quantities to be developed from the Eastern Aquifer". These flows were understood to provide for the "future needs of the Palestinians in the West Bank [which] are estimated to be between 70–80 mcm/year" (Article 40, Para. 6). Suspicion about the derivation of such figures are inspired primarily by this close matching of the estimated capacity of the aquifer with the definition of future Palestinian water needs.

Following a decade of extensive development efforts of the EAB by the Palestinian Water Authority and USAID, it is generally acknowledged that this 'extra 78' MCM/y is not really available. Updated estimates of the safe but untapped yield of the aquifer vary. Based on the results of their multi-year, multi-million dollar well-drilling programme, a senior USAID water programmer estimates it at 45 MCM/y, (Newman 2004, pers. comm.). A senior hydrogeologist places the estimate at roughly 65 MCM/y, drawing attention to the fact that much of this is in fact prohibitively expensive to develop due to the fractured nature of the Karst geology (Messerschmid 2004). There are, furthermore, important doubts about the motivations behind the calculation of the figure, with Selby (2003a) stating that it is a

> strange coincidence that at a time when the Israeli state was searching for new water supplies for the Palestinians and for a way of denying the Palestinians their rights to develop the Western and North-eastern aquifers, that it suddenly managed to conjure up a sparkling new and until then barely noticed water resource [(the Eastern Aquifer Basin)] (Selby 2003a: 127).

What is more, the 'extra 78' figure does not seem to be based upon any agreed-upon estimate of future Palestinian water needs. Notwithstanding what was agreed to by the PLO signatories of the Oslo II Agreement, the PWA for their part have identified the 'unobstructed' water needs of Palestine at over 700 MCM/y by the year 2010[90] (NSU 2005b).

There is scant information explaining the methodology used to determine the 'future needs' identified by the Oslo Accord. Wolf papers over the topic, explaining how "a formula for agriculture and per capita consumption determined future Palestinian water needs at 70–80 MCM/yr. and Israel agreed to provide 28.6 MCM/yr. towards those needs" (Wolf 2000b: 138). No further information about the "formula" is offered, so a deeper investigation is required. One question that arises, for instance, concerns how analysts would perceive the terms of the Oslo II Agreement if Israeli water needs had been calculated with the cited formula.[91] Wolf's statement may also mislead through inaccuracy. The Accord in fact obliges "both sides" to supply the 28.6 MCM/y referred to. The bulk of these flows (19.1 MCM/y) are in fact to be provided by the Palestinian, not the Israeli side.[92] As Ines Dombrowski (1998: 100) states, "the agreement [over additional extractions from the EAB] places a much larger financial and administrative burden on the

Palestinians", because the much lower water table level of the EAB requires a relatively greater pumping effort. Reading between the lines of the terms of the Oslo II Agreement (and of leading analysts' interpretations of it), one is forced to conclude that the Palestinian side was meant to be satisfied with whatever water it was given, and to let the Israeli side plan its sector.[93]

Desalination for the Land-locked West Bank?

A second instance of Israeli *master planning* for Palestine is the case of the proposed 'Hadera–Tulkarem' project, shown in Figure 7.1. The project proposes that a desalination plant to serve both Israeli and Palestinians be built at Hadera on the Israeli coast. Desalinated water would be sent from the coast to demand centres in the West Bank, through transmission lines several hundred kilometres long (IWC 2004). The project reveals to just what lengths the proponents of the *Needs, not Rights* discourse will go in order to assist with the supply to meet Palestinian domestic demand, while avoiding the issue of Palestinian water rights.

The first public declaration about the project was made by then Israeli Water Commissioner Noah Kinnarty in August 2002, when he confidently identified US-funded desalination projects as the "solution" for water in Gaza, , and more "American" wells as the solution for the southern West Bank (Kinnarty 2002). As to Palestinian water demand in the northern West Bank, Kinnarty states:

> I have proposed that the international community build a desal [sic] plant at Hadera with a supply pipeline to the northern West Bank. The Americans will build the facility and the additional donor countries perhaps will lay the distribution pipe for the Palestinians (Kinnarty 2002).

The statement is telling as much for its confident tone as for its irrationality. Hydraulic engineers scratch their head at the idea, which proposes to solve the water shortage on the West Bank by using one of the most distant and expensive water sources available. The absurdity is not lost on the residents of the Palestinian villages intended to receive the water. The proposal suggests that the residents of Barta'a, for example, pay for desalinated seawater arriving from the West, while the readily exploitable water under their feet is taken by Israeli pumps for Israelis in the East. Prohibited from securing a water source from groundwater within the village borders, and prevented from securing its own springwater by violent menaces from the settlers in Yitshar, the residents of Madama are even more embittered by the promotion of the project as a 'goodwill gesture'. Were the project to be implemented, they would be facing bills for water up to three times more than other residents of the West Bank, and up to five times more than the Israeli settlers that have destroyed their traditional source.

The pre-feasibility engineering report on the project (*Supply of Water to the Palestinian Authority from the Desalination Plant at Hadera* (see IWC (2004)) estimates the transmission costs alone at US$1.15 per m³. Including production and capital investment costs, the price of the water is expected to be near US\$1.85 per m³. This cost compares with the roughly US\$0.50 per m³ that targeted West Bank consumers currently pay, and the roughly US\$0.35 per m³ that it would cost to produce water from the WAB, were it not prohibited by the terms of the Oslo II Accord to do so.

Figure 7.1 Proposed route of the 'Hadera–Tulkarem' project of desalination for the West Bank, showing existing Palestinian and Israeli water pipelines.

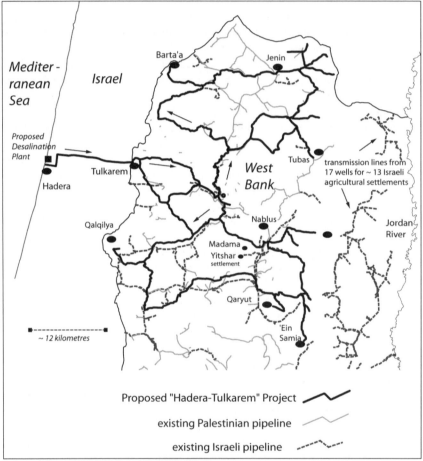

Adapted from IWC (2004) and WBWD (2003).

Tracking the development of the project offers insight into how exploitation of asymmetrical power leads to apparently illogical outcomes. The Israeli water engineering company Tahal was commissioned in 2003 by the Israel Water Commission (IWC) to undertake the pre-feasibility report on transmission costs. The report was completed and delivered by the IWC to the PWA in January 2004. It was also presented by Uri Shamir to the US House of Representatives in May

2004 (Shamir 2004). The idea was promoted to the PWA by the USAID office in Tel Aviv sometime following the Washington meeting. During the same period, the Head of the Planning Division of the Israeli Water Commission publicly promoted the idea before at least two international conferences,[94] claiming that the cost of the water to Palestinians would be US$ 0.50/m^3 (Dreizin 2004, IWC 2004), or at least cheaper than the price that Mekoroth currently charges the Palestinians (which varies from roughly US$ 0.40 to US$ 0.70/ m^3).

Official and unofficial Palestinian reaction to the project raised the expected concerns about security, sovereignty and cost (Pearce 2004). Some of these issues were dealt with in a direct manner by Israeli and American officials. There were, for instance, discussions between USAID officials and the Israeli Prime Minister on making the route of the transmission line inside Israel US sovereign territory (as is an embassy) in order to alleviate Palestinian concerns about Israeli sabotage (Arlosoroff 2004, pers. comm.). Other Palestinian concerns were dealt with in a less direct manner, as we shall see shortly.

The PWA hesitated in its response to the Israeli/US proposal. Anonymous sources in the PWA state that the project was initially accepted on the condition that control of the plant is not in the hands of the Israelis and that it would "not compromise Palestinian water rights". The PWA has since refuted any such agreement, both publicly and behind closed doors. The project had still not been implemented by January 2006, though persistent promotion by the Israeli and American sides continued until the election of the Hamas government.[95]

From a power-based perspective this case has several interesting aspects. Firstly, the idea for the project came from the Israeli side. This instance of *master planning* the Palestinian water sector entirely disregarded stated Palestinian interests, not least of all their call for the implementation of the water rights that Israeli had agreed to in 1995. Secondly, the PWA's position of subordination and its inability to achieve its interests is further exposed by their initial acceptance of the project, however conditional it may have been. Third, and perhaps most importantly, is the support for the project that the Israelis were able to ensure from agencies on the American side, including the State Department in Washington as well as the US Embassy and USAID office in Tel Aviv. By convincing the water policy-makers of Palestine and of Palestine's most important donor that the project holds merit, the Israeli side successfully exerted a form of ideational power. The success in having the argument accepted was accomplished, in part, through deliberate public misrepresentation of the project's real water production costs by the Israeli Deputy Water Commissioner. Promotion of the project was ultimately halted not because of Palestinian refusal, but because of a shift in US State Department policy towards development assistance for the Palestinian people, following their election of Hamas in January 2006.[96]

In terms of costs to its reputation, foreign relations and sheer effort, these exertions of ideational power are far more efficient than coercive or incentive-based means of securing Palestinian compliance. This method, furthermore, effectively eliminates the (Palestinian) issue of inequitable allocations by presenting an image of Israeli cooperation and goodwill. The "élites of power" do not only make history by shaping our understanding of the past: their capacity for *master planning*, means that they can also make the present.

Sanctioning the Discourse

The élites of power can also sanction discourse, as we saw in Chapter 2. Whether or not it is fully aware of the extent of their utility, the most powerful riparian actor can employ the tools at its disposal to ensure a position of discursive hegemony is maintained. The extent and influence of the Israeli *Needs, not Rights* discourse is a strong case in point. We now turn to an examination of precisely *how* this came about, following the clues found in two mechanisms of power – donor funding to the PWA and influence over public opinion.

Influence of the sanctioned discourse over USAID

The US Government is by far the largest source of bi-lateral assistance in the water sector, primarily through the development efforts of USAID (Chapter 4). The water and wastewater sector, furthermore, was re-affirmed by USAID in 2005 as one of the main areas of "assistance to the Palestinian people" (USAID 2005), thereby sustaining the significance of the PWA–USAID client–donor relationship. The support of the US Government and USAID is all the more important to the Palestinians because of the role that USAID plays as the mediator of the Palestinian–Israeli interaction over water issues.

Palestinian dependency on American financial and political support through the apparatus results in an asymmetrical relationship and ensures that the PWA cannot afford to ignore USAID policies and activities (even if it were to challenge them). As such, the PWA as a whole has not realised the significance of that gem of insight into donor hydropolitics: 'the World Bank needs Egypt more than Egypt needs the World Bank'.

We have noted the transformation of the official Palestinian discourse during the Israeli Hegemony Era. The PWA essentially abandoned its *Rights First* discourse in favour for a *Cooperation* discourse that aligns itself with the US and Israeli-sanctioned discourses. This harmonisation of discourses ensures that Israeli interests prevail in any outcome, given the Palestinian compliance produced through the normative and ideational methods discussed above. The negative reaction of USAID and the Israeli water sector to the Palestinian *Rights First* discourse reveals, however, that total Palestinian compliance is not always assured, and must be obtained through other means. At 'water-cooler' meetings and informally after work, the routine and open discussions amongst USAID decision-makers follow the lines of 'the Palestinians have got to learn that they are the loser, and that the winner writes history'. The implication is that the PWA, and Palestinians in general, are wasting their efforts when they pursue Palestinian water rights in seeking redress for the inequitable allocation of transboundary waters.

Supporting evidence for this comes from an examination of the types of projects that USAID chooses to promote. Consider, for example, the USAID attitude to Palestinian concerns over the previously discussed proposal for the 'Hadera–Tulkarem' desalination plant. The opinion of the then highest-ranking resident water official at USAID towards the concerns raised by the PWA is telling:

> The PWA are afraid to show public support for the Hadera–Tulkarem project but we think it's a great idea since a) donors will fund it, b) it's easy to build (since it's mostly in Israel) and, c) the land is not an issue (we may deem the parts of the project running through Israeli sovereign territory as US property). But politically we know the Palestinians cannot support it. But they will support it, they say, as long as it doesn't pre-empt their water rights. So USAID and the Israelis will say "fine, it doesn't pre–empt your water rights" and then we'll build it anyway. (Newman 2004, pers. comm. (paraphrased)).

The pragmatic approach taken by the donor is less striking than the disregard shown for the needs and interests of its client. At one level, this is simply a case of a high-stakes donor-driven agenda, an objectively corrupt phenomenon experienced with monotonous regularity around the world. Considering that this US discourse also aligns very neatly with the Israeli *Needs, not Rights* discourse, however, the effects are further reaching. USAID actions fuel the formation of a coalition of discourses, with all of the predictable consequences that could be expected to entail. The Israeli *Needs, not Rights* discourse, which purposefully avoids the issue of resolution of the Palestinian–Israeli water conflict through negotiations of water re-allocation, has, at some point over the course of the Israeli Hegemony Era, become the 'sanctioned' international discourse. This was achieved contrapuntally by the most powerful riparian state through its influence on the extremely powerful main donor and mediator of the conflict.[97]

Influence of the sanctioned discourse beyond the basin
The effects of Israeli hegemony in the water sector are not confined to the Jordan River basin. International public opinion and academia are no more likely than the Israeli public to 'hear' the Palestinian *Rights First* discourse, given the limited avenues of expression open to its advocates. What these audiences are likely to hear are such statements as:

> [The 'Hadera–Tulkarem' proposal is stalled right now because] some of [the Palestinians] are still insisting on water rights from aquifers that in any case are empty and becoming saline. In other words, some of the Palestinians who deal with this issue are in the ideological phase, not the phase of pragmatic solutions (Kinnarty 2002);

and;

[T]he only treaty in which existing uses were relinquished is the 1995 Israel/Palestine accord on West Bank and Gaza aquifers ... By recognising and quantifying Palestinian needs, and by agreeing to provide 28.6 MCM/yr. towards those needs, the 1995 accord represents the only case in which prior rights are explicitly relinquished (Wolf 2000b: 140).

The discourse presented by then Israeli Water Commissioner Noah Kinnarty could be expected to be warmly received by USAID officials, caught up in a pragmatic spirit that facilitates their work by depoliticising it. Kinnarty's statement is deceptive, however, and requires analysis. He misleads first by obscuring a key fact. The aquifers that the Palestinians are demanding water rights from are the NEAB, EAB and WAB, which are not really "empty and becoming saline" (though, to be sure, water quality remains a concern for both sides). Secondly, in characterising his Palestinian counterparts as "ideological" for advocating the fulfilment of clauses agreed to by the Israeli side under the Oslo II Agreement, the Palestinian discourse is portrayed as problematic. In such a discursive climate Palestinian demands and Israeli obligations alike are more easily by-passed, put down or ignored altogether.

Though considerably different in tone, Wolf's assertion also warrants a closer examination. He suggests that the terms of the 1995 Oslo II Agreement form a unique case of notable cooperation, for Israel's 'explicit relinquishment' of its prior water rights to Palestinians. The pitch and content of the statement is likely to strike a chord with the international public, donors, scholars and others who would see or promote a 'water peace' discourse (see Chapter 4). It is hardly inconsequential to the Palestinian side, however, that the rights referred to have not been quantified, much less acquired in real terms. A disproportionate amount of focus may be being placed on the *spirit* of the Agreement, while the very limited impact it has had satisfying Palestinian demand is downplayed. In other words, the water conflict is de-emphasised as the benefits of cooperation are over-emphasised.

The manner in which the discourses shape the presentation and reception of depictions of the world is important. The Palestinians who speak in terms of the *Rights First* discourse are portrayed as illogical and obstructionist, while those who adhere to the Israeli *Needs, not Rights* approach are upheld as exemplars of ground-breaking goodwill and cooperation. Through such methods, hegemonic Israel is able to influence the ideas and opinions of the professional, donor, diplomatic and academic communities, including many of those in Palestine. The status quo is thus readily perpetuated and the low-intensity Palestinian–Israeli water conflict lingers on unresolved.

Conclusion

This chapter has shown something of the extent and influence of Israeli ideational power in international water conflicts. Some of the tactics used to wield ideational power have been identified as securitisation, master planning and sanctioning of the discourse. The curious fact that the Palestinian Water Authority did not initially reject the Israeli/US proposed 'Hadera–Tulkarem' desalination scheme is worth singling out as an instance of the effectiveness of ideational power. There is no doubt that the ideas promoted through the dominant discourse of the Palestinian–Israeli water conflict are compelling: 'there is simply not enough water for everyone'; 'we are all in this together, don't obstruct goodwill with an ideological fixation on rights'; 'too bad, so sad – the winner writes history'. Such ideas are reinforced by the mechanisms of a system that rewards compliance and punishes dissent. Groups holding such ideas will be met with open doors, ears and chequebooks. Dissenters are likely to remain on the fringes of the debate, oscillating between varying intensities of outrage, frustration, fear, despair and a sense of defeat.

It is apparent that there exists a form of Gramsci's "hegemonic apparatus," a mechanism for manufacturing consent, propagating the system and maintaining the power asymmetry. This is explored in greater detail in the final chapter, but Nussbaum's reflections on the relation between power and consent are worth considering briefly here. Following her study of women's oppression in India, Nussbaum suggested that: "[if] someone who has no property rights under the law, who has no formal education, who has no legal right of divorce, who will very likely be beaten if she seeks employment outside the house, says that she endorses traditions of modesty, purity and self-abrogation, it is not clear that we should consider this the last word on the matter" (Lukes 2005 [1974]: 146). Any analysis devoid of consideration of such an apparatus and its effects is considerably limited in its utility. At best it provides a distorted view of the world. At worst, such analysis can be inflammatory, recklessly preserving the conditions under which conflict and grievances continue to flourish.

Power, consent and projected lack of alternatives is just as relevant in our case. If the head of an important ministry in a crumbling donor-dependent government, who has inherited a deliberately weakened institution and a 'joint' management structure designed to prioritise his counterpart's military and political interests over his developmental ones, and whose shreds of legitimacy hang not on dedicated service to his own people but on continued participation in a coercive *modus vivendi*, consents to inappropriate infrastructure projects presented as the only alternative by his counterpart, we should not consider this the last word on the matter.[98]

An element missing from most analysis is an appreciation of the degree to which the ministry and minister alike are themselves subjects of the discourse they sustain. Both are bound in the chains of donor politics and entangled in an elaborate apparatus that quite effectively maintains control over the transboundary resources in the hands of the more powerful. This is so despite any number of loud declarations to the contrary, as these emanate from within the discursive structures of the apparatus itself.

So far, this analysis has revealed aspects of the hidden politics behind the Palestinian–Israeli water conflict and something of the extent of Israeli hegemony. The following chapter provides a detailed examination of the effects that these forms   of   power   have   on   water   production   and   consumption.

8

Hydraulic Power – Dominance of Production

PUMPING, power and politics combine to weave a tale in this chapter. By capitalising on over fifty years of water abstraction records kept by the Hydrological Survey of Israel, the quantitative hydraulic analysis undertaken complements the qualitative analysis of power-plays in previous chapters. The hidden politics and covert expressions of power we have reviewed would not be 'seen' by a classical hydraulic analysis. Conversely, a purely qualitative analysis would be weak on the ability to detect trends or flesh out its assertions. Combining the two approaches allows for the structured, conclusive, analysis of the nature of Israel's control of the conflict, which is presented in the final chapter.

Our analysis plots the figures against a time-frame of political, climatic and hydropolitical history, and adds an intriguing element to story of the water conflict. It will quickly become apparent that actual water production is not determined solely by official Israeli water policy. Strong domestic groups like the Agricultural lobby, or emblematic events like the 1967 Six-Day War or drought periods, have a powerful informal influence on the policy. Flows consumed by the Palestinian water sector are shown to be little more than an inconsequential fraction of the much larger picture – which is primarily shaped by Israeli pumps.

Several analyses employing consumption graphs have been made of Israeli water policy. These include: Kay et al. (1998); Allan (2001); Thomas (2004); Feitelson (2005a); and Fischhendler (forthcoming–a). The efforts have produced a fairly well-documented history of the hydrological negotiations, and the hydropolitical drivers, that have shaped the policy. There are at least three good reasons to repeat the exercise here. First, previous analyses have not been conducted within a power analytical framework. Secondly, Israeli consumption figures will be compared with *Palestinian* consumption figures, enabling a parallel view of markedly different water development trajectories. Thirdly, previous analyses have been limited to the study of Israeli *consumption* figures: they are therefore lacking in the insights that come from considering Israeli water *production* rates and – more importantly – the water sources themselves (i.e. surface or groundwater). Israeli production data is presented in Figure 8.1, Israeli consumption data in Figure 8.3, and Palestinian consumption data in Figure 8.4.

A note on the analytical frame and data used in this chapter's analysis
The frame used in Figures 8.1, 8.3 and 8.4 has multiple layers. Our examination of consumption figures requires their sub-divisions into the three main sectors of consumption, i.e. domestic, industrial and agricultural. Domestic consumption rates are also broken down into a further sub-layer of population data. Production figures are likewise divided into the two main sources of water, i.e. surface water and groundwater. The categories for time scale of the frame are the four hydropolitical eras that were employed in our review of the hydropolitical history[99] (Chapter 4). The bulk of the data employed for the following analysis comes from the Israel Water Commission (IWC) report *Consumption and Production 2001*, and other sources offered in Appendix C.

Water and the Oslo II Agreement
Paragraph 3a of Article 40 of the Oslo II Agreement lays out the principles of the water-sharing agreement according to the "existing quantities of utilisation", plus an additional 78 MCM/y that the Palestinian side could develop from the Eastern Aquifer Basin (Chapter 7). The unstated rationale for such an arrangement was that all basins (except the EAB) were being fully exploited by 1995, and could not / should not be further developed. Schedule 10 of the Agreement also details "existing extractions, utilization and estimated potential" of each aquifer. As we saw in Table 3.3, these were 145 MCM/y for the NEAB; 94 (+78) MCM/y for the EAB and 362 MCM/y for the WAB.

Schedule 8 of the Agreement further stipulates that "the increase of extraction from any water source, by either side, shall require the prior approval of the JWC", referring to the previously discussed Joint Water Committee. Taken together, the provisions of Article 40 and Schedules 8 and 10 render the usage quantities of Table 1 *effective limits* on abstraction for each side, within the West Bank. Additional wells in the same aquifers in Israel are not subject to JWC deliberations. Abstraction above and beyond the Oslo-II defined usage quantities without the approval of the JWC are subsequently considered violations of the Agreement. The effective limits – and potential violations of – abstraction should be borne in mind as we continue with the analysis.

Israeli Water Production 1948–2003

As the flows being contested in the Palestinian–Israeli water conflict are *fresh* water flows, analysis of production based on the source of production is important. The source is either from boreholes (i.e. groundwater) or surface water (including springs), according to the terms of the Israel Water Commission and as shown in Figure 8.1. 'New' water sources such as treated wastewater and desalinated brackish or seawater are excluded from the analysis, as it is the competition over freshwater flows that concerns us most. The pumping record serves to tell the story of Israeli national development, hydropolitics and power. A combined reading of both sources of production serves to highlight yet more outcomes deriving from the asymmetry in Israeli–Palestinian power relations.

Description and analysis of Israeli Groundwater Production

Perhaps the most striking aspect of the production curves in Figure 8.1 is the great increase in Israeli groundwater production during the 'Ideological Era' from 1948 to 1968. The middle curve of the figure shows that groundwater production increased from roughly 300 MCM/y to 1,000 MCM/y, during a period characterised by Israeli national and Zionist ideological objectives and by contestation with Syria and Jordan over control of the region's main surface water (see Chapter 4).

The only source of water to which the State of Israel had uncontested access during this period was the groundwater located within its own political borders. The bulk of this was developed through shallow and deep wells in the Coastal Aquifer Basin (CAB) and the Western Aquifer Basin (WAB), extraction from both of which had begun to exceed the estimated sustainable yields as early as the 1970s. The levelling-off of the groundwater production curve during the 'Israeli Domination Era' from the 1970s reflects attempts by Israeli water professionals to preserve the natural resource, and the increased ability of the state to meet the water demand through the pumping of surface water (particularly from 1964 onwards, as we shall see). The same period also marked the beginning of the highly contentious internal Israeli allocation debates.

The significant drought event of 1985 and the corresponding initial cuts in allocation to the agricultural sector are indicated in Figure 8.1 by the first drop in groundwater production. The events also mark the beginning of the widely varying Israeli groundwater pumping volumes that continue until the present. The 1989–91 drought period accounts for the even greater drop in production in 1992, down to pre-1962 levels. The reduction in groundwater production at this point reflects rational resource water management practices.

Analysts have offered explanations for the steady growth in groundwater production during the 1990s, which reached its highest peak in 1999, from two perspectives. A rational water management response to the rapid recharge of the karst aquifers following the heavy rains of 1992, appears to offer an explanation from a hydrological perspective. Tony Allan (2001: 210), by contrast, approaches these changes from a hydropolitical perspective. He suggests that the increase in groundwater withdrawals were a response to Israeli perceptions of a heightened risk of losing control of some of this water, in light of the negotiations it was entering with both Jordan and the Palestinians. Whether or not it is politically motivated, Israeli production from the Western Aquifer Basin has since 1991 consistently surpassed the estimated renewable abstraction limits which were later agreed to under Oslo II, as we will explore in Figure 8.2. Groundwater production has dropped steadily since the 1999 peak.

Description and analysis of Israeli Surface Water Production
Unlike the rapid and unobstructed development of groundwater during the
'Ideological Era', Israeli development of surface water sources was obstructed by
clashes with Syria and the political wrangling of the demands of the Johnston
mission. Surface water production (lower curve of Figure 8.1) increased
dramatically upon completion of the Israel National Water Carrier (NWC) in 1964,
nearly doubling over the following eight years. Following the relative peak reached
in 1971 near the beginning of the Israeli Domination Era, surface water production
continued to vary while levelling off in much the same manner as groundwater
production.

Surface water production also decreased with the first cuts to the agricultural
sector in 1986 and reached an extreme low following the 1990 drought, one year
ahead of the low in groundwater production. Both sources continued to be
produced and managed in concert until the late 1990s. As with groundwater
production, surface water production climbed steadily following the 1989–1991
drought, until reaching a peak in 1998, one year ahead of the groundwater
production peak. Surface water production has remained highly variable
throughout the rest of the Israeli Hegemony Era.

Analysis of Total Water Production
Comparison of the groundwater, surface water and total production curves of
Figure 8.1 reveals the extent of Israeli dominance over neighbouring Palestine. The
upper curve shows that there is a strong relation between total water production
and each of the four distinct hydropolitical eras identified in Chapter 4. Total
freshwater production increased steadily during the 'Ideological Era', levelled-off at
the beginning of the 'Israeli Domination Era' and has been erratic since that time,
hovering widely around 1,750 MCM/y. Though one should not read too much into
the link between Israeli freshwater production and hydropolitical events, it cannot
be explained away as mere coincidence, as we shall see below.

Figure 8.1 also shows how the two main sources of freshwater have been
produced in concert – at least until 1999. Coordinated management of different
water sources is common water management practice. Surface water is typically
more responsive than groundwater to droughts and changes in administration, not
least of all simply because the flows are more visible and thus prone to public
pressure. It is widely acknowledged that the water levels in the Lake of Tiberias, for
instance, are as closely followed by environmental groups and the media as they are
monitored by the scientists at the Kinneret Limnological Laboratory. Of greater
relevance from a power-analytic perspective is the fact that the water demand of
the various Israeli sectors *will* be met – whether through groundwater or surface
water sources. In other words, water management in Israel is driven by internal
demand, not by the sustainable limits of the resource, or out of concern for the

grievances of neighbouring riparian states. And internal demand, as we have seen, is driven mainly by the agricultural sector.

Further evidence that the Israeli water sector operates according to a supply-side management paradigm is given by the split in the common trend between groundwater and surface water, in 1999. The sharp decrease in surface water production by the late 1990s , driven in part by dropping Tiberias levels (Thomas 2004), was made up by increased production of groundwater. In order to meet the inelastic national Israeli water demand, the strain was borne by the less visible but equally sensitive groundwater resources, particularly those of the Western Aquifer Basin.

Israeli over-abstraction from the Western Aquifer Basin

Israeli reliance on the Western Aquifer Basin (WAB) has come at the double cost of over-abstraction of the stated sustainable limits of the resource and violation of the terms of the 1995 Oslo II Accord. Figure 8.2 surveys Israeli abstractions from the WAB, based on official figures and a similar graph provided by the Hydrological Service of Israel. Israeli abstraction of groundwater from the Western Aquifer Basin (WAB) is presented in Figure 8.2, which is based on a similar graph provided by the Hydrological Service of Israel. We observe that Israeli abstractions from wells and springs exceeds the 340 MCM/y – stipulated as the effective limit of Israeli abstraction in Oslo II – on average by 88 MCM/y from 1995 to 2003. This quantity does not include Palestinian production from the same aquifer, which was roughly 22 MCM/y before considering the effects of the Wall. Just as sombrely, the unceasing production is much greater than the "estimated potential" defined in Oslo II as 362 MCM/y (see HSI (2004: 138)). Israeli abstraction from the WAB in 1998/99 alone was 582 MCM/y. This is more than 1.5 times the suggested capacity of the resource, and nearly equivalent to the entire volume of water consumed by Palestinians from all sources during the same year (as we will see in Figure 3.1).

The evidence leads to several potential conclusions. First, several Israeli and international hydrogeologists agree that the WAB's Oslo II-defined "potential" of 362 MCM/y is considerably lower than the basin's actual safe yield. The implication is that the limit was set deliberately low – either for ultra-cautious environmental reasons, or political reasons, or a combination of the two. Fischhendler attributes the "over"-abstraction to successful pressure from the Israeli Agricultural lobby to modify the criteria for compensation from the Emergency Decree, the emergency policy set up as a response to the beginning of the 1999–2002 drought: "Ultimately, the 40 per cent cutbacks in the agricultural sector [for 1999] … dwindled to 27 per cent. The difference was provided by overexploitation from the Mountain [Western, Eastern and Northeastern] Aquifer [s]" (Fischhendler forthcoming–a: 9).

Figure 8.1 Freshwater Production in Israel, 1948 - 2003.

IWC (2002b) (see Appendix C). Freshwater figures do *not* include production from wastewater re-use or desalination techniques.

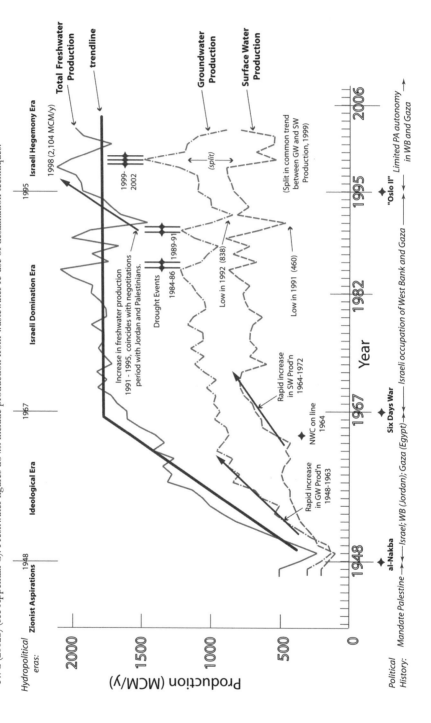

In the event that the 362 MCM/y figure cited in the Oslo II Agreement was not deliberately set low, the quantity may reflect the Israel Water Commission's best guess at the aquifer's long-term safe yield. In that case, Israeli abstractions since the endorsement of the Agreement would be consistently – and dangerously – high.

Whether or not the yield of the aquifer was set deliberately low, the spirit and the letter of the agreement signed with the Palestinians are breached. The pumping record of Figure 8.2 betrays the notion that the Palestinian-Israeli water agreement has led to rational water management of the most important transboundary resource. Selby's (2005)characterisation of the JWC as a forum for "joint mismanagement", it would appear, holds fast. It is perhaps not surprising to find in a recent poll taken of members of the Israeli Water Engineers Association that "over 96% of all respondents thought the water sector is in crisis, and over 91% thought that severe or very severe damage was caused to the water resources" (Feitelson 2005a: 417).

Figure 8.2   Israeli over-abstraction of the Western Aquifer Basin, 1970–2003.

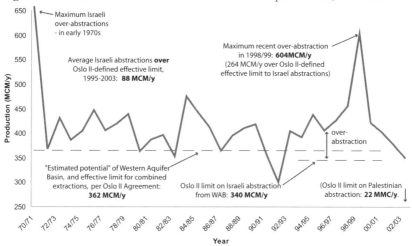

Data from Hydrological Survey of Israel, HSI (2004: 138).

These Israeli violations of the letter of the Oslo Accords are made possible by virtue of the fact that the broader political context is structured more by power asymmetry than by the rule of law or a balance of powers. While the JWC is mandated to monitor abstractions within the political borders of the West Bank, it is not mandated to monitor – let alone control – abstractions from within Israel. Sole responsibility for monitoring or reducing the abstractions lies with the Israel Water Commission.

A final, but significant, point that can be made about the violations of the Oslo II Agreement on the Western Aquifer relates to the Palestinian response. While the data is officially in the public domain, there is no detectable outcry about over-abstraction. No demand for an enforcement mechanism to deal with the violations has been voiced by either the official Palestinian side or Israeli and Palestinian civil society. Perhaps as was the case with the Wall, the Palestinian Water Authority may not want to raise the issue and risk losing what little legitimacy the Israeli side grants it. Israeli and Palestinian human rights groups may be too pre-occupied in their documentation of more acute issues, such as land confiscation, house demolitions, assassinations and massacres, to attempt to draw attention to the more chronic hydrologic violations. The 'hegemonic apparatus' is quite efficient here, serving to organise some issues out of an otherwise vigorous debate. The more powerful position enjoyed by the Israeli side affords it the luxury of being able to choose between abiding by the terms of the agreement it has signed or meeting its domestic demand driven chiefly by the agricultural sector.

Israeli and Palestinian Water Consumption 1948–2003

The story emerging from an examination of Israeli water *consumption* through time (Figure 8.3) is of the effects on water management policy of the various lobby groups, and the internal tensions that exist between them. As was the case with Israeli water production from 1948 to 2003, an analysis of Israeli water consumption data reveals the extent of its hegemony – or domination – over its Palestinian counterpart.

Analyses similar to that found in Figure 8.3 have recently been produced from hydraulic perspectives (in Thomas 2004) and political economy perspectives (in Feitelson 2005a). Though these studies do not consider the effects of power asymmetries on water policy, their findings serve to complete the broader picture. The following discussion focuses on the effects of hydropolitical events and exercises of power, particularly on the Israeli Domestic and Agricultural sectors.[100]

Description and analysis of Israeli Domestic Water Consumption

There are three main attributes to note from the Israeli Domestic consumption curve in Figure 8.3. The first is the steady increase since 1948. Accounting for roughly 15 per cent (~211 MCM/y) of total water consumption in 1967, the Domestic sector accounted for over 30 per cent (~672 MCM/y) by 1998. Given the predicted steady population growth, it is likely that Domestic sector consumption will continue to increase. It is also likely to increase in relation to the other sectors, and to acquire a greater influence over national-level water policy than in the past.

Secondly, there is the sector's direct relationship with the Israeli population. Although such a relationship is to be expected, the parallel rates at which the curves develop is nonetheless striking. Based on the quantities presented, Israeli per capita domestic consumption rates are substantially unchanged since the creation of the state, having consistently ranged from 240 to 300 litres per person per day (87–110 MCM per person per year).

Lastly, we see the *drop* in consumption in 1990–91, which occurred despite the rapid increase in population due to the wave of Russian immigration in 1989.

Decreased domestic consumption during a time of increasing population reflects the potential responsiveness of the sector to national water policies and to the water-saving measures taken during the drought. The Israel Water Commission announcement in 2006 of a Master Plan for saving up to 135 MCM/y by 2020 on Domestic consumption (FOEME 2006b), will be counting on this responsiveness to meet the challenge.

Description and analysis of Israeli Agricultural Water Consumption
By far the largest consumer of water, the Israeli Agricultural sector has always been the main force driving, shaping and obstructing Israeli water policies. The most striking feature of Figure 8.3 is the rapid increase in Agricultural Consumption during the 'Ideological Era', which corresponds with the rapid increase in groundwater production (from Figure 8.1). Agricultural consumption rose nearly five-fold from 260 MCM/y in 1948 to roughly 1,200 MCM/y by 1968. The continued growth – albeit slower – towards the end of the Ideological Era was fuelled by increased surface water production, made possible in large part by the hydraulic capacity of the National Water Carrier and related Lake of Tiberias water works.

Of note also are the three significant drops in Agricultural consumption in the wake of drought periods. Cuts to the sector made following such emblematic events reveal that the Agricultural sector – much more than the Domestic or Industrial sectors –has been affected by uncertainty in supply volumes.[101] Such 'excess' water beyond the Agricultural consumption freshwater cap of 530 MCM/y is readily obtained by the sector through exemptions to the cap (Arlosoroff 2005, pers. comm.) and continuous agricultural lobbying to reduce the rationing (Fischhendler forthcoming–a: Figure 3). The irregular exploitation of high variability by the sector (the flows range from ~ 800 to 1,300 MCM/y) have led to it being characterised as Israel's "strategic reserve" in Allan's words, or "de facto buffer" to cite Feitelson once again. The terms reflect the role these flows play in mitigating conflict over internal Israeli distribution.

Analysis of Total Israeli Water Consumption
Israeli per capita water consumption rates vary widely. They reached a peak of 980 litres per person per day (358 MCM per person per year) in 1998 with a rough average similar to the 2003 rate of 753 litres per person per day (275 MCM per person per year).

As with the Production graph, the Total Consumption curve is distinguished by three distinct phases. While there is an evident relation between water consumption and important political events, this may be less direct than with the production data. Water consumption rates did not level off at the beginning of the 'Israeli Domination Era', for example. In fact, despite the variable consumption rates reflecting the changing Israeli policy in the agricultural sector toward the end of the 1970s, total consumption rates have never really stabilised.

Figure 8.3 Total Water Consumption in Israel, 1948 - 2003.

IWC (2002b) (see Appendix C). Total Water Consumption and Agricultural Consumption figures *include* water produced through wastewater re-use and desalination from 1993 onwards (roughly 200 MCM/y), explaining why these are sometimes greater than the production figures of Figure 8.1.

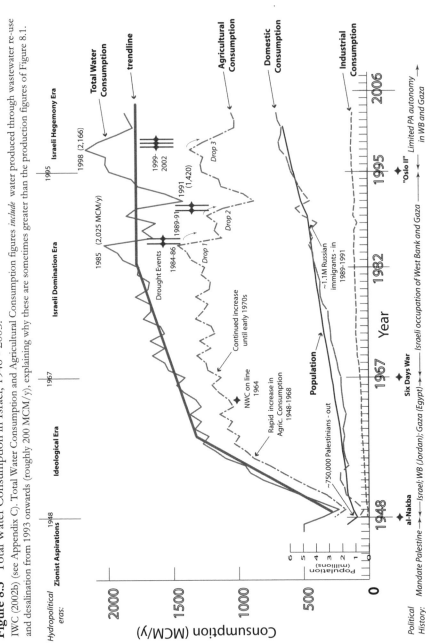

The persistent variability reveals that it is water *production* (i.e. pumping) rates that are determined by policy, while consumption is determined in turn by how much is produced. Another way to express what may be a self-evident conclusion is all the water that can be produced will be consumed (or vice versa). While this may be expected for drinking water, it is not a foregone conclusion for agricultural water policy. The allocation of the 'strategic reserve' flows is determined by the Israel Water Commission and Water Council, in a highly politicised process. During drought periods, internal allocations will favour the domestic and industrial sectors. Allocation of the buffer flows during wet years is competed for by numerous sectors: the Agricultural sector; flows for aquifer recharge; flows for the environment; and flows deemed to satisfy future Palestinian domestic demand. We turn now to briefly examine the consumption of this latter, Palestinian 'sector'.

Description and analysis of Palestinian Water Consumption

Figure 8.4 plots the estimated Total Palestinian Water Consumption against the Israeli Consumption curves of Figure 8.3. Total Palestinian Consumption pales in significance to the Israeli Agricultural or even Domestic sectors. But a closer look reveals an even more imbalanced story. Firstly, whereas Israeli pumping rates have been accurately monitored and recorded (at least since 1959), Palestinian pumping rates remain disaggregated and are readily contested. The paucity of reliable data reflects in part the state of affairs in the Palestinian side's management of the resource - and their lack of real control over it. The second feature to note is the consistently very low rate of increase in total consumption since 1948. There are no sharp increases in consumption (or in production) during periods of British, Egyptian and Jordanian, Israeli or Palestinian Authority rule. Despite efforts by the PWA and the international donor community, Palestinian efforts to embark on a 'hydraulic mission' have failed. One symptom of this is *decreasing* Palestinian per capita water consumption rates, with roughly the same volumes of water allocated to an ever-growing population. Based on the quantities presented, Total Palestinian *per capita* consumption rates hover around 260 litres per person per day[102] (95 MCM per person per year). Chapter 9 discusses other consequences of the failed development efforts.

The most conspicuous feature of Figure 8.4, however, remains the significant disparity between Palestinian and Israeli consumption. Total Israeli consumption is consistently five–six times greater than Palestinian consumption. Perhaps more significantly, Total Palestinian consumption – including all the irrigation water used by farmers in Palestine – runs to less than half that of Israeli *Domestic* consumption. Maintained at such a relatively small share, Palestinian consumption in the current order of affairs bears minimally on Israeli water policy and is insignificant, to all intents and purposes, to Israeli water policy-makers. This point is elaborated upon in the 'Aside' following, and will be developed as we proceed with the analysis.

Figure 8.4 Comparison of Israeli and Palestinian Water Consumption, 1948 - 2003.
IWC (2002b) (see Appendix C). Total Water Consumption and Agricultural Consumption figures *include* water produced through wastewater re-use and desalination from 1993 onwards (roughly 200 MCM/y). Palestinian production through these methods is currently neglible.

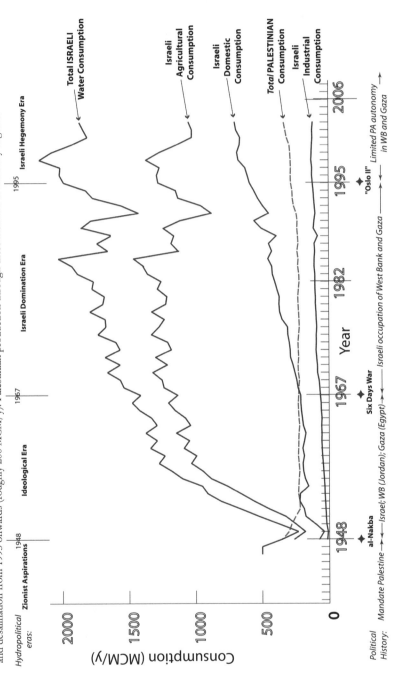

Box: On the data of the Israel Water Commission

An assessment of the methodology used by the Israel Water Commission (IWC) for the bulk of the data of Figures 8.1 and 8.3 can inform our power-based analysis of the Palestinian–Israeli water conflict. The 2002 IWC report states clearly that its production and consumption figures *include* the quantities supplied by Israel to the Palestinians (which it states as 39 MCM/y in 2001 (34 MCM/y for the WB and 5MCM/y for Gaza)).

The 2002 IWC report figures do not include flows produced by Palestinian sources, which it estimates outside of the tabulated figures in the West Bank as roughly 30 MCM/y (IWC 2002b: 7). This figure presumably includes the flows to Palestinians from the PWA wells, municipal wells and WBWD wells, and corresponds to the figures of Table 3.3. The report makes no mention of Palestinian production figures in the Gaza Strip, nor does it distinguish between Palestinian and Israeli *consumption* figures throughout the decades. While the consumption figures given prior to 1967 in the report are known to reflect solely Israeli use, it is not clear whether the figures post-1967 include the consumption of the Palestinian inhabitants of the West Bank and Gaza, for whom Israel had by then acquired responsibility. As all Palestinian wells therein came under the control of the Israeli authorities, one might expect to observe a jump in the volumes of water produced 'suddenly' under Israeli control. This increase would be expected to be roughly equal to the volume of water that was being produced until that time under Jordanian and Egyptian rule.

The IWC reports during this period (including the publications dated 1969, 1970 and 1978) reveal, however, that the West Bank and Gaza were not considered part of the IWC 'planning regions'. It is apparent that Israeli-controlled Palestinian production and consumption in the West Bank and Gaza were *not* included with the published figures, at least until the date of the 1978 publication. The West Bank and Gaza did become part of the IWC's planning regions at some point between the 1978 and 2002 IWC reports, however. By 2002, Gaza was included in the 'Negev' region while the West Bank is included in the 'Jordan Valley'; 'Judean Desert and Dead Sea'; and 'Judea and Samaria' regions. The shift in recording methods reflects the shift in Israeli policy as an occupying and dominating force. It would be interesting to determine how, why and at which point between 1978 and 2002 did Palestinian land become an Israeli water planning region. Of further relevance would be an exploration of how Israeli hegemony was encouraged by official use of ideology, such as the Zionist labels 'Judea and Samaria' for parts of the West Bank.[103]

The quantities supplied by Mekoroth through the WBWD and Palestinian municipal wells is known to vary from zero in June 1967 to 26–28 MCM/y by the time of the 1995 Oslo II Accord and the handover of responsibility to the Palestinian Authority (from Table 3.1). Few wells were dug by Israel in the Gaza Strip during this period (within which production decreased from roughly 120 MCM/y in 1967 to roughly 100 MCM/y by 1995 (el Musa, 1997).

It is noteworthy that the bulk of the water consumed by Palestinians during the decades of Israeli occupation came from traditional sources, i.e. private agricultural wells and springs. Although these were monitored and controlled by Israeli authorities, the 'production' of this water was not directly through Israeli efforts, nor was it counted by the Water Commission as such. [104] Water consumed by Palestinians from these sources was similarly not counted in the published Israeli consumption figures. The recording methods and magnitude of the flows explain why no drop is observed in either consumption or production following the handover of the responsibility of water supply to the PWA in 1995. In other words, the flows currently produced and consumed by Palestinians have *no demonstrable effect on Israeli policy*. In the Gaza Strip, these flows are downstream and completely outside of the Israeli sphere of concern. In the West Bank the flows are relatively small enough to be lost within the accounting margin of error of the IWC.

Summary Analysis of Water Production and Consumption

This section provides a power-based combined analysis of the production and consumption figures. Several dimensions of the Palestinian–Israeli water conflict are unearthed, the most significant of which are shown in Figure 8.5. Three of these are related to a reduced uncertainty of flows for Israel – which are here labelled 'risk dimensions' – while the final one is of a hydropolitical nature. It is argued that each dimension is in part consequential on the pervasive imbalance of power between the sides.

Risk Dimension #1: Greater Assurance of Supply
One intriguing feature of Figure 8.5 is the levelling-off around 1967 in both Total Production and Agricultural Consumption rates. Although Agricultural Consumption rates vary greatly from 1967 onwards (in response to cuts when obliged to, or by drawing on the strategic reserve whenever possible), there is an apparent mean of approximately 1,200 MCM/y, first reached in 1968. Similarly, and as was noted in Figure 8.1, Total Production rates are seen to level off at roughly 1,750 MCM/y in 1969. From a resource management point of view, the levelling-off of production rates is a rational reaction to peaks in over-abstraction (most notably in the Coastal and Western Aquifer basins). Certainly, this is the sanctioned discourse on the subject, and has been argued for by numerous academics.[105]

There may be an under-emphasised dimension to the hydropolitical history of the 1967 war, however. Israel's conquest of the entire territory on both shores of the Upper Jordan River, the headwaters of the Banias River, the west shore of the Lower Jordan River and the Western, North Eastern and Eastern Aquifer Basins has had demonstrable effects on Israel water planning and practice. The effects of the conquest of land are observed in the greater assurance of supply afforded to Israeli water policy-makers.

Without the relative guarantee of supply provided by the 1967 Israeli resource capture, two scenarios could be expected to have developed: either a) a levelling-off of production and consumption at rates substantially lower than the actual ones, as further development would have been compromised by continued skirmishes with Syria and Jordan; or b) spiralling production levels far exceeding the estimated sustainable yields, in a typical response to the absence of an assured supply.[106] That neither scenario has occurred reflects the new-found confidence in Israel's capacity to exploit the flows following 1967 and it ability to sustain the supply-driven management paradigm ever since.[107] This is confirmed by the pumping and consumption record, whether or not it forms part of the sanctioned discourse or is in the active consciousness of water policy-makers.

Turton has suggested that the reduction of uncertainty in this case is a key instance of desecuritisation: a process which may create an opportunity to address the fundamental drivers of a conflict (2003: 175). The drop in the Israeli public's interest in water issues following the 1967 resource capture reflects the desecuritisation. The basic drivers of the conflict were unfortunately *not* addressed, however, subsequent to the war. Water issues were (re)securitised when they served ulterior political goals, as we shall see.

Risk Dimension #2: Control Over Allocation of 'Strategic Reserve' Flows
A second feature to note from a combined reading of the water consumption and production graphs is – once again – the high variability. We have described the flows available from wet years above the estimated sustainable yields of all transboundary sources as *strategic reserve* or *de facto buffer*, allocated by the Israel Water Commission. How Israeli water policy-makers view these 'excess' flows in light of the needs of Palestinians is revealing.

Consider, for instance, the experience of the good rains of 2004 and 2005, whereby surface water levels in the Lake of Tiberias rose to the point of nearly over-spilling the Alumot dam (see photographs, Appendix A). Contrary to Israeli custom of halting pumping from the National Water Carrier during the Passover period,[108] the pumps in 2004 operated at their full capacity around the clock. The break with tradition was justified by the Israeli Minister of Infrastructure in terms of the cost of the water that would be 'wasted' if it were to overflow into the Jordan River. The head of the Planning Division of the IWC furthermore commented on the effect of such rainy seasons, stating that they would result in the temporary halting of the more expensive water produced by future desalination plants (Cohen 2004b).

What is the likelihood of this 'reserve' of water being considered for allocation to Palestinians? One must consider it in light of the fierce competition between the Israeli Agricultural lobby, water professionals, the Ministries of Infrastructure and Finance, and environmental groups.

Figure 8.5 Four Power-Related Dimensions of the Water Conflict.

IWC (2002b) (see Appendix C). Total Water Consumption and Agricultural Consumption figures *include* water produced through wastewater re-use and desalination from 1993 onwards (roughly 200 MCM/y). Total Freshwater figures do not.

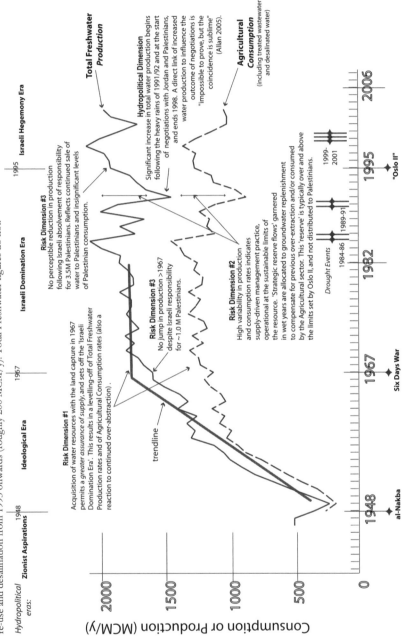

Israeli allocation policies are expected to continue to exclude Palestinian water needs so long as they remain based on ideological arguments and not on international obligations (Chapter 4). The water needs of the Palestinians are generally regarded solely under economic arrangements. Viewed as a sector willing to pay for it, the Palestinian side has a chance to compete with the Israeli agricultural sector, for instance. With no representation at any decision-making levels, the outcome for the Palestinian side is subject to the pressures of the broader political context. As we have seen in many instances, it has little ability to bring about any such pressure. The hegemonic apparatus continues to function silently and efficiently, as the PWA commits to purchase more from Mekoroth. Reserve flows may not be up for negotiation under a context of re-allocation and resolution of the conflict, but they may happily be purchased under economic terms written by the Israeli side.

Risk Dimension #3: Maintaining Insignificant Levels of Palestinian Consumption
The third power-related dimension to note from Figure 8.5 highlights the irrelevance of the Palestinian position even further. Palestinian water demand, like Palestinian consumption and production rates, has little to no impact on Israeli water policy. Palestinian flows in fact are small to the point that they fit within the margins of error of Israeli record-keeping, and the water sold to Palestinians does not visually alter the Israeli water production curves. The 'peace dividends' generated by these otherwise marginal economic transactions are surely greater than the economic rewards. The official discourse is replete with highly principled declarations that the Israeli side is 'providing' the Palestinian side with water in a spirit of cooperation. The spirit could be expected to change were the Palestinian side able to exert more pressure than the Agricultural lobby, for instance, and purchase volumes of the same magnitude. Indeed, if the Palestinian side were able to consume quantities that might threaten the interests of any of the Israeli sectors, the intensity of the conflict might be felt by the Israeli side as it is on the Palestinian side. The scenario, however, is actively prevented.

Israeli-measured consumption rates did not change with the added responsibility of providing water to roughly one million Palestinians in 1967. Nor were Israeli consumption rates affected by the loss of this responsibility in 1995, as Israeli-supplied water going to Palestinians at that time was in the order of only 30 MCM/y (or one per cent of total Israeli consumption). The oppressive water-related Military Orders imposed during the Israeli occupation have in effect been replaced (and legitimised) by the terms of the Joint Water Committee. These arrangements have ensured that Palestinian water consumption is kept at a level which the Israeli side can accept, forecast and contain. This element of control serves to further reduce the uncertainty of the physical scarcity of the flows – at least for the Israeli side. The pumping record testifies to Israel's 'careful' policy towards Palestinian consumption.

Hydropolitical Dimension: The Effect on Negotiations
Of the several apparent paradoxes that can be read from Figure 8.5, one of the most relevant to the water conflict is the steady increase in both Total Production and Agricultural Consumption following the 1989–1991 drought period. Developing in the wake of the IWC's success in curbing the agricultural sector's thirst by the early 1990s, it is somewhat surprising to see the upward surge on the heels of the heavy rains of 1991. Increased Agricultural Consumption is in part due to the yearly renewals of the exemptions of Agricultural allocation caps, plus a lowering of rationing targets, as we have seen. The surge also coincides with the period of negotiations prior to the signing of the political agreements with Jordan and Palestine. By the time inter-*state* allocations were determined by 1994 and 1995, Israeli freshwater production levels had risen sharply to 1,918 MCM/y up from the 1991 low of 1,450 MCM/y. Freshwater production continued to rise in the years following the signing of the agreements, reaching a record peak of 2,103 MCM/y in 1998. It is worth reiterating the point that the discussion centres around *fresh* water flows, and excludes the 'new' water derived from desalination or wastewater treatment techniques.

Considering that the agricultural sector was associated with less than two percent of Israeli GNP by this time, the surge during the negotiations period cannot be explained by any economic arguments. The surge is also difficult to attribute to rational water management policies. A hydrogeologist from the British Geological Survey points out the very rapid recharge rate of the karst aquifers of the WAB, for example, as shown in Figure 8.6.

Figure 8.6 shows the elastic relation between groundwater (aquifer) levels and rainfall, most poignantly revealed by the dip in abstraction with the heavy rains of 1992. The increased abstraction rates that also follow the heavy rains may be rationalised by reference to the sudden relative abundance of groundwater. In other words, after increasing their reliance on surface water or other aquifers, Israeli water managers may want to 'relax' abstraction from other sources and draw from the now full Western Aquifer. This deduction is tempered by considering two other aspects of groundwater management, however. Firstly, groundwater abstraction rates typically *drop* following heavy rains, as there is less dependence on groundwater (as more soil water is available and less irrigation is required).[109] Secondly, if groundwater abstraction from the WAB were suddenly called upon to relieve the pressure on other water resources, we would expect to see a corresponding decrease in production from other sources. As we noted in Figure 8.1, however, both surface water *and* groundwater production *increased* from 1991 to 1995, giving yet more credence to a political explanation to the phenomena.

The possibility that Israeli consumption rates were increased in order to improve the Israeli position at the negotiations table with Palestinians and Jordanians was first raised by Tony Allan (2001: 210, 250). Given that the prospect of Israeli goverments losing some of their control over water was perceived as a security issue in previous eras, (Chapter 4), there does seem to be some justification for the claim. It is further supported by further consideration of the anti-negotiations stance taken by proponents of the Israeli hydrostrategic discourse, along with the timing of the renewal of such discourse.

In any case, the sudden increase in Agricultural consumption following years of effort directed to reducing overall consumption is not explained on economic or scientific grounds. A weak explanation may be that the sudden feeling that water was in abundance, following the 1992 rains, may have reduced the will to maintain the politically costly cuts to the Agricultural sector. Without judging intentions, it is impossible to identify which elements of the Israeli water sector drove the increase, and whether it was intentional or not. After repeatedly testing his hypothesis – that Israeli water production increased to improve its negotiating position – on Israeli water professional, however, Tony Allan maintains that "it is impossible to prove, but the coincidence is sublime" (Allan 2005).

Figure 8.6   Rainfall, groundwater levels, and abstraction rates in the Western Aquifer Basin.

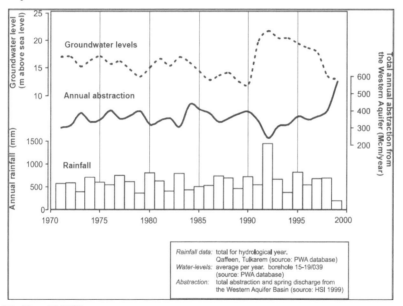

(MacDonald 2002).

Conclusions

Our review of the relations between the Israeli and Palestinian hydro-economies and their respective hydraulic power has revealed several key features which add to the qualitative analysis of the previous chapters. We have seen that the supply-side water management paradigm in Israel continues to be dominant: whatever source is available to meet the demand of its various sectors will be used. Scrutiny of Israeli consumption figures has revealed how Domestic consumption continues to grow in importance, reaching 30 per cent of all of the water consumed. The Israeli Agricultural sector continues to drive water policy despite persistent efforts by Israeli water professionals and the Ministry of Finance to address the situation. The focus on water supply is shown to come at the double cost of over-abstraction of the aquifers and violation of the Oslo II Agreement. The policies of Israel are marginally, if at all, affected by Palestinian policy in the sector, while all Palestinian use, consumption and planning are tightly bound to Israeli policy decisions. The Palestinian side is 'free' to purchase water from the Israeli side, only so long as the latter is willing to sell it and even then only under its conditions. There are, furthermore, strong indications that Israeli water production is, at least partially, tied to negotiations in the broader political context.

The significant differences between the pumping and consumption records of each side reflect the extreme power asymmetry between them. The significantly determining role of power disparity can be seen, at this stage, amidst other aspects of the water conflict. The features reviewed to this point – control of the transboundary flows, allocation of the flows, hydraulic capacity, donor assistance, persceptions and analysis of the conflict – have all been moulded to an extent by power asymmetry. The asymmetry and outcome were more overt and measurable when Israel officially occupied the West Bank and Gaza from 1967 until 1995. Since the 1995 Oslo II Agreement, they have been maintained through more subtle, hegemonic means. The following (and final) chapter examines this shift to hegemony – and its damaging effects – more explicitly.

9

Israeli Hydro-Hegemony

The cold reality of power is, of course, that it has to be endured. Even when it is culpable and seen to be so, its effective reality is that it cannot be escaped for a duration.
Wole Soyinka (b. 1934)

THE Israeli side's control over transboundary freshwater resources is complete, at many levels. Whether enforced through military orders, enshrined in agreements, or held in place through arguments of pragmatism and threats, the degree of control in the hands of the more powerful affords little space to the less powerful. The established 'order of things' between the two sides in the water conflict is the result of extremely varied but systematic endeavours by one of the parties to perpetuate and extend their superiority over the other. If hegemony is control by a mix of coercion and consent, the rule maintained along the Jordan River and the transboundary aquifers is some form of 'hydro-hegemony'. This final chapter pulls together the qualitative and quantitative analysis of the forms of power at play to conclude that – in essence – the real politics behind the water conflict are veiled by the very hegemonic relations they reproduce.

The following review of each side's measure of power in all its forms reveals the extent of the asymmetry. The entire body of evidence presented up to this point is then deployed in an evaluation of the form and effects of Israel's hydro-hegemony. The status quo may favour the Israeli side, in the short term, but the effects harm both sides, with the fragile and precious resource facing a perpetual threat of contamination. International donors also lose out, as their development assistance is invested and re-invested in projects that are inherently unsustainable. In addition, Palestinian state-building efforts are thwarted, and the lingering water conflict continues to exacerbate the on-going political conflict. Of course the real losers are the most vulnerable people on the weaker side. Hundreds of thousands of Palestinian residents – like those in Madama – are still obliged to purchase water from unsafe tankers, while their Israeli settler neighbours engaged in industrial agriculture have it piped into their homes at a subsidised cost. Though a fairer future is entirely possible, the analysis of current interests, legitimacy and power guards against it.

Power Asymmetry Measured

The following assessment of the 2004 power balance between Palestine and Israel is conducted with a full awareness of the difficulties inherent in the task. Any assessment of power requires two kinds of judgements, and judgements are likely to be limited in their perspective, and therefore prone to fallibility. One judgement concerns the *scope* of the power that is being assessed while the other relates to the *significance of the outcomes* that agents are capable of bringing about. This second judgment, furthermore, requires an examination of the *interests* of those agents.

Measurement of inter-state power may be particularly open to question as there is no consensus on a method for doing so. A common approach is to make a simple "capability analysis" by comparing specific aspects of the hard power of states (Evans and Newnham 1998: 447). Figure 9.1 expands upon the capability analysis to include the second and third dimensions of power – bargaining and ideational. The sub-structure of the figure attempts to incorporate the scope and the significance of the outcome of each dimension of power.

Comparison of relative hard power

A glance at the category of hard power in Figure 9.1 confirms our intuition – of a significant disparity favouring the Israeli side. The asymmetry in hard power between Palestine and Israel is nowhere more evident than in the Economic sector. The State of Israel dominates both in terms of gross national product per person (US$15,000 compared with US$1,650 for Palestine (IMFA 2004a)) and the form and shape of its economy (which is reflexive, diversified and adaptive, compared with a Palestinian economy which is either asymmetrically contained by Israel's economy or is its client (Khan 2004b). Military capabilities are similarly skewed, with the well-trained Israeli military amounting to over 4,300 tanks, 474 warplanes, 51 warships and over 600,000 soldiers (IMFA 2004b), while the Palestinian security forces created after Oslo II limited to hundreds of poorly trained and poorly armed policemen. The power balance also tilts over to the Israeli side in terms of their relative ability to draw upon International support, particularly the US, although Palestine does have a minimum of political support from Arab States and a steadily weakening United Nations. The very high level of education in Israel is reflected in its industrialised economy and its high degree of human capital, particularly in the field of water resource development. The enduring power indicator of Riparian Position is the only aspect of hard power in which the riparians have similar footing. Israel is downstream of the aquifers that straddle the West Bank, just as Gaza is downstream of Israel on the Coastal Aquifer. While Israel is downstream of Lebanon and Syria on the Jordan River, it has the upstream advantage there over Palestine.

Comparison of relative bargaining power

Analysis of the relative bargaining power of each riparian reveals a more even-handed situation than our intuitions might suggest. We have seen in

Figure 9.1   Indicative comparison of Israeli and Palestinian state power (2004).

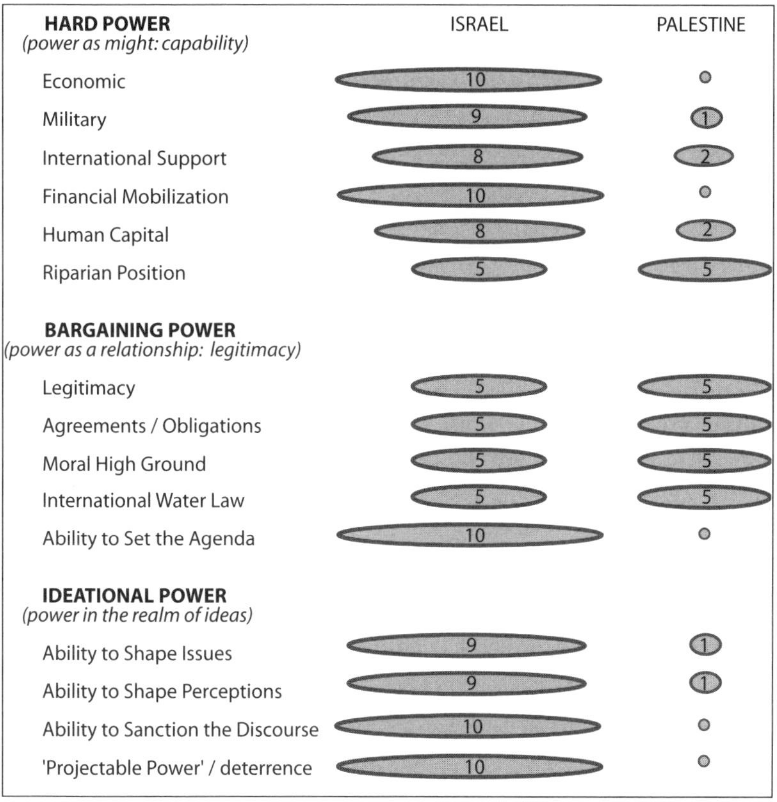

HARD POWER (power as might: capability)	ISRAEL	PALESTINE
Economic	10	○
Military	9	1
International Support	8	2
Financial Mobilization	10	○
Human Capital	8	2
Riparian Position	5	5
BARGAINING POWER (power as a relationship: legitimacy)		
Legitimacy	5	5
Agreements / Obligations	5	5
Moral High Ground	5	5
International Water Law	5	5
Ability to Set the Agenda	10	○
IDEATIONAL POWER (power in the realm of ideas)		
Ability to Shape Issues	9	1
Ability to Shape Perceptions	9	1
Ability to Sanction the Discourse	10	○
'Projectable Power' / deterrence	10	○

Figure is indicative only. Measures are made in relation to each party, on a basis of 10.

Chapter 2 that bargaining power is garnered primarily by being a legitimate actor in a relationship. The 1995 Oslo II Agreement, to which both Palestine and Israeli are party, gives each an equal measure of legitimacy and obligations. The two sides have formal equality. International Water Law, in theory, also treats both sides equally, with Israel demanding Palestinian conformity to the principle of 'no significant harm' while, for their part, Palestinians call for Israeli compliance with the principle of 'equitable and reasonable utilisation'. The gap between the theory and the practice of international water law, however, cannot be over-emphasised. The discussion of Chapter 2 demonstrated the extent to which the law is subordinate to the effects of other forms of power, and to politics more generally. Finally, we have a rather imprecise measure of the ability to set the agenda, which is primarily a feature of discourse. Our review of the goings-on behind the scenes at the Joint Water Committee (Chapter 6) demonstrated that not only does the Israeli side have the ability to set the agenda of JWC meetings, it has on occasion also been so confident of the outcome that the minutes of meetings have been written ahead of time.

Comparison of relative ideational power

The abstract concept of ideational power is difficult enough to conceive, and even more difficult to measure. An example of Israeli ability to shape issues and perceptions was the hype surrounding the Wazzani Springs incident in 2002 (Chapter 7). Lebanon successfully countered the threats by presenting evidence to neutral third parties – a tactic that has never worked for the Palestinian side. Furthermore, we have seen the effectiveness of the Israeli side's ability to sanction the discourse in our review of the contention between Palestinian and Israeli discourses. The Israeli *Needs, not Rights* discourse prevails, essentially unchallenged. The asymmetry of projectable power is exemplified by Israeli ability to back up any threats it makes, given its significant reserves of hard power. In other words Israel has both the covenant *and* the sword. By way of contrast, Israeli non-compliance with Palestinian demands or threats is commonplace, as may be expected from a realist perspective.

The pumping and consumption graphs of Chapter 8 demonstrated how Israeli internal and transboundary water policy has been influenced by the asymmetry in power. Expressions of hard, bargaining and ideational power have all contributed to maintaining the current order of things. The following section summarises these events, and demonstrates how Israeli control is growing ever more efficient.

The Evolution of Control

Another form of classification reduces the water conflict to a variety of kinds of 'event', with each event coming to be understood in the terms of *compliance-producing mechanisms*, as described during our review of hegemony theory (Chapter 2). The increasing efficiency of the mechanisms was noted there, as one moves from (I) coercion → (II) utilitarian exchange → (III) inducing normative agreement → (IV) inducing ideologically hegemonic beliefs. We had theorised at that point that an effective manipulation of the mechanisms would enable the construction of a situation of hegemony. Table 9.1 shows how Israel has accomplished this in fact, by providing a partial inventory of events related to the water conflict, along with their associated compliance-producing mechanism.

From empire to hegemony

The summary of methods used by the Israeli side to ensure Palestinian compliance in Table 9.1 reveals an evolutionary process towards increasingly efficient means of securing compliance, from Types I to III and IV. This confirms the shifts revealed by different forms of analysis elsewhere. In terms of hegemony theory, the Israeli side has shifted from dealing with the conflict by contestation to empire/domination and, more recently, through hegemony.

Table 9.1   Partial inventory of events from the Palestinian–Israeli Water
Conflict, and associated Compliance-Producing Mechanisms.

Year	Event	CPM	Chapter
1948	Acquisition of land	I	4
48-58	GW development in Israel	I	4
1964	Damming of Lake Tiberias and construction of the National Water Carrier	I	4
1967	Acquisition of land	I	4
1967	Military Orders restricting Palestinian development	I	4
67-95	Israeli development of EAB	I	6
67-95	Legislation restricting Palestinian development	I	4
67-95	Minimal Israeli development in Palestine	II	4
1981	Weakening of WBWD	I	4
90-95	Negotiations over water with Jordan, Palestine, ending in bi-lateral agreements	III	8
2002	Wazzani Springs Dispute	III, IV	7
2002	Destruction of water infrastructure in WB	I	5
2002+	Construction of the Wall over WAB	I	5
95-06	Creation of JWC	I	6
95-06	JWC – threats of non-cooperation	I	6
95-06	Manipulation of WBWD	II	6
95-06	JWC – denial of permits	I	6
95-06	JWC – coercive *modus vivendi*	II	6
95-06	Continued Israeli exploitation of EAB	II	7
95-06	Defining/maintaining legitimacy of PWA	I	4
95-06	Recognition (but not fulfilment) of Palestinian Water Rights	III	4
95-06	Over-Abstraction in WAB (above Oslo limits)	III	8
95-06	Agenda-Setting	III	6
95-06	Master-Planning	IV	7
95-06	Sanctioning the Discourse	IV	7

Abbreviations: **CPM** = corresponding compliance-producing mechanism, according to
Lustick's (2002) classification of increasingly efficient compliance-producing mechanisms: **I**
- coercion; **II** - utilitarian exchange; **III** - instigating normative agreement; **IV** - inducing
ideologically hegemonic beliefs; **Ref** = reference to corresponding Section in this book. GW
= groundwater; WB = West Bank; JWC = Joint Water Committee; PWA = Palestinian
Water Authority; EAB = Eastern Aquifer Basin; WAB = Western Aquifer Basin; WBWD =
West Bank Water Department.

As we noted in Chapter 2, the crucial difference between 'imperial' and hegemonic
rule was the institution of *formal equality* and its associated political practices. Where
there is no formal equality, the control over the 'order of things' by the more
powerful group is explicitly understood in terms of hierarchical relations of
domination and subordination. With formal equality, control is exercised through

hegemony. Hegemonic control is, by definition, maintained using the formula of force + consent; swords and covenants; hard and soft power.

Israeli hegemonic rule has emerged from the latest stage of a lengthy battle. The very coercive and physical measures that were employed against the Arab States during the Ideological Era (1948–67) reflected the fact that neither adversary had full control of the resource and that both held roughly equal measures of hard power. Rule during this period was contested. Following its territorial conquest of 1967, the Israeli side enjoyed more or less full control over the resources, and employed hard power to maintain it. Palestinian compliance during this 'Israeli Domination Era' was ensured primarily by the use of force, though there is also evidence of the use of 'carrots' and other consensual tactics which served to legitimate the Israeli settlement project.

The shift from 'imperial' domination to hegemony was completed in 1995 with the signing of the Oslo II Agreement. With the formally equal Palestinian side committed to the norms of a treaty that cemented the status quo of the Domination Era, the Israeli side developed more efficient methods with which to ensure compliance. Clauses that may have benefited the Palestinian side (like Israel's recognition of Palestinian water rights) were neglected, while clauses that enshrined Israeli control (like the definition of the West Bank into Areas A, B, C) were emphasised, even after the death of the Oslo process. What is more, with the legitimacy of the Palestinian Water Authority tied to the agreement, the more powerful side was able to structure the Joint Water so that it guaranteed the perpetuation of the asymmetric water distribution. The great success the Israeli side has had in sanctioning the discourse that surrounds Palestinian water development efforts, and the conflict in general, has cornered the PWA into a position of subordination and subjugation.

Under hegemonic rule, the Israeli side can see that its interests are advanced merely by reminding the PWA of their obligations, and it rarely encounters any resistance to the *modus operandi*. Though perhaps not motivated by ever greater control of the transboundary flows (or 'accumulation through dispossession', to return to Harvey's phrase), Israeli deployments of hard power continue throughout this period, inflicting extensive damage on Palestinian water infrastructure and constructing the Wall over significant portions of the Western Aquifer Basin. This mix of force with the 'consent' generated through bargaining and ideational power is the strongest indicator that the situation has shifted from 'empire' to the more efficient hegemonic form of control.

A representation of the shift in the form of Israeli control is given in Figure 9.2. The graph reveals how Israeli control over water resources was at the "contested" level prior to its acquisition of new resources along with the land in 1967, after which it progressed to "full" at some point during its occupation of the West Bank and Gaza. While chiefly coercive 'Type I' methods were used to produce compliance during the first decades of the conflict, these were gradually replaced (or complemented) by more efficient normative and hegemonic methods. The variety of Israeli discourses on water policy towards Palestinians also reflects this evolution. The more belligerent hydrostrategic discourse of the 1950s dissipated due to lack of interest after the waters had been somewhat secured by the 1967 territorial capture, only to regain importance when water issues once again became captured public attention during the early 1990s negotiating period.

The *Hydrostrategic* discourse has survived through to 2005, though it remains subordinate to the *Needs, not Rights* discourse. As the now-sanctioned discourse, the latter has held considerable sway over Palestine's donors – and helped to ensure that the Palestinians remain with very little 'wriggle room.'

Maintaining the Hegemonic Apparatus

The sanctioning of the *Needs, not Rights* discourse is by far the most common and efficient method employed by the Israeli side to maintain its position in water conflict during the hegemony era. A continuous sanctioning and re-sanctioning of the discourse contributes to the self-perpetuation of the asymmetric status quo. More broadly, the extent and form of Israeli control over the Palestinian water sector is best understood in terms of the reflexive powers of a 'hegemonic apparatus', to return to Gramsci's term.

Hegemonic relations do not confine those involved to the zero-sum games of domination and resistance. Rather hegemony, like capital, is a form of self-expanding power which generates resources even as it accumulates control over them. The mix of coercive and consensual means through which the more powerful side exerts its predominance does not have to unilaterally determine the outcome of competition over resources. Instead it sustains the conditions under which outcomes are decided politically. At the commanding heights of this particular hegemonic apparatus is a complex system of legislation, military orders, treaties, conferences and press releases. Its foundations are a more visible, but equally complex, system of wells, pumps, dams and walls. The entire system capitalises on existing power asymmetries, utilising them to reproduce and deepen the poor state of Palestinian governance and to maintain the structural constraints in the international context which make others unable or unwilling to challenge the status quo. Palestinian resistance to Israeli attempts to impose ideas and plans through the sanctioned discourse is located chiefly within civil society and expressed in terms of the *Rights First* discourse. The official Palestinian *Cooperation* discourse, however, coincides with the Israeli and US-sanctioned discourse, weakening the voice of those seeking fulfilment of Palestinian rights.

Israeli *master planning* and *agenda setting* is that much easier when it goes unchallenged by a compliant official Palestinian 'partner', and faces a Palestinian water sector divided on how to respond to its sole competitor. The apparatus may also be exploiting and encouraging a mutation of the Palestinian government's already weak separation of powers. The legislature, judiciary and executive in the Palestinian water sector are effectively merged and focused on water project implementation and the donor funding that accompanies it (see Figure 4.1).

Figure 9.2 Relation of Total Israeli Water Production and Agricultural Consumption to form and level of Israeli control, main discourses, compliance mechanisms adn the efficiency of these.

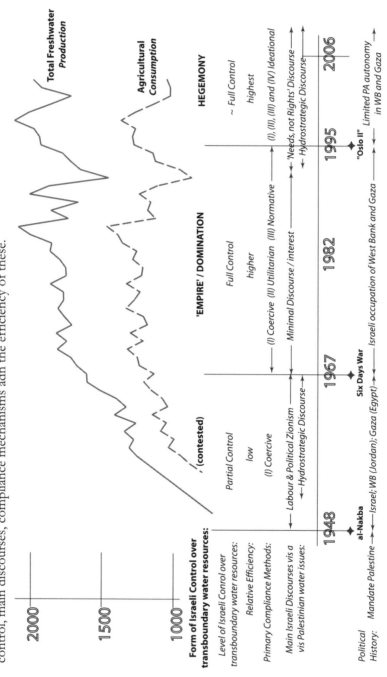

The effects of enduring asymmetry seep ever deeper into the decisions and non-decisions of the Palestinian water authorities. Demands from the Israeli side that simply go unchallenged today may go altogether unquestioned tomorrow. Maintaining a 'careful' policy towards Palestinians may require the hegemonic apparatus to evolve from enabling the imposition of ideas to ever closer control over patterns of thinking. One indicator of such a transformation would be a gradual shift in the official Palestinian discourse towards complete subordination to, if not complete integration with, the Israeli water sector. The flip side reaction could be a growing resentment from Palestinian society (or water officials) about the status quo, with consequences that are difficult to predict. Such a challenge to Israeli hydro-hegemony would be evidence of the limits of its reach: the hegemony may extend to the PWA, for instance, but not to the general public. We return to informed speculation on the future after an evaluation of Israeli hydro-hegemony and its effects.

Evaluating the Form of Hydro-Hegemony

We recall that the Greek root of 'hegemony' is *to lead*. In the epistemic sense of the word, hegemony may thus be evaluated positively, as in the case of a benevolent dictator – or negatively, in reference to an autocratic and oppressive dictator. While any evaluation depends on where you stand when you make it, there are examples which may help to render a more objective evaluation.

'Hegemonic stability theory' credits the occurrence of cooperation to the presence of an overwhelmingly more powerful player (see Lowi 1993). South Africa, as the unquestioned hydro-hegemon along the Orange River, may be taken as an example. The sharing of benefits between it and Lesotho from the Lesotho Highlands hydro-electric project that South Africa has helped to build in upstream Lesotho, and the water-sharing arrangements it has worked out with downstream Namibia, both support claims that it is playing the role of a 'benevolent' hydro-hegemon (Turton and Funke 2007). The riparians and the river itself would be worse off without the overwhelming presence of South Africa, though evidently such a claim should (and is) debated from upstream and downstream positions (see Heyns (2005), Horta (2007)).

The form of hydro-hegemony established by Israel, on the other hand, gives less generous benefits to the weaker partner. Largely unimpeded by Palestine, the Israeli side enjoys a privileged position which allows it a wide degree of freedom to form its own policy and to manage its endogenous and transboundary resources. Those who support the current asymmetry between Palestine and Israel over water issues, for whatever reasons, are likely to judge the current state of affairs positively: emphasising Palestinian 'free riding' and Israeli prowess with water technology. Some may defend the inequity simply by rejecting any consideration of Palestinian interests, as do those promoting the anti-negotiations hydrostrategic discourse. Others may take an approach that emphasises the stability and cooperation (through the JWC) that results from Israel's hydro-hegemony, and can readily provide evidence to support their view.

Those who resent the current state of affairs over water issues, on the other hand, are more likely to evaluate the hydro-hegemony negatively. They may tend to emphasise Israeli oppression in the sector, or decry Israeli interference of in Palestinian affairs and the denial of Palestinian rights, citing the coercive aspects of hegemony their primary evidence. Those looking a little deeper will highlight the ways in which Palestinian attempts to develop the sector are routinely restricted or obstructed. Whatever the reasons that may be given to explain and justify the situation, the Palestinian side remains – virtually – powerless to manage the resource as it would intend. The situation of hydro-hegemony will be viewed by some Palestinian officials as one of compromise under asymmetry. It will be viewed more bitterly by Palestinian civil society as one of extreme frustration, or of 'domination dressed up as cooperation' to return to Selby's observation.

The problem with position-based perspective evaluations is, of course, that they do not consider the complete picture. The primarily coercive (and currently, covert) methods through which Israel maintains its hegemony leave little room for doubt that the conflict is maintained through a mixture of methods. The 'hegemonic apparatus' ensures that the Israeli side is able to pursue its fundamentally careful policy towards Palestinian use of transboundary waters. Control takes priority over cooperation, while collaboration is more valued than contestation. Low-intensity conflict with the Palestinians is tolerable, so long as it can be contained. Furthermore, we will see that the effects of the form of hydro-hegemony are felt primarily (but importantly, not solely) by the Palestinian side – whether or not we may view this as 'positive' or 'negative'.

Questioning the Evaluation

We expect our evaluations to be contested by other analysts. They may question the applicability of a study that sheds a negative light on a state that has recently signed water-sharing agreements with two of its historic enemies, and maintains a vocal and eloquent discourse of cooperation. It is anticipated that such claims can be countered by the facts and events that have been presented herein. Such questioning is, furthermore, considered both as a testament to and, indeed, strengthens the power-based analysis. It was noted in Chapter 2 that writing on hegemony and on water conflict analysis in general tends to be the political science of the winners, just as the victor writes history. By pursuing a method that classifies and analyses several forms of power – including covert forms – this study explores the unquantifiable extent and depth of a hegemonic state of affairs: thoughts are created, then controlled; the power of ideas neutralises pressures for accountability over the destructive effects of war; the discourse is dictated, then sanctioned; representations of the exact opposite are accepted by proponents and antagonists alike. Any study shedding light onto such a state of affairs is bound to challenge prevailing perceptions about the 'truth' or 'reality' of the situation. Questions and debates about the utility of the approach are therefore as expected as they are welcome.

The Effects of Hydro-Hegemony

The effects of these socio-political power asymmetries on 'shared' transboundary resources manifest themselves at different levels and in various ways. From an environmental perspective, the resources continue to be recklessly managed and squandered. At the international level, a hidden (but lingering) conflict persists, continuing to drain the resources and threaten intervention from the international community. The Palestinian side feels the effects through the continuing inequitable distribution of the flows which will lock the Palestinian agricultural sector into under-development for decades. These effects are suffered, not least of all, by the Palestinian residents of Madama and other villages who are condemned to collect their water in ways their ancestors – and the belligerent Israeli settlers perched on top of their water source – would never imagine.

A Squandered Resource

Those who study the 'cost of non-cooperation' from an environmental perspective need look no further than the West Bank and Gaza for evidence to back their theories. One views the scorched earth in all of its literal meaning as one drives along the Jordan River valley and tries to look out for the river. The area between the highway and the river has been a closed military zone ever since Israel occupied the West Bank in 1967. The fact that this real estate was never developed may have made of it a sanctuary for a wildlife squeezed out everywhere else by human activity. Though a tiny number of elegant gazelles can still be observed by those the Israel Defence Forces permits to enter the area, the bulk of the land – all undergrowth, shrubs, trees and other habitat – is intentionally (and routinely) burned clear to the ground.

The environmental sceptic could cynically point out that the scorched earth does at least permit a nice view of the river for the tourists and settlers using the highway (though not for Palestinians, who have been forbidden from driving on it since January 2005). But the Jordan River is a small stream of sewage at this point, and can be smelled before it can be glimpsed. It has been like this since Lake of Tiberias was dammed in 1964 in order to assure a steady inflow to the Israeli National Water Carrier. Further downstream, the Dead Sea is dying as a consequence, having split into two bodies in the 1980s through evaporation. Like the better-known Aral Sea catastrophe, that is now an undergraduate textbook case study of environmental mismanagement under the Soviet empire, the waters of the Dead Sea pull away from the hotels and cafes built on its shores at the rate of one metre every year (see Photograph A5, Appendix A). The groundwater level has dropped along with the Dead Sea's surface, and no longer supports the spongy earth that make up the sea's floor. Large portions of Israeli roads built upon the drained seafloor have been sucked in by the resultant spectacular sinkholes. These have subsequently become a menace to any future development of the area. NGOs, such as Friends of the Earth, are actively engaged in attempts to restore the Jordan River, and refer to the dangerous sinkholes with sly smiles as 'nature's revenge'. Considering that the land was taken from Palestinians in 1967 and that they alone are barred access to it, it is not surprising to find that some of the original inhabitants of the valley also refer to the sinkholes as the 'land's revenge'.

Such acts may intimate Nature's capacity for defiance. She is currently proving no match for men consumed by politics and pre-occupied with power and ideologies. A high cost of hydro-hegemony has been borne by those extinct and endangered species whose habitat has been wiped out. Yet we would do well to be wary of nature seeking retribution. If she is dying anyway, might she not take some men along with her? That is not an unlikely outcome of the continuous poisoning of the precious groundwater aquifers.

Of all the Israeli settlements and Palestinian towns perched above the transboundary aquifers of the West Bank, only the municipality of al Bireh, near Ramallah, has a functioning wastewater treatment plant. Friends of the Earth is trying to draw attention to what they call the 'seeping time bomb', though their efforts are continually undermined by higher politics on both sides. Raw sewage from homes, restaurants and hospitals pours out of the structures into the wadis and, eventually percolates into the aquifers. Though the depth of the aquifer in most places and the natural filtering effects of the karst limestone help the situation, biological contamination of the aquifers is something all hydrogeologists agree is a question of 'when', not 'if'. The wastewater generated by the Israeli settlements is proportionately much greater than that generated by Palestinians. This is to be expected, since the settlers are supplied with much more water than their Palestinian neighbours. The flow of wastewater is naturally in the same proportion, with 350,000 settlers generating a full quarter of all sewage flows in the West Bank (Tagar, et al. 2004b).

The number of wastewater treatment plants stalled for approval by the Joint Water Committee is a further testament to the failures of the institution. Pushed by donors, the PWA has sought and secured funding for such projects in a number of locations. A large-scale wastewater treatment plant *was* approved by the JWC for Hebron. Two years of project preparation work were abandoned by donor USAID, however, following Hamas' election victory. Israeli over-abstraction of the Western Aquifer may be further aggravating the situation. Israeli supply-driven water policy will meet domestic demand from whatever source is available. When the level of the Lake of Tiberias is too low, the difference is not made up through reduced consumption, but through increased reliance on the hidden groundwater resources of the aquifers (Chapter 8). The less water in the basin, the more easily it is contaminated by the untreated waste trickling down from above.

Hydrogeologists are tired of reminding us that by the time they detect such contamination, it will be too late to do anything about it. Far from providing effective 'joint management' of the shared resources, the Joint Water Committee was born crippled by politics, and has prevented neither over-development of the resource on the Israeli side nor under-development on the Palestinian side.

Unsustainable Development Assistance

If the costs of poor cooperation over transboundary water resources are borne in large part by Nature, they are also paid for by the international community. While there will be no war solely for control of the Jordan River, the effects – and the root causes – of the conflict continue to drain coffers.

International humanitarian aid agencies have proven quite effective at dealing with the consequences of disaster, war and acute conflicts. International 'development' agencies have a much tougher time meeting the goals they set for themselves. Both humanitarian aid agencies and 'development' agencies admit that their greatest failures are in instances of chronic conflicts. The water component of the Palestinian–Israeli struggle is a case of a chronic conflict within a chronic conflict.

Donor assistance for Palestinian water sector development, since 1996, had reached nearly three-quarters of a billion dollars by 2004. While USAID provided the bulk of such funds, Japan, Sweden, Finland, Norway, the EU and the World Bank were all also actively engaged. The donors took pride in the assistance they provided to Palestinians for the development of a rather professional water ministry (the PWA), the merging of municipalities into the Coastal Water Utility in Gaza and the improved capacities of Palestinian water technicians. Five or six deep wells in the Herodian valley and partial wastewater treatment plants in Gaza are other visible effects of the donations.

Yet no single donor expresses more satisfaction than frustration. For all of the hundreds of millions of dollars and buckets of sweat spent, the sector is less developed a decade on from the Oslo II agreement than it was at the outset, with Palestinian per capita water consumption having actually fallen. The ambitious water master plans designed by the PWA and international donor agencies in the late 1990s laid around on desks in Ramallah, Washington, Tokyo or Berlin for several years as efforts to start implementing them persisted. The plans were literally shelved as the noose of the power politics active at the JWC began to tighten.[110]

The long-term development efforts of donors started to shift around the year 2000 with the heightened violence and extensive destruction that accompanied the recurrent incursions of the West Bank and Gaza. After months of agony trying to implement 'development' type projects, building from the ground up, donors shifted their programmes to dealing with emergencies, applying 'band-aids' and attempting to mitigate the effects of the fighting.

A compromising fact is that donors in the water sector never seemed to fully comprehend the context in which their efforts were meant to be implemented. At least, if it was understood, it was either ignored or navigated around. Both the acute broader political (and very violent) conflict and the chronic (and low-intensity) water conflict have rarely been acknowledged. Subscribing wholeheartedly to the idea of cooperation and the norms of the Joint Water Committee, donors are unable or unwilling – even after January 2006 – to consider any project that does not pass the obstacles the committee sets up through its licensing procedure. The inevitable result is piecemeal development of the sector, with projects approved here and there, mere tatters of the original master plans. By failing to address the root causes of the conflict, donors have inevitably misallocated their treasured aid dollars to projects that are unsustainable by design.

What is perhaps even more surprising – unless one takes a power-analytic perspective on things – is that the conflict itself has been veiled from view. The base elements of the conflict have been either avoided by, or are invisible to, the international planners of the Palestinian water sector. Amid the hopeful glee that permeated development agencies and international conferences on the heels of the Oslo II Agreement, the asymmetries in power and water distribution have been wilfully ignored in the mistaken hope that real change was about to happen. The second and third round of international consultants that were sent out to assist with development efforts in the wake of Oslo's glory years had no pretensions to evening out the playing field – they were working, after all, from within a hidden hegemonic apparatus designed to maintain the status quo.

Unless they were to step back and look at the broader political picture, those international agencies still interested in developing the Palestinian water sector remain doomed to myopia. If and when they do see the wider perspective they will likely then re-focus on the narrow, pragmatic, path more travelled by. The institutions and those who work in them will invent cheap lies and be thankful for the conscience-soothing falsities [111] offered by the hegemonic apparatus. The gloss on the development agencies' brochures remains after the individuals who have tried to change this system from within eventually leave it, to be replaced by the latest round of international consultants. Watch this space for hundreds of millions more mis-spent development assistance. The economic costs borne by wealthy capitals, however, pale in comparison with the environmental degradation their efforts barely mitigate. They are also incomparable with the effects on Palestinian state-building efforts and Palestinian individuals.

Containment at the National Level
At the Palestinian national level, the effects of Israeli hydro-hegemony manifest themselves first and foremost through the highly asymmetric distribution of transboundary flows. The severity of the inequality is perfectly evident, no matter which yardstick it is measured by. *Use* of the transboundary resources, we have seen, is skewed roughly 1,600 MCM/y to 275 MCM/y in Israel's favour (Table 3.3). As was noted at that point, none of the qualifications to these figures mitigates the skew to any significant degree; if anything, per capita consumption is even more skewed in Israel's favour.[112]

The distribution of *control* over the allocations is just as one-sided. Figure 3.3 showed that Israeli-controlled water consumed by Palestinians inside of the West Bank is roughly equal to the amount of water controlled by the PWA in the West Bank. Likewise, our discussion of the Israeli master-planning and agenda-setting activities through the JWC has underlined the extent to which that Israeli policy influences Palestinian decisions. The reverse is emphatically not the case.

If the legitimacy of the Palestinian Water Authority is undermined by its inability or unwillingness to react to traumatic events like the Wall or the large-scale destruction of water infrastructure, the continuing situation of extreme inequity in distribution may prove to be the final nail in its coffin. We have seen already, however, that the legitimacy granted to the PWA through cooperation with Israeli and international water professionals has thus far proven more significant than any challenges to it by Palestinian civil society or other ministries.[113] That delicate balance of power is likely to hold until a) either there is a revolution within Palestine against all government trappings, or b) PWA and Israeli interests no longer align. Considering the efficiency of the hegemonic arrangement for the Israeli side, there are likely be conscious efforts to ensure that the interests remain aligned. The less attractive alternative for the Israeli side is to return to the 'imperial' type of rule, whereby it would have responsibility for the sector and be obliged to coerce the Palestinian side into compliance. This would entail re-managing what was not previously manageable, and spending considerable sums on pollution-prevention projects, for example. Better to have a compliant and subservient Palestinian counterpart to fulfil Israeli interests in the sector, with international donors footing the bill, as the ex-head of Mekoroth has made clear (Chapter 7).

The extent of Israeli influence on Palestinian water policy extends to governance, in what may be an effective reversal or mutation of the separation of governmental powers. The legislature, judiciary and executive of the Palestinian water sector (Figure 4.1) actually combine to serve the 'fundamentally careful' Israeli policy. Having thus divided the Palestinian administration, the Israeli side may reap the benefits of an ever weaker Palestinian governance of the sector – at least in terms of a lack of any challenge to its control, but not in terms of the burden it may have to bear as consequence. The effects of structurally under-developed governance contradict whatever political maturity Palestine may have garnered through its decade of democracy.

The PWA thus finds itself in a very hard place if it intends to contribute to sustainable Palestinian state-building efforts. The late 1990s national water master plans, for instance, called for a 'water link' to feed Gaza with freshwater from the West Bank. Without Israeli agreement to traverse Israel, however, the PWA has no ability to implement such plans, even if they were permitted to extract the water from the Western Aquifer Basin (which they are not). The sole remaining large-scale option for the PWA in Gaza, then, is to desalinate. As we have seen, however, the desalination plant planned by USAID was halted for political reasons (see footnote 57), and most donor funding since then has run dry. So it is that Palestinian water development plans in Gaza are either directly prevented by Israel, or indirectly aborted due to politics with the US.

If one hears USAID or the Israel Water Commission stating that 'cooperation' is the only way forward, it must be understood that the terms of the arrangement are dictated by the Israeli side. Thus is the PWA offered the chance to purchase water for Gaza, from either the Israeli desalination in Ashqelon or the intended Hadera–Tulkarem project. Without proper consideration of the original Palestinian intentions, these 'offers' appear generous indeed: and the Palestinian side can be reasonably chided in public for not embracing them. Apart from efficiently assuring consent, the hegemonic apparatus also has the ability to selectively filter out divergent perceptions to represent 'reality' in the form most convenient to the powerful.

Relations between the PWA and Palestinian civil society are understandably acidic. Palestinian water NGOs are not caught up in the hegemonic apparatus, and are thus freer to acknowledge the extent of the sector's enslavement. Being on the fringes of all decision-making, however, they are relatively powerless to address the situation. Their continued efforts to do so in the forms of reports, conferences and film documentaries are commendable counter-hegemonic strategies that may eventually give rise to a less oppressive hydro-hegemonic regime. Should that day come, it might bring with it the resolution of the conflict and end the reality endured by the Palestinian residents of towns still unserved by water networks.

Box: Still Dry in Madama

Detailed explanations of the fragile legitimacy of the PWA and agreements violating the principles of International Water Law must sound like excuses to the residents of Madama village. Like hundreds of thousands of other Palestinians in other villages yet to be served by drinking water or irrigation networks, their patience may be running out. But lack of patience is a luxury afforded only to those who have the power to address their grievances. The extent of this capacity for the villagers of Madama is to lobby their representatives for services; and they are still waiting for the well promised by the PWA in 2002.

The Rujeib well, we recall from Chapter 6, was dropped from USAID plans in 2002, despite the fact that it had already been granted approval by the Joint Water Committee. Having decided to "punish" the PWA for their refusal to allow a new Israeli well in the Eastern Aquifer Basin, the colonel in charge of 'humanitarian affairs' at the Israel Civil Administration refused to allow the drill rig to be established on the Rujeib site. The PWA did not muster enough bargaining power to counter the punishment. The USAID office in Tel Aviv, which was intent on drilling wells at the time, looked elsewhere to complete a project, leaving Rujeib – and Madama and six other villages – behind.

At a certain level, the residents of Madama are simply the victims of an unfortunate series of events. They have been caught up in a political web consisting of the personal politics of an arrogant Israeli army officer in addition to the internal politics of the JWC. The residents are furthermore under-represented by a still weak fledgling national water institution. This version of the villagers' plight is the received wisdom on the subject, and is regularly put forward with compassion by hand-wringing proponents of those who advocate development of the sector, but not resolution of the water conflict.

This narrow view of affairs may soothe some consciences, but excludes the nature and effects of the hegemonic power structures that have been spelled out by this book. It leaves out, for example, the fact that the internal politics of the JWC are as they are only because the institution's founding treaty asymmetrically structures them in favour of the Israeli side. Furthermore, the idea that residents of Madama are simply the hapless victims of an unreasonable Israeli army officer blocks off the possibility of questioning why that officer would have such an influential say in such matters in the first place.

An even more fundamental issue is the unquestioned assumption that the residents of Madama would be best served by a well at Rujeib. The most logical place to drill a well for Madama is not dozens of kilometres away in Rujeib, but within the village limits. However, the residents of Rujeib sit atop of the confluence of the Eastern and Western Aquifer Basins, and have been prevented from drilling since 1967: first through the military orders imposed by the predecessors of the ICA general who prevented the drill rig from going to Rujeib; then by the terms of the Oslo II Accord which froze the status quo of 1995 indefinitely thereafter.

Stepping back yet further, one must question the very need for a well. The main reason one is being considered at all is because the village's main source of water remains subject to threats of contamination by the Israeli settlers perched on the hilltop above. The spring that has fed the village for centuries is now subject to sabotage and poisoning by the extremist residents of Yitshar settlement.

The proposal for a well at Rujeib to feed Madama is in fact an exercise in perverse logic. If the settlers won't leave – so the logic goes – the residents should drill a well. If the residents are barred from drilling a well, the Palestinian authorities should drill one for them. If the Palestinian authorities are prevented from doing so because of an agreement which they endorsed, they should drill somewhere further away where they are permitted to, and pump the water to Madama. If the Palestinian authorities are prevented from this by an element of the occupying Israeli army, the residents shall remain without water. If on the other hand the residents are 'lucky', the Israeli authorities will permit the construction of a well dozens of kilometres away (the third-best alternative), the Palestinian authorities will find funding for it, and the water will flow. At least, that is, until a lack of maintenance, Israeli army bulldozers or settler sabotage disrupts it, and yet another layer of 'logic' is worked through to resolve the problem.

The view that the residents of Madama are victims of a breakdown in a system otherwise intended to serve them hides the politics at the very root of the conflict.

The Future

A civilization that proves incapable of solving the problems it creates is a decadent civilization.

Aimé Césaire (b. 1913).

There is scant supporting evidence for claims that the cooperation over transboundary water issues between Palestinians and Israelis is based on anything other than a gesture of sharing of responsibilities. Certainly, the extent of that cooperation has barely developed beyond joint data collection. Without proper data sharing (whereby the Israeli side would disclose water use in settlements, for example) or jurisdiction over the entire resource, any institution professing to manage the aquifers responsibly is deluding itself. Without equal decision-making power and responsibility, wasted development funds, environmental degradation, dry taps and lingering conflict will endure. Such overt power-sharing appears unlikely under the current conditions of Israeli hegemony in the sector, whereby power is wielded in efficient, covert ways.

This message is not intended for those advocates of unilateral Israeli actions seeking ever greater separation from their Palestinian neighbours. Such advocates are not likely bothered by the hidden politics played out through the various forms of power. The message may, though, resonate more deeply with those advocates of continued cooperation who may have, up to now, missed what lies under the veil.

Although this study precludes any claims to prediction, the analysis can inform our observation and evaluation of future trends. It directs our attention onto the reproduction or transformation of the form of hydro-hegemony Israeli currently maintains. This is of no less significance for the Israeli water sector, as the benefits it currently draws from hegemony are likely to remain short-term, insofar as the conflict lingers on unresolved and hydro-relations remain unstable.

We have noted how internal Israeli tensions (Chapter 4) have lead to conflicting and largely unsuccessful attempts at demand-management, increased desalination production and potential freshwater imports from Turkey. These chronic tensions and confusions tend to foil attempts to predict future trends – the future shape of the sector depends primarily on how the internal Israeli water conflict plays itself out. While that outcome may be unpredictable, this study's analysis implies that the future will remain largely unaffected by Palestinian water needs or recognised rights, let alone ambitions.

This is, at least, the most likely outcome in the absence of a permanent negotiated agreement with the Palestinians. Given existing Israeli desalination plans, and subject to the successful performance of the 2005 desalination plant in Ashqelon, it can be expected that an Israeli supply-side management paradigm will continue for some time.[114] Physical scarcity will most likely continue to be dealt with through technology, not through modified water resources management (such as demand management), or the acquisition of the upper reaches of the Hasbani in Lebanon. Demand will continue to increase, thereby putting a further squeeze on opportunities for a negotiated resolution of the water conflict with co-riparians.

The Israel Water Commission forecasts for the future certainly seem to indicate as much. The Commission identifies a need to meet both the demand of the Israeli Agricultural sector (through "lower-grade" water) and that of the continually growing Israeli and Palestinian Domestic sectors (IWC 2002b: 50), but not that of the Palestinian Agricultural sector. This latter will have to compete with a new sector – that of the 'environment'.

The Commission's 2002–2010 Transition Plan gives the same weight to environmental demands as it does to those of other "consumption sectors", though it stops short of defining allocation targets (IWC 2002a: 3). The Palestinian agricultural sector finds itself on a par with this new sector, and will have to compete with it for allocations at the Israeli Knesset against the much more strongly represented Israeli agricultural sector. The environmental lobby's political influence in the Knesset pales in comparison, but is better represented than the (non-existent) Palestinian agricultural lobby.

In any and all cases, progress on the water conflict will be determined by events in the broader political context. A negotiated permanent agreement with the Palestinians would not necessarily resolve the water conflict, just as the Oslo political process simply shifted Israeli control over the flows from an imperial to a hegemonic form. Improvements in the water sector would only be possible following a change in the broader political policy of asymmetric containment, though – again – such a shift would not automatically translate to the water sector. Nevertheless, the possibility of a more 'benign' form of hydro-hegemony, wherein control over the water resources was the responsibility of all riparians (including Palestine and Jordan, and eventually Lebanon and Syria) is worth considering. An indispensable condition for such Israeli leadership would be a significant restructuring – if not replacement – of the Israeli–Palestinian Joint Water Committee.

Also, the security concerns of those Israelis still advocating an anti-negotiations hydrostrategic discourse would have to be put on the table along side the concerns over sovereignty that Lebanon and Syria have with the Hasbani and the Banias. The Palestinian side has, in fact, already appealed both publicly and behind the scenes for Jordan River basin-wide re-negotiation to end the conflict. The opportunities offered by desalination and wastewater re-use technology would have to be drawn upon to ensure an equitable and reasonable distribution of freshwater resources in accordance with International Water Law (see e.g. Phillips et. al. (2006)). Riparians' domestic needs would have to be prioritised over agricultural consumption. The sustainability of any such agreement would, naturally, depend on the commitment and capacity of each party to implement rational water management, with supply-side policies being replaced by demand-side management, and all sources of contamination being brought under control.

The more likely, and less rosy, scenario is of heightening unilateralism by the more powerful side. Under such circumstances, transboundary resources are likely to be increasingly contaminated, with the Western Aquifer becoming worthless to all. Palestinians in the West Bank will be obliged to rely on local privately–owned and expensive desalination units, like their compatriots in Gaza. Israelis will have recourse to endogenous sources of water and build up a greater reliance on desalination technology. The Palestinian agricultural sector will dry up slowly, as whatever good water remains is devoted to the cities. The intensity of the water conflict will increase along with the inequity, and the power plays that are currently hidden may eventually be challenged in a more overt and aggressive form.

Appendices

Appendix A

Diagrams and Photographs

Figure A1 Plan of the southern shore of the Lake of Tiberias, Degania Gates, Alumot Dam and Lower Jordan River.

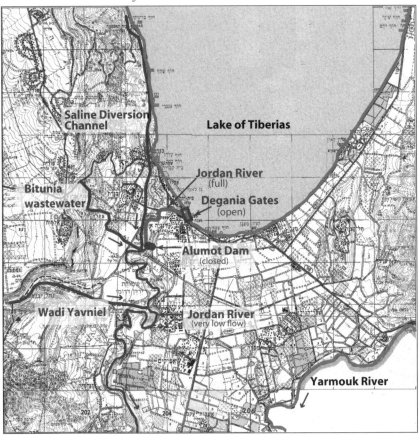

Photograph A1 Saline Diversion Channel just upstream of Alumot Dam, 21 February 2005. (*All photos by author*)

Photograph A2 View of Alumot Dam at high water level, 21 February 2005.

Photograph A3 View of Alumot Dam at high water level, 21 February 2005.

Photograph A4 The dying Dead Sea, June 2006.

Appendix B

Supporting Documents for Damaged Water Infrastructure of Jenin

Table B1 Source and supply of drinking water for the Municipality of Jenin (1998–2003).

Water Source	Owned by	Capacity [m3/h]	Actual supply [m3/month]		Share of water [per cent]		Operated by
			worst case	*best case*	*worst case*	*best case*	
Municipal Well	Municip.	25–90	9,000	45,000	9	18	Municip.
Mekoroth Line	Mekoroth	20–80	10,000	30,000	11	4	Mekoroth/ WBWD
PWA Well	PWA	170–200	50,000	120,000	55	50	Municip.
Jalame Filling Pt.	Mekoroth		8,550	15,000	9	6	Mekoroth
Agric. Wells	private	——	12,000	30,000	16	22	Municip.

(Laboud 1998, KFW 2000, WBWD 2003, Shawi 2003, pers. comm.)

Photo B1 Jenin Refugee Camp, following IDF partial and total destruction of 450 buildings (~800 homes), April 2002.

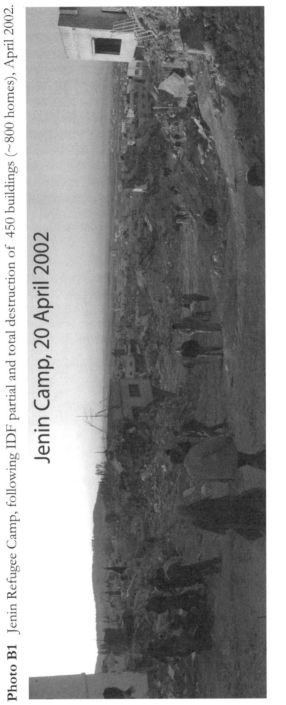

Jenin Camp, 20 April 2002

Photograph B2 Jenin PWA Well; IDF Merkava–3 Tank, 28 March 2003.

Photograph B3 IDF bulldozer, Jenin, 20 April 2002.

Photograph B4 Jenin Municipality water crews repairing valve (for third time in two weeks) at al Sharkiya, 20 April 2002.

Table B2 Classification of damages to water infrastructure in Jenin, April 2002.

Type	Description	Example
Infrastructure (indiscriminate)	Unintentional damages to infrastructure suffered under stated IDF rules of engagement (tank or bulldozer traffic, digging of trenches, stray bullets, shrapnel)	• crushed manholes or fire hydrants • crushed pipe (when exposed) • pin-hole or joint leaks in pipes (when buried) • watermains broken over a short span • bullet-pierced rooftop reservoirs and booster pumps.
Infrastructure (deliberate)	Deliberate damages to infrastructure due to IDF military activity	• watermains dug up lengthwise • destruction of municipal water crew repairwork (when carried out under close coordination with the IDF) • destruction of repair crew equipment (backhoes, compressors, etc.) • threats to municipal crew impeding repairwork.
Developmental / Economic	Financial or opportunity costs	• water infrastructure projects halted mid-way • lost opportunities for new development projects due to donor's reluctance to invest • water un-billed for due to physical damages to network • lack of water production due to dismissal of well operator • increased break-down due to interruption of routine operations & maintenance (O&M)
Political	Impact on Cooperative agreement between Israeli and Palestinian water technicians (e.g. the Joint Water Committee).	• crippling of established bi-lateral cooperation through the JWC • crippling of Municipality's water-provision capacity and corresponding degeneration of authority • revelation of incapacity for action of PWA, and corresponding lack of authority • slow-down of development projects (e.g. well-drilling)

Appendix C

Israeli and Palestinian Water Production and Consumption Data

The data on Israeli and Palestinian water production and consumption used to produce Figures 8.1, 8.3 and 8.4 are presented in Table C1. Discussion on the sources of the data follows.

Table C1 Israeli Water production and consumption, and Palestinian water consumption data, 1946–2003 (MCM/y).

	Israeli Total Water Consumption				Palest'n Total Cons'n	Israeli Freshwater Production		
YEAR	DOM	IND	AG	TOTAL		BH	SW	TOTAL
1947					500			
1948	75	15	260	350	350	200	150	350
1949	40	10	180	230	300	130	100	230
1950	104	21	250	375	280	150	225	375
1951	176	24	325	525	250	275	250	525
1952	188	27	450	665	218	365	300	665
1953	220	30	560	810	220	460	350	810
1954	217	33	660	910	230	535	375	910
1955	155	35	760	950	228	500	400	1000
1956	179	38	883	1100	225	625	425	1050
1957	192	42	946	1180	220	675	425	1025
1958	195.6	46.1	1032.3	1274	225	833.7	470.1	1303.8
1959	185.9	51	993.2	1230.1	230	784.9	486.7	1271.6
1960	197	54	1087	1338	228	869.8	468.1	1337.9
1961	184	56	1047	1287	227	834	422.6	1256.6
1962	173.8	55.1	1144.2	1373.1	225	950.8	456.9	1407.7
1963	192.6	57.2	1038.6	1288.4	220	902.1	423.7	1325.8
1964	199.1	54.4	1075.4	1328.9	225	861.9	531.3	1393.2
1965	206.4	59.2	1152.9	1418.5	228	882.3	624.1	1506.4
1966	210.7	60.8	1203	1474.5	230	966	629.9	1595.9
1967	211.4	66	1133.3	1410.7	227	925.8	673.2	1599
1968	231.2	70.2	1235.4	1536.8	225	973.6	694.8	1668.4
1969	239.7	74.9	1249.3	1563.9	220	957.4	753.3	1710.7
1970	253.7	86.3	1319	1659	228	1024.2	781.7	1805.9
1971	267.6	87.1	1210.1	1564.8	230	954.2	785.3	1739.5
1972	285.9	92.4	1297.3	1675.6	225	1043.4	769.8	1813.2
1973	288.2	97	1179.9	1565.1	228	1110.6	593.1	1703.7
1974	294.7	94.4	1207.1	1596.2	230	1042.1	714.4	1756.5
1975	305.4	94.5	1327.9	1727.8	225	1139.5	661.4	1800.9
1976	307.3	91.2	1271.2	1669.7	220	1048.1	713.5	1761.6
1977	347.6	94.3	1231.5	1673.4	222	1051.6	711.2	1762.8
1978	365.5	96.2	1325	1786.7	225	1161.5	692.1	1853.6
1979	370.1	100.1	1220	1690.2	228	1119.6	623.7	1743.3

1980	367.6	99.7	1211.6	1678.9	230	1028.6	718.6	1747.2
1981	385.1	103	1281.7	1769.8	225	1040.3	748.2	1788.5
1982	400.9	103.2	1254.6	1758.7	220	1092.4	762.9	1855.3
1983	418.8	103.2	1355.7	1877.7	222	1129.1	715.1	1844.2
1984	422.4	109	1388.7	1920.1	230	1191	798	1989
1985	451.5	108.1	1464.7	2024.3	227	1213.1	864.9	2078
1986	423.1	103.8	1125.3	1652.2	235	1064	665.1	1729.1
1987	446.5	107.5	1178.7	1732.7	227	1015.7	834.5	1850.2
1988	388.6	83	1157.8	1629.4	230	942.1	715.5	1657.6
1989	500.6	113.8	1236.8	1851.2	235	1109.9	887.5	1997.4
1990	554.8	108.4	1113	1776.2	233	1209	654	1863
1991	444.8	100.4	874.8	1420	240	990.4	459.8	1450.2
1992	490.1	105.8	955.3	1551.2	260	837.8	805.6	1643.4
1993	527	110	1125.4	1762.4	268	990.3	721.9	1712.2
1994	555.5	113.9	1143.6	1813	270	996.5	773	1769.5
1995	588.1	119.4	1273.8	1981.3	280	1089.2	829.5	1918.7
1996	604	124.4	1284.3	2012.7	282	1081	847.3	1928.3
1997	621.2	122.8	1263.8	2007.8	280	1093.3	873.3	1966.6
1998	671.7	129.2	1364.9	2165.8	282	1222.6	881.1	2103.7
1999	681.8	126.5	1264.6	2072.9	285	1474.4	527.6	2002
2000	662.1	124.2	1137.4	1923.7	290	1181.6	669.1	1850.7
2001	658.4	120.1	1021.9	1800.4	310	1164.6	542.9	1707.5
2002	688	122	1021	1831	320	1086	538	1912
2003	698	117	1045	1860	331	830	852	1970

Notes: All figures in MCM/y, except population figures which are in millions. DOM = Domestic sector consumption; IND = Industrial sector consumption; AG = Agricultural sector consumption; BH = Borehole production; SW = Surface water production. Israeli Production figures are for freshwater only, and do *not* include water generated by wastewater re-use or desalination techniques. Israeli Consumption figures from 1993 onwards *do* include water generated by wastewater re-use or desalination, the large majority of which are used in the Agricultural sector (roughly 200 MCM/y until 2005). This explains why 'consumption' figures are sometimes larger than the 'production' figures.

The source for the bulk of this data is the Israel Water Commission's (IWC) report 'Consumption and Production 2001', records of which date only from 1959. Numerous other sources have been employed to update and verify the data. These include: the Israeli Central Bureau of Statistics 2004 Report on Agriculture (ICBS 2005) as well as their 2005 Annual Statistical Review (ICBS 2005: Table 21.6); the Israeli Ministry of Agriculture 2003 Report on Agriculture (IMOA 2001: Table 12); the 2002 Israeli Parliamentary Inquiry into the Water Sector (PCIIWS 2002: Table 2); the Hydrological Service of Israel's Annual Report (HSI 2004); and older Water Commission reports such as IWC (1969, 1970, 1978).

Figures from 1948 to 1959 (the start date of HSI record-keeping) were taken from Galnoor (1978), Kahhaleh (1981), Stork (1983) and Schwarz (2004) (Kahhaleh (1981) and Stork (1983) both cite Arlosoroff (1977), which was unseen.). Pre-1948 data was taken from the British Mandate Palestine's 1947 Memorandum on the Water Resources of Palestine (GOP 1947), and secondary sources such as Stork (1983); Allan (2001); and Thomson (2004).

A detailed list of data sources follows (where no data source is specified, the figures have been interpolated or interpreted based on sourced data).

Israeli Consumption Figures

1948. These figures are cited by Schwarz (2004: 17) and Kahhaleh (1981: 13), both of whom cite Arlosoroff, Saul (1977) *Water Resources Development and Management in Israel*, Kidma (Jerusalem), III, 2 (No. 10), pp. 4–10.

1949. Galnoor (1978: 339). Galnoor cites Israel (1972), *Development of the National Economy 1948–1971*, Israel Economic Planning Authority, Jerusalem, p.12.

1953. Total Consumption figure – Kahhaleh (1981: 15). Kahhaleh cites the Tahal Seven Year Plan (Tahal (1959)).

1955. Galnoor (1978: 339). Galnoor cites Israel (1972), *Development of the National Economy 1948–1971*, Israel Economic Planning Authority, Jerusalem, p.12.

1958–2001. Israel Water Commission – IWC (2002b).

2002. Agricultural Consumption – Israeli Central Bureau of Statistics Report *Agriculture in Israel* (ICBS 2004: Table 12). Total Consumption – Israeli Central Bureau of Statistics Report *Agriculture in Israel* (ICBS 2004: Table 12). Domestic and Industrial Consumption – Hydrological Survey of Israel (HSI (2004)).

2003. Hydrological Survey of Israel (HSI (2004)).

Israeli Production Figures

1947. British Mandate Palestine Governmental Report (GOP (1947)).

1953. Total Production figure – Kahhaleh (1981: 15). Kahhaleh cites the Tahal Seven Year Plan (Tahal (1959)).

1955–1957. Total Production figures – Kahhaleh (1981: 34). Kahhaleh cites Kariv, Zeef, *Israel Water Economy*, Tel Aviv: Mekoroth Water Co. Ltd., p. 11.

1958–2001. Israel Water Commission – IWC (2002b).

2002. Total Production – Israeli Central Bureau of Statistics Report *Agriculture in Israel* (ICBS 2004: Table 12). Surface Water and Borehole Production – Hydrological Survey of Israel (HSI (2004)).

2003. Hydrological Survey of Israel (HSI (2004)).

Palestinian Total Consumption Figures

As discussed in Chapter 4, the data for Palestinian consumption and production figures is scarce and of questionable accuracy. The margin of error in the overall quantities consumed, however, is expected to be minor, given the relatively small absolute quantities involved.

1947. The figure shown for 1948 is matched from British Mandate Government of Palestine's estimate of production at that date (GOP (1947)), with 300 MCM/y from boreholes and 200 MCM/y from wells. This includes water counted throughout historic Palestine (today Israel, West Bank and Gaza).

1948. The drop for the year 1948 is matched from the Israeli consumption figures for the same year, from Schwarz and Kahhaleh (see above). This interpretation is open to discussion.

1952. This figure is calculated based on the estimated population figures (667,000 in West Bank, 250,000 in Gaza) multiplied by an estimated *per capita* consumption of 237 MCM/y. This *per capita* consumption figure itself is matched from the per capita consumption from 1967 (based on 227 MCM/y consumption (the level calculated from the mid- 1980s) and a population of 954,898 (see below).

1967. This figure is matched from the mid-1980s figure, on the assumption that most development in the sector in the West Bank and Gaza during the occupation period was conducted after 1982.

Mid-1980s. This period is taken as roughly 1980–93 by Attili (2004). Attili cites the United Nations 1992 *Water Resources of the occupied Palestinian territories*.

2003. The figure was calculated from several sources, as explained in Table 4.3.

Notes

1 Water Wars or Water Conflicts?

1   The destruction that fighter jets heap upon water infrastructure or resources in *non-*water conflicts *is* significant, however. This was most recently demonstrated in summer 2006 by the Israel Air Force's destruction of the Gaza electrical power plant (which supplied electricity for one third of the wells) and (along with artillery from Israel Defense Forces) over fifty water towers in southern Lebanon (Unicef 2006).

2   The American West's water conflict is meticulously documented and eloquently described in Mark Reisner's *Cadillac Desert*. From the turn of the twentieth century, the relatively much more powerful state of California was able to set the agenda with its weaker neighbours. Describing mid-1960s attempts to enforce the Colorado River Basin Storage Act, Reisner notes "what California demanded as the price for acquiescence was simple – devastatingly simple. Before Arizona received a drop of its entitlement, it wanted its full 4.4-million-acre-foot entitlement guaranteed. As far as California was concerned, there would be no equitable sharing of shortages, no across-the-board cuts in times of drought; it wanted satisfaction no matter what" (Reisner 1986: 294).

3   Of course the case is not so simple. China's interests in the dams is to profit on the topography to produce hydro-electricity. A large portion of the best market for electrical power is the downstream riparians themselves. China is also interested in keeping the river navigable, so that cargo ships can reach the remote regions. We thus see that, despite its overwhelmingly superior military, economic and political power, China is not completely 'free' to disregard the interests of its fellow riparian states. Thailand, Cambodia and the other 'weaker' states may capitalise on what is conceived, in Chapter 2, as their 'bargaining power' to ensure the best possible outcome of the conflict.

4   Nasra Abu Oteiq, 70 years old, Fatma Abu Safra, 65, Suheir Abu Ghrara, 17, Jamal Abu Safra, 2 and Mohammad Otieq, 11 months, died when the levees of the sewage lake burst in early April 2007. The cause is attributed to limited Palestinian capacity to maintain the wastewater treatment system, Israeli restrictions on the movement of goods into Gaza, Palestinian infighting and international donor politics. See Zeitoun (2007).

5   British geographer David Harvey (2005: 75) analyses the extent of US hegemony in geopolitics, noting that its success largely depends "upon whether the US can persuade the world that it is acting in a leadership role, concerned to develop collective power by acting as guarantor of global oil supplies to all, or whether it is acting out of narrow self-interest to secure its own position at the expense of others".

6   Ex-World Bank Chief Economist Joseph Stiglitz states that "today even the IMF agrees that it has pushed [the liberalisation] agenda too far – that liberalizing capital and financial markets contributed to the global financial crises of the 1990s and can wreak havoc on a small emerging country" (Stiglitz 2002: 59).

7 The theoretical work of Gramsci and Lukes is systematically applied to the realm of water conflicts in that regard, as we will see in Chapter 2. The approach taken is catalysing into what is becoming known as the 'Framework of Hydro-Hegemony', promoted primarily by the 'London School'.

2 *Understanding Power and Water*

8 The suite of theory is not complete. Regime theory is one neglected element. Readers are directed towards the theoretical work of Robert Keohane (1980), the criticism of Susan Strange (1982) and application in the water sector by Jägerskog (2001) and Kibaroglu (2002) to name a few.

9 A dozen alternative viewpoints are offered in the 2005 *Special Issue on Power* of *Millenium: Journal of International Studies* Volume 33, No. 3.

10 Lukes' theories have attracted criticism. The bulk of the criticism concentrates on the subjective nature of the role that interests play in power structure, and how these cannot be readily measured by social science methods. Hutchings (2005) for example, notes that pluralists argue that social science cannot act as an adjudicator of real interests, and that post-structuralists question the grounds on which genuine and non-genuine interests can be determined (2005: 890). Lukes responds to the criticism by arguing for the effects of the *covert* nature of power (see Lukes (2005 [1974])).

11 Strange's analysis draws implicitly on the 'knowledge is power' work of Foucault. Readers interested in Foucault's work are directed to Barnett (1999), Horrocks (1999), Burawoy (2003) and many others.

12 At the personal level, this may be made possible through notions of inferiority and questioned identity. The servility of black Africans to their colonial 'masters', for example, may have been one result of the application of this third dimension of power, as the quote from Aimé Césaire implies. The idea that a group is unaware of their own interests – known as *false consciousness* – is understandably open to considerable criticism. "Serious problems arise out of this [concept of *false consciousness*], as Lukes notes, because 'to say such power involves the concealment of people's 'real interests' by 'false consciousness' evokes bad historical memories and can appear both patronising and presumptuous'" (el Khairy 2006).

13 In the words of Jones (2006: 10), "Gramsci's major contribution to knowledge is to challenge a simplistic notion of opposition between domination and subordination or resistance. Instead he recasts ideological domination as hegemony: the process of transaction, negotiation and compromise that takes place between ruling and subaltern groups".

14 Another reason there is confusion with the term 'hegemony' may be the result of different interpretations developed on either side of the Atlantic Ocean, as described in the Oxford Concise Dictionary of Politics: "When one social class exerts power over others beyond that accounted for by coercion or law, it may be described as hegemonic. …Thus the bourgeoisie was regarded as hegemonic within capitalist society by Gramsci, who believed their power depended on the permeation by bourgeois values of all organs of society … Among contemporary North American international relations theorists, the term has been used rather differently [in the dominative, subjugative sense]." (McLean and McMillan 2003: 239).

15 In other words, "to maintain its authority, a ruling power must be sufficiently flexible to respond to new circumstances and to the changing wishes of those it rules. It must be able to reaching into the minds and lives of its subordinates, exercising its power on what appears to be a free expression of their own interests and desires" (Jones 2006: 3).

16 Article IV of the Helsinki Rules states that "each state is entitled, within its territory, to a reasonable and equitable share in the beneficial uses of the waters of an international drainage basin" (IWL 1966).

17 The 1997 UN Convention Seven refers to seven factors relevant to the definition of equitable and reasonable utilisation: a) Geographic, hydrological and other factors of a natural character, b) the social and economic needs of each state for the watercourse, c) the population dependent on the watercourse, d) the effects of use of the watercourses on other states, e) existing and potential use of the watercourse, f) conservation, protection, development and economy of use of the watercourse, g) the availability of alternatives of comparable value to an existing or planned use.

18 As the London Water Research Group is demonstrating, 'a treaty does not co-operation make', particularly through the work of Elisabeth Kistin.

19 A perceptive and comprehensive analysis of narratives on water throughout history can be found in Hamlin (2000).

20 The effect of unquestioned discourse can be exemplified by the development of the Integrated Water Resources Management (IWRM). Wester and Warner (2002) show how use of the watershed as the base unit for administration has become accepted to the point that its weaknesses are not even acknowledged, much less considered. Such weaknesses include the reinforcement of existing inequities through the depoliticising of water management issues, and issues of representation with stakeholder participation. Supporting evidence for this claim can be found in the topics chosen for discussion at international conferences (see e.g. the program of the SIWI conference in Stockholm, August 2005), and in the literature (e.g. Biswas 2001, Allan 2003).

3   An Asymmetrically Distributed Resource

21 Diversion structures operated by Israeli farmers on Wadi Gaza mean that only the flood flows ever reach Gaza, and the wadi within Gaza is primarily, like the upper reaches of the Lower Jordan River, a stream of sewage.

22 The term 'aquifer basin' refers to the geological (i.e. rock) formation which holds groundwater. Aquifers may be naturally recharged through rainfall infiltrating from the earth's surface, or artificially through pumping known as 'aquifer injection'. The geology and hydro-geology under the earth's surface in Palestine and Israel is very complex. In the West Bank, the karst limestone formations have been driven by tectonic plate movement, resulting in thousands of fractures, dips and rolls. Cross-sectional views of the geology vary enormously depending on the location taken. General representations such as in Figure 3.1 do not capture this complexity, but serve to provide an adequate idea of the dynamics of underground water flows.

23 Dozens of low-capacity wells were drilled illegally by Palestinian civilians during the most intense periods of recent violence (2000–2003), particularly in the North Eastern Aquifer Basin.

24 The situation contrasts with that in Gaza, where there are over 4,000 agricultural and private wells producing an estimated 140 MCM/y. Most of these wells proliferated during the post-Oslo period, when the PWA was unable/unwilling to control drilling. The effects of this loss of control are often exaggerated. The total extraction from within Gaza, has not substantially increased from pre-1994 levels, when Israeli-managed agriculture, such as strawberry and orange production, kept water consumption near the same levels.

25 The private tankers seek water where they will. When access to a Palestinian water source is barred by any of the hundreds of temporary or permanent Israeli checkpoints that dot the West Bank, the Palestinian tanker drivers purchase water from obliging Israeli settlers. The settler making the deal sells water provided to him at a subsidised

rate from the Israeli government. The irony is not lost on the Palestinian villagers, as in the case of the residents of Madama – see Box, Chapter 1.

26 World Bank (2004).

27 WBWD (2003). Average for year 2002.

28 USAID (2002b: Tables A1, A2, A3). Averages taken from years 1980–1999.

29 SUSMAQ (2001a: (Table 4.1 in this study)). Includes estimated flow from the Israeli-controlled brackish springs near the Dead Sea. These flows are *not* computed in the freshwater consumption figures, although they do have industrial uses (from Table 3.1, Palestinian abstraction (65.9 MCM/y) + Israeli abstraction (88.3 MCM/y) = 154.2).

30 Calculated from Avg. Production of WBWD Wells (10.4 MCM/y (this table)) – Israeli Consumption from the same source (4.5 MCM/y (this table)) = 5.9 MCM/y.

31 Based on 2005 bills from Mekoroth to the PWA (Mekoroth 2005).

32 SUSMAQ (2001b: 213). The figure compares with 50 MCM/y from Table 3.1.

33 Calculated from Average Total Israeli Production (55 MCM/y (this table)) – Palestinian Consumption from this source (6.9 MCM/y (this table)) = 48.1 MCM/y.

34 Calculated from Israeli Consumption from this source (9 MCM/y) + Average Palestinian Consumption from this source (~29 MCM/y) = 38 MCM/y.

35 Calculated from Average Total Consumption charged to WBWD (~46MCM/y (Mekoroth 2005)) – Average estimated Production of WBWD wells (10 MCM/y (this table)) = 36 MCM/y.

36 Calculated from Total Israeli Settler Consumption (57 MCM/y (Arlosoroff 2005, pers. comm.) (see also Dillman (1998: 57)) minus Israeli Consumption from Israeli wells inside the WB (48.1 MCM/y (this table)) = ~ 9 MCM/y.

37 The figure does not include the roughly 180,000 settlers located in the West Bank near Jerusalem (PASSIA 2004), whose water is supplied through the same system as the Israeli residents of Jerusalem.

38 Several systematic attempts have been made to determine the Palestinian share that would result from application of the principle. Ziad Mimi (2003) calculates the Palestinian equitable and reasonable share from the Jordan River System in the range of 175–225 MCM/y (Mimi and Sawalhi 2003). The 1955 Johnston Plan figure allocated 215 MCM/y (Johnston 1955, Phillips, et al. 2005: 6), matching El Musa's figure based on the 1953 Baker–Harza engineering study assessment of irrigable lands on the western ghor, flood plain, of the Jordan River Valley (1998: 310). Official Palestinian estimates of the Palestinian share of the JRS waters vary from 100 MCM/y (el Musa 1998: 309) to 350 MCM/y (NSU 2005c).

39 SUSMAQ (2001b: Table 5.1). This includes all sources from the Upper Jordan River, but not the return flows from groundwater into the Lower Jordan River. Estimates of the amount abstracted by Israel from the Lake of Tiberias for local or out-of-basin use via the NWC vary from 345 (HSI 2004: 288) to 400 (Markel 2004a) to 460 MCM/y (Jridi 2002: 24) to 500 MCM/y (UNEP 2003: 11). The maximum pumping capacity of the NWC is elsewhere cited as 1.5 MCM/day, or 550 MCM/y (Cohen 2004a). Local use of Tiberias water is estimated at 70 MCM/y (SUSMAQ 2001b: Table 5.1) to 230 MCM/y (IWC 2002b).

40 Wadi al Far'a is technically not a transboundary resource as it lies completely within the political borders of the West Bank (Figure 4.1). An estimated 6 MCM/y is captured by Israeli sources inside the closed military zone through the 'Tirzah Reservoirs', which are observable from Highway 90 in the Jordan River Valley (NSU 2005c: 21).

41 SUSMAQ (2001b: 150). Estimated average annual flow. This flow in particular is highly variable, ranging from 0–100 MCM/y, depending on climatic conditions.

42 Official allocation figures from the Oslo II Interim Agreement, Article 40 (Oslo II 1995).

43 This figure excludes the eastward flowing springs in the EAB, as these are not transboundary. The Oslo II allocation (including the 'extra 78' MCM/y (see Chapter 7)) is 132 MCM/y. Subtracting the eastward flowing springs (63.8 MCM/y (Table 3.1)) leaves 68 MCM/y.

44 Allocations from the Coastal Aquifer were not specified by Oslo II. The figure of 429 MCM/y is actual Israeli abstraction in 2002/2003 (HSI 2004: VII); the Palestinian figure of 135 is actual consumption, estimated at 80 MCM/y over the estimated sustainable yield (NSU 2005b: Table 2.1).

45 The concept of 'water footprint' was developed by Arjen Hoekstra, at the Delft Institute for Water and Education.

46 Israel was to purchase the water from Turkey and ship it through super-tankers or 'Medusa Bags' to Haifa (Cohen 2004c). The estimated cost of one dollar per cubic metre was conflated, according to several Israeli water professionals, with savings derived from a tied return deal for Israel to retro-fit Turkish army personnel vehicles. The 'arms for water' deal, as it came to be known never fully materialised, though there is a more recent push for a Turkey–Israel underwater 'corridor' of pipes transporting oil, natural gas, electricity and water.

4   Highly Politicised Hydropolitics

47 USAID contributions to the water sector in the West Bank were more than double the second largest donor in absolute terms (the World Bank), and triple the other large contributors like Norway, France and Germany (PWA 2003b: Fig. 5). A similar situation exists in Gaza, where USAID had committed to undertaking key large infrastructure projects such as the Gaza Desalination Facility and the North–South Carrier.

48 Though the Litani River (but not Mount Hermon) did eventually come under Israeli control from 1978 to 2000, the Litani was not diverted for Israeli use. See discussion in Chapter 7.

49 The 'hydraulic mission' of a state has been conceived of as the official policy that seeks to mobilise water and improve the security of supply as a foundation for social and economic development (Turton 2003: 10). Eric Swyngedouw (1999) documents the legitimacy that the Spanish government derived through such hydraulic efforts. Harvey's (2005) Marxist analysis refers to a similar dynamic in different terms. He refers to the role played by "fixed capital" embedded in the land. In the nineteenth century, Harvey notes, "states built roads and communications systems primarily for the purposes of administration, military control and protection of the territory as a whole (2005: 105).

50 The engineering efforts required to sustain the refugee re-settlement plans have been characterised by Italian anthropologist Mauro van Aken (2003)as instruments in the depoliticization of their plight.

51 Although there has been much debate over the allocations that Johnston arrived at (and apparently much misunderstanding (see Phillips, et. al. 2005b), the Johnston Plan is still regularly cited in as the most comprehensive attempt to distribute the JRS waters.

52 Other sources make a more direct link between the 1967 war and water resources. As Anthony Turton points out: "In his capacity as Chief of Staff of the Northern Command of the Israeli Defence Forces, Ariel Sharon offers an insight: "People generally regard 5 June 1967 as the day the Six-Day War began. This is the official date. But in reality the Six-Day War started two and a half years earlier, on the day Israel decided to act against the diversion (initiated by upstream Arab states) of the Jordan". (Bullock & Darwish, in Turton (2003: 49)). Sharif el Musa comments "the fact that Israel has benefited enormously from the water it seized in 1967 does not necessarily make the "water imperative" in this instance plausible. The outcome of the June 1967

war was by no means as certain at the time as it appears in retrospect, just as the fact that Israel benefited tremendously from cheap Palestinian labour does not suggest that it would have fought a war for it (el Musa 1997: 218).

53 Feitelson (2002) credits the invisibility of the issue (until 1995) to the dissipation of the threat from Arab states, the institutionalisation of the water sector into the hands of a select few (with the creation of the Water Commissioner's Office in 1959) and the subsequent shift in water policy from the high-profile security issues to the relatively "mundane" issues of internal allocation.

54 These include, but are not limited to Military Orders 92 (1967); 158 (1967); 457 (1974); and 498 (1974). The control exerted by Israel over water resources in the occupied Palestinian territories through legal means has been explored in great depth by several authors. Suggested readings on the subject are el Musa (1997: Ch. 4), Messerschmid (2005) and the comprehensive report by Centre for Housing Rights and Evictions (COHRE) and BADIL (COHRE 2005). The resultant legal environment was one of "legal dualism", with one system of law for Israeli settlers and one for Palestinians (Eyal Benvenisti, in el Musa (1997: 263)).

55 Yet another indicator of the discrepancy in development during this period between Israeli settlers and Palestinians living in the West Bank is the number of wells that were developed. The number of Israeli wells inside the West Bank increased from 0 to 32 (most of them very high capacity) while the number of Palestinian wells (all of which are low capacity) decreased from 413 to 364. The decrease is attributed to dropping water levels or increased states of disrepair due to lack of maintenance (Trottier 1999: 100).

56 The severe drought period that ended in 1990/91 certainly contributed to the resignation of the pro-agriculture Water Commissioner Psemach Ishay (Ben-Zvi, et al. 1998) and the heightened public awareness of the woes of the Israeli water sector.

57 Articles in the Israeli newspaper Ha'aretz concerning the Palestinian–Israeli water conflict numbered only eight in 2000, compared with 30 in 1995. There were over 300 *internal* Israeli water-related news items in 2000 (Feitelson 2002: 309).

58 The institutional structure, for instance, enables the influence of non-water related factors such as inequalities built-in as administrative divisions and unequal access to checks and balances (Fischhendler forthcoming–a: 25).

59 The upper management PWA was staffed primarily with ex-PLO exiles who had been living in Tunis since their eviction by Israel from Lebanon in 1982. The much larger staff of the WBWD, in contrast, was completely staffed by 'insiders' who had lived through the trials of the Israeli occupation. Though the WBWD is officially under the PWA (as we have seen in Chapter 3), resentment continues until this day.

60 Bossier (2006) views the lack of communication as evidence of discursive power, noting that the PWA's "discursive power is felt, even if there is a wide gap [between the planners of the Water Law and the Palestinian people], a discrepancy that flies in the face of the planners and the actual process" (Bossier, 2005: 16).

61 Zaslavsky (2002: 4) claims, for instance, that an Israeli withdrawal from the Golan would be followed by intensive Syrian development for up to half a million people, which "would undoubtedly turn the Sea of Galilee into a polluted, sewage-infested pool." The radical views expressed therein also fit with the definition of what Allouche (2004) refers to as "water nationalism".

62 Instructive critique of constructed knowledge active in the Palestinian–Israeli water sector, including analysis of Sherman's point of view, is offered in Allan (1999).

63 Fischhendler (Fischhendler forthcoming–b: 6) demonstrates how this turn of language was a deliberate use of ambiguity that permitted the Jordanian negotiators to satisfy their own politicians (and hence the Jordanian public) while permitting Israel not to

concede on any issue that would otherwise follow from its recognition of proper Jordanian water "rights".

64 One Palestinian negotiator, on the other hand, credits the "accomplishment" to persistence and hours of intense negotiations (Haddad 2005, pers. comm.).

65 Donors have often been criticised for not tackling the political aspects of development. The World Bank, for example, states in the 2002 UK House of Commons Select Committee Report on International Development: "removing the 'access controls' imposed by the Israelis would have increased real GDP by 21%, whereas a doubling of development assistance – without easing closure – would only reduce the number of people living in poverty by 7% by the end of 2004. The situation in the [West Bank and Gaza], in other words, is not one which donor assistance alone can resolve" (CARE 2005). For more on this subject see e.g. Brynen, (2000), World Bank (2003), Hanafi and Tabar (2004), Keating et. al. (2005).

66 The steadfastness of USAID was severely eroded when the office in Tel Aviv saw their policy determined by the US Embassy in response to the killing of three American bodyguards in the Gaza Strip, November 2003. The US Embassy decision to suspend the work on the Gaza desalination plant and North–South transmission line until Palestinian officials handed over the killers, backfired. The killers were never handed over and the projects were halted indefinitely. The embassy's use of the multi-million dollar widely touted solutions to Gaza's water crisis were used as carrots for ulterior political motives was resented by the USAID officials, who are otherwise keen to label their assistance with stickers claiming "A gift from the American People for the Palestinian people". All US assistance and most of USAID's activities were halted when the Palestinian people elected the Hamas government in January 2006.

67 While Israeli advances into desalination and wastewater re-use technologies make possible an ever-increasing supply, these flows do not come at the cost of dispossession to the Palestinian side.

68 The 'fundamentally careful' nature of Israeli policy in the water sector is intuitively analogous to the Israeli *security first* approach to negotiations at the broader political level (See Hilal and Khan 2004).

5   Hard Power – Coercing the Outcome

69 This section is based on Zeitoun, Mark (2005) Conflict and Water in Palestine – The Consequences of Armed Conflict on Drinking-Water Systems in Jenin, West Bank. In: Khatib, I., K. Assaf, D. Clayes and A. al Haj Daoud, *Water Values and Rights*. Ramallah, Palestine: Palestine Academy Press. Much of the evidence presented herein was acquired through unpublished sources available to the author who was working as a water engineer in the relief effort at the time of the events.

70 There are furthermore several cases of destruction inflicted by Israeli *settlers* against Palestinian water infrastructure, notably in the villages of Bani Zaid Al Gharbyeh (PHG 2004b). In Madama, we may recall, settlers repeatedly damaged the village spring and once poisoned it with soiled diapers (Oxfam 2003b). This destruction was carried out despite attempts from the IDF and Mekoroth to prevent it. The discussion in this chapter is limited to damages inflicted by the Israeli state, which are more extensive but different in nature from the evidently deliberate acts of sabotage by settlers.

71 The three settlements were evacuated in 2005 as part of the Likud government's 'Disengagement Plan'.

72 The effects of the Wall have been particularly well documented by the UN Office for the Coordination of Humanitarian Affairs, as well as numerous Palestinian and Israeli legal and human rights organisations. The construction of such a visible sign of oppression in such an age of transparency and mass communication has led to the

common parlance of those involved in the conflict that this is the 'best documented case of ethnic cleansing in history'. The amount of information is indeed impressive – as shown in the UK newspaper website Guardian Unlimited's interactive feature.

73   Trottier (2007)offers a deeper and coherent account of the effects of the Wall on internal Palestinian power structures. She notes, for instance that "the varied impact the fence is having on inter-Palestinian power relations means that it is strengthening simultaneously a power, the PA, and its counter-power, the traditional power structure. This is leading to a specialisation of responsibilities for each whereby centralisation of power in the hands of the PA sometimes happens when it is in the interests of the Israelis" (Trottier 2007: 125).

6   *Bargaining Power – The Joint Water Committee*

74   A senior WBWD engineer describes, for example, the frustrations in 1999 with siting a reservoir for the Palestinian village of Beit 'Ur al Fauqa, west of Ramallah. The preferred site of a nearby hilltop was already occupied by an Israeli settlement and immediate excluded from consideration. The compromise alternative location, determined along with an Israeli employee of Mekoroth, was halfway up the hill outside the limits of the Israeli settlement. This location was rejected by the Israeli Civil Administration for 'being too close to the settlement'. The infeasible third alternative suggested by the Mekoroth representative was near Tira, over 3 kilometres away. The distance of the project from the town made it economically infeasible for the Palestinian side. Beit 'Ur al Fauqa remains to this day without any water storage capacity (Aish 2005, pers. comm.).

75   The German-funded wastewater plant of Salfeet, for example, was intended to be built in Area C, just outside of the municipal boundaries. Despite approval for the project by the technical committee at the JWC, Israeli settler and military interests intervened, resulting in a reversal of the approval (Messerschmid 2003).

76   In fact the opposite is possibly the case. There is growing evidence that the high sources of salinity within Gaza's groundwater is due as much to natural contamination stemming from Israel as it is from seawater intrusion (Vengosh, et al. 2005).

77   The relation between apparent equity between the two sides and the effective Israeli veto at the Joint Water Committee was identified soon after the beginning of the JWC, as noted in Newton (1999: 37).

78   Such was the case with the drilling of a well started by a US engineering company hired by USAID in 2000, in a location of the West Bank classified as Area B. The employees were confronted by an IDF military patrol requesting a well-drilling permit. The maps held by the contractor and soldiers revealed slight differences, with the IDF map showing the well-site to be in Area C. The jurisdiction of the well site remained contested, and the well was never drilled (Phillips 2004, pers. comm.).

79   The quote is attributed to Colonel Oded Hermann, Head of the Humanitarian Liaison office of the ICA, as stated to PWA Deputy-Director Fadel Kawash (Barghouti 2005, pers. comm.).

80   The quote is attributed to Deputy Water Commissioner Yossef Dreizin in 2004 (Anon, 2005).

81   This is not to downplay the instructive importance of the negotiation process that led to the letter of the water article of the Oslo II Agreement. As was the case at the Camp David II negotiations in 2000 (see Chapter 4), there was significant pressure (though from the Palestinian leadership) on the water negotiators to reach any sort of agreement (Haddad 2005, pers. comm.). 'High politics' regularly trumps 'low' political issues like water, with the results usually felt most acutely long after the 'high' political decision-makers are out of office.

82 Israeli Deputy Water Commissioner Jossef Dreizin admits that "here and there, there are examples of Israeli projects in the West Bank without JWC approval", adding that these pale in comparison beside similar Palestinian violations of the procedures (Dreizin 2006, pers. comm.).

83 Palestinian breaches of the JWC procedures are typically in the form of shallow wells drilled by family farms in the Northeastern Aquifer Basin, around Jenin. These are neither sanctioned nor controllable by the PWA, though the responsibility for the breach lies with them. The quantities of water involved pale in comparison with the deep wells intended for industrialized agriculture on settlements.

84 The Israeli side's unwillingness to hand over the wells (*Dothan 1*, *2* and *3*, the wells that partially feed the city of Jenin – Figure 5.1) may stem from the fact that they still serve nearby Israeli military camps. It may also be due to the stated Israeli intention not to alter the Oslo II designation of the sites from Israeli-controlled 'C' to Palestinian-controlled 'A'.

85 Further evidence of contradictions in JWC meeting minutes is provided in Newton (1999: 38)

7   *Ideational Power – Imposing Ideas*

86 Taken in part from Zeitoun, Mark (2007) Violations, Opportunities and Power along the Jordan River: Security Studies Theory Applied to Water Conflict. In: Shuval, H. and H. Dweik, *Water Resources in the Middle East – the Israeli-Palestinian Water Conflict*. Heidelberg, Germany: Springer Verlag.

87 Israel sought US mediation while Lebanon preferred UN mediation; the EU worked under the auspices and with the agreement of the UN. The core issues of the dispute, however, were not addressed by the mediators, a fact that first manifested itself during the summer 2006 war between Israel and Hezbollah. Along with the extensive damages to water towers (Chapter 5), the IDF also damaged the three main components of the Wazzani Springs project (the intake, the booster station and the Taibe treatment plant). At the first level of analysis, it seems the dispute 'lost' by Israel in 2002 to Lebanese bargaining power was addressed four years later by a less efficient but more assured source of hard power. The damages to the project in 2006 were slight, however, and easily repaired – discrediting implications of deliberate destruction. The Wazzani Springs and the Hasbani River remain a latent issue in a conflict that will heighten in intensity at times the politicians find opportune. In his first public speech after the war, Hezbollah leader Hassan Nasrallah mentioned transboundary water issues on five occasions (IC 2006).

88 In terms of pollution such threats are very real, as with the case of the Western Aquifer (see Tagar (2004b) and FOEME (2006a)).

89 There is furthermore considerable evidence in the literature of over-abstraction by Israeli wells in the EAB along the Palestinian portion of the Jordan River Valley. This has been blamed for reducing the flow of the 'Ein al Sultan' spring which feeds Jericho (Snowdon 2006).

90 Other authors have offered more conservative estimates, calculating the 2025 Palestinian water demand at 400–631 MCM/y (USAID 2002a: App. C, World Bank 2004). Actual water demand is necessarily a function of irrigable land, population growth, development plans and other factors. As such, water demand is notoriously difficult to define, and subject to extensive politicking.

91 A similarly opaque reference to 'a formula' is found in an position paper by the Israeli Ministry of Foreign Affairs which states that through the Oslo Accords "a formula was decided upon for increasing the water allocation gradually over the interim period" (IMFA 1999). The ambiguity is less damaging than the statement's fallaciousness, as a

reading of the Oslo Accords will reveal. There is no reference to a gradual increase found in Article 40 of the Oslo II Accords.

92 Paragraph 7 of Article 40 states "In this framework, and in order to meet the immediate needs of the Palestinians in fresh water for domestic use, both sides recognise the necessity to make available to the Palestinians during the interim period a total quantity of 28.6 mcm/year". The paragraph then details specific sources for the Israeli (9.5 MCM/y) and Palestinian (19.1 MCM/y) shares. The clause furthermore does not mention Palestinian agricultural allocations, despite Wolf's assertion.

93 A further example of unilateral Israeli determination of Palestinian needs is provided in the 2002 Israel Water Commission report on Production and Consumption, whereby the estimated "future consumption" of the PA from Israeli sources is "based on an average increase of 4% per year" (IWC 2002b: 52). This is over and above the flows that were to be supplied by Israel under the terms of the Oslo II Agreement. In judging the merit of this increase, one must consider that a) it is a unilateral decision made without consideration for or consultation with Palestinian water professionals, b) the water is being sold as an economic transaction, and could be expected to hold lower priority than water provided to Israeli customers, and c) it responds only to Palestinian domestic demands, disregarding Palestinian plans for agricultural and industrial development.

94 The SIWI International Water Week in Stockholm, August 2004, and the Israel–Palestine Centre for Research and Information 'Water for Life' Conference in Antalya, October 2004.

95 At least one half of the project seems bound to continue, with a call for bids to build the 100 MCM/y plant placed in December 2006. It remains to be seen whether Palestinians in the West Bank or Gaza will be intended customers of the plant. Covering investment of such large infrastructure is best done through a guaranteed market. As was the case of the Ashqelon plant, the market is not guaranteed, particularly in wet years, when more affordable water of better quality is available (Talhami 2005).

96 It is worth following whether the Hadera–Tulkarem project will be re-promoted by USAID following a change in the government in Palestine.

97 A more recent example of Israeli manipulation of donors comes following the August 2005 Israeli 'disengagement' from the Gaza Strip, and claims that Palestinian sewage from Beit Lahia may contaminate the intake of the Ashqelon Desalination Plant (in Israel). In the absence of a military presence in Gaza, the Israeli authorities were obliged to find other means to ensure Palestinian compliance in halting the pollution. Israeli journalist Ze'ev Schiff gives insight into how this might be accomplished, citing "sources in the [Israel] Water Commission [that] say that one way to pressure the Palestinians to avoid laying the sewage pipe is by means of the donor states" (Schiff 2005).

98 One is reminded of Aimé Césaire's observation of the subjugation of Black Caribbean's to their European colonial conquerors (see discussion on ideational power, Chapter 3). When the 'order of things' is arranged by the powerful, the weaker subjects bent on survival or maintenance of their relatively privileged positions within a subjected society know exactly what to do – comply. This is what Lebanese poet Kahlil Gibran understood when he wrote "they are the slaves for whom time has exchanged rusty chains for shiny ones so that they thought themselves free" (Gibran 1965).

8   Hydraulic Power – Dominance of Production

99 No era can be either sharply started or ended with a single and brief hydropolitical event, or even within the span of one year. The limits of the eras define relate more to a diffuse set of events and time period that surround the particular date chosen.

100 The relative share of the Israeli Industrial sector has not risen significantly, from 5 to 8% of the total volume of water consumed in Israel (Figure 8.3), and is not discussed in further detail here.

101 For a deeper discussion on the uncertainties surrounding the Israeli water sector, refer to Dery and Salomon (1997).

102 Based on a Palestinian population in the West Bank and Gaza of 2.98 million in 1997 and 3.5 million in 2003 (PASSIA 2004). See also Lautze (2005) for a discussion of Palestinian per capita consumption.

103 Allouche's (2006) exploration of Wolf's concept of water-nationalism may well reveal further insight into this point.

104 A further reason these flows may not have been counted by the IWC is that several of the wells produce water from perched aquifers. Perched aquifers are located above the transboundary aquifers, and are typically small, responsive to rainfall events and not transboundary. This last feature means that – as for the case of groundwater in Gaza – Palestinian production from them does not adversely affect Israeli water supplies, and may not be a matter of concern to the IWC.

105 See for example Ben-Zvi, et al. 1998, Wolf 2000a, Feitelson 2002, Medzini and Wolf 2004, Schwarz 2004, Thomas 2004, Fischhendler forthcoming–a.

106 The dynamic is partially described by the common understanding of the *Tragedy of the Commons* parable. For application to the water sector, see Hartmann (2002), Dietz and Olstrom (2003) and Lindemann (2005).

107 A proponent of the Israeli hydrostrategic discourse concurs with the facts, stating that the outcome of the 1967 war "enhanced Israel's degree of control over the water sources and their amounts … Any peace process can only leave Israel worse off" (Frisch 2002: 10).

108 Due to concerns raised by the orthodox community that this water may contain prohibited leavened foodstuffs.

109 Evidence of this established water management practice is given by Bachmat and Abdul Latif: "Correlation between the depth of annual rainfall and the annual volume of pumpage has shown that years of low rainfall are accompanied by high rates of annual pumpage and vice versa. Indeed, the highest record level of rainfall in 1991/92 was accompanied by the highest historic drop of 26% in the pumped volume, whereas the lowest level of rainfall in 1998/99 carried a record increase of the pumped volume by 30% in one year" (Bachmat and Abdul Latif 2006: 812).

9   *Israeli Hydro-Hegemony*

110 One of the most professional and extensive plans was conducted by USAID, entitled *West Bank Integrated Water Resources Management Plan*. Starting from scientifically rational base data, the two-volume document and CD recommend alternatives to the PWA for West Bank – wide integrated development of the water sector. USAID does not deny that it shares data from their projects in Palestine with their compatriots and colleagues at the US Embassy in Tel Aviv, as well with Israeli water authorities. According to US engineers hired to work on the plan, the Israeli water authorities rejected some of its base assumptions and data. USAID officially never published the plan as a consequence, wasting years of work and missing an opportunity to address the root causes of the Palestinian under-development of the sector – politics.

111 The term is borrowed from Mark Twain, who in his book *Mysterious Strangers*, wrote: "Before long you will see this curious thing: the speakers stoned from the platform, and free speech strangled by hordes of furious men who in their secret hearts are still at one with those stoned speakers – as earlier – but do not dare to say so. And now the whole nation – pulpit and all – will take up the war-cry, and shout itself hoarse, and mob any

honest man who ventures to open his mouth; and presently such mouths will cease to open. Next the statesmen will invent cheap lies, putting the blame upon the nation that is attacked, and every man will be glad of those conscience-soothing falsities, and will diligently study them, and refuse to examine any refutations of them; and thus he will by and by convince himself that the war is just, and will thank God for the better sleep he enjoys after this process of grotesque self-deception" (Twain 2004 [1916]).

112 A further measure of equitability may be through consideration of the distribution of benefits derived from the flows or through consideration of which state has control over them. There are currently no applications of shared benefits between Palestine and Israel, although one hopes that future hydro-electric or distribution schemes may be conceived and constructed within a spirit of mutual interest.

113 Various elements of Palestinian civil society in any case are caught up in the same trappings that Oslo laid down, with many NGOs following donor-driven agendas similar to those followed by the ministries (see Hanafi and Tabar 2004).

114 It is worth considering that in the hypothetical situation that desalination technology was as feasible in the 1960's as it was in 2005, the National Water Carrier may never have been built, and the June 1967 war may have been less intense.

Bibliography

Adalah (2006) Appeal to the Supreme Court against Policy of not Providing Drinking Water to Arab Bedouin Living in the Unrecognized Villages in the Naqab. *Adalah - The Legal Center for Arab Minority Rights in Israel - Newsletter*, 30. November 2006,

Aish, I. (2005, pers. comm.) *On the History of Cooperation through the JWC.* Personal communication with author, Ramallah, West Bank, 12 September 2005.

al Farra, Amani (2005) Health Effects due to Poor Wastewater Treatments in the Gaza Strip. *Water for Life in the Middle East: 2nd Israeli-Palestinian International Conference*, Antalya, Turkey, 20-12 October 2004, Israel/Palestine Center for Research and Information.

Allan, J. A. and C. Mallat, Ed. (1994) *Water in the Middle East: Legal, Political and Commercial Implications.* London, I.B. Tauris.

Allan, J.A. (1999) Middle Eastern hydropolitics: interpreting constructed knowledge. *SOAS Water Issues Study Group, School of Oriental and African Studies / King's College - London* (Occasional Paper 18).

Allan, J.A. (2001) *The Middle East Water Question: Hydropolitics and the Global Economy.* London, UK: I.B. Tauris.

Allan, J.A. (2003) IWRM/IWRAM: a new sanctioned discourse? *SOAS Water Issues Study Group, School of Oriental and African Studies / King's College - London* (Occasional Paper 50).

Allison, G. (1971) *Essence of Decision - Explaining the Cuban missile crisis.* Boston, USA.

Allouche, Jeremy (2004) Water Nationalism: An explanation of the past and present conflicts in Central Asia, the Middle East and the Indian Subcontinent? Institut universitaire de hautes études internationales. Ph.D. Thesis. Université de Genève, Geneva, Switzerland.

Amery, Hussein and Aaron Wolf, Ed. (2000) *Water in the Middle East: A Geography of Peace.* Austin, USA, University of Texas Press.

Amnesty International (2002) *Shielded from Scrutiny: IDF Violations in Jenin and Nablus.* MDE 15/143/2002, Amnesty International, November, 2002.

Anon. (2005, pers. comm.) *Briefing on the JWC Meeting of 11 September 2005 in Tel Aviv.* Personal communication with author, Ramallah, West Bank, 12 September 2005. 12 September 2005.

Ari, Shavit (2001) Sharonis, Sharonis, Sharonis. *Ha'aretz Daily (English).* Tel Aviv, Israel, 12 April 2001.

ARIJ (2000) *Israeli Violations in the North of the West Bank - Palestine: Update 30 November 2000.* Land Research Center. Bethlehem, Applied Research Institute of Jerusalem.

Arlosoroff, Shaul (1998) *Israel - Policy Issues in Water Resources Management,* Paper submitted to the IGCC (UCSD) Conference: Water and Food Security in the Middle East, Cyprus, 20-23 April 1998. Published by The Truman Institute, Hebrew University, Jerusalem.

Arlosoroff, Shaul (2000) Water Resource Management in Israel. *In:* Feitelson, E. and M. Haddad, *Management of Shared Groundwater Resources: The Israeli-Palestinian Case with an International Perspective.* Ottawa, Canada: International Development Research Council.

Arlosoroff , Shaul (2004, pers. comm.) *On the Israeli relationship with PWA.* Personal communication with author, Tel Aviv, Israel, 7 September 2004. 7 September 2004.

Arlosoroff, Shaul (2005, pers. comm.) *On Israeli Water Use - Past, Present, Future.* Personal communication with author, Tel Aviv, Israel, 2 September 2005. 2 September 2005.

Attili, Shaddad and David Phillips (2004) *Israel and Palestine: Legal and Policy Aspects of the Current and Future Joint Management of the Shared Water Resources.* Ramallah, West Bank, Negotiations Support Unit, Negotiations Affairs Department, Palestine Liberation Organisation, June 2004.

B'tselem (2000) *Thirsty for a Solution: The Water Crisis in the Occupied Territories and its Resolution in the Final-Status Agreement.* Jerusalem, B'tselem - The Israeli Information Center for Human Rights in the Occupied Territories, July 2000.

B'tselem (2001) *Not Even a Drop: The Water Crisis in Palestinian Villages Without a Water Network - Information Sheet.* Jerusalem, B'tselem - The Israeli Information Center for Human Rights in the Occupied Territories, July 2001.

Bachmat, Yehuda and Mohammed Khalid Abdul Latif (2006) The 1999 Drought and its Hydrologic Impact. *In:* Shuval, H. and H. Dweik, *Proceedings of the 2nd Israeli-Palestinian International Conference Water for Life in the Middle East, Held in Antalya, Turkey 10-14 October 2004.* Jerusalem: Israel/Palestine Centre for Research and Information.

Barghouti, I. (2004, pers. comm.) *On current Water Issues in Palestine, and Hadera-Tulkarem.* Personal communication with author, Ramallah, West Bank, 8 September 2004. 8 September 2004.

Barghouti, I. (2005, pers. comm.) *On Cooperation at the JWC and the Dynamics of Power.* Personal communication with author, Ramallah, West Bank, 4 September 2005. 4 September 2005.

Barnett, Clive (1999) Deconstructing context: exposing Derrida. *Transcripts of the Institute of British Geographers* (24): 277-293.

Ben-Zvi, Arie (1996) Effects and Yield of the Proposed Kinneret Bypass Project. *Water International* 1996 (21): 30-34.

Ben-Zvi, Arie, Emanuel Dlayahu, Mendel Gottesmann and Avner Passel (1998) Evolution of the 1990-1991 Water Crisis in Israel. *Water International* 23 (2): 67-74.

Benvenisti, Eyal (2002) *Sharing Transboundary Resources - International Law and Optimal Resource Use*. Cambridge, UK: Cambridge University Press.

Biswas, Asit (2001) Integrated Water Resources Management: A Reassessment. *Third Forum on Global Development Policy*, Henrich Boll Foundation.

Bossier, Wilfried (2005) Issues of Legitimacy and Governance in the Palestinian Water Sector. PhD Upgrade Submission. King's College London, June 2005, London, UK.

Brynen, Rex (2000) *A very political economy: peacebuilding and foreign aid in the West Bank and Gaza*. Washington, DC, USA: United States Institute of Peace.

Burawoy, Michael (2003) For a Sociological Marxism: The Complementary Convergence of Antonio Gramsci and Karl Polanyi. *Politics & Society* 31 (2): 193-261.

Burges, Sean (2005) Review of Lobell, Steven E., The Challenge of Hegemony: Grand Strategy, Trade and Domestic Politics. *Millenium: Journal of International Studies* 33 (3).

Buzan, B., O. Waever and J. de Wilde (1998) *Security - A new Framework for Analysis*. London, UK: Lynne Rienner Publishers, Inc.

CARE (2005) *Access to Water in a Conflict Situation: Case Study of the Occupied Palestinian Territories (draft)*. Ahamed, R. London, UK, CARE International.

Carles, Alexi (2006) Power asymmetry and conflict over water resources in the Nile River Basin: the Egyptian hydro-hegemony. Department of Geography. Master's Thesis. King's College London, University of London, London, UK.

Cascao, Ana (2005) Hydro Hegemony in the Nile River Basin. *Presentation given at First Workshop on Hydro-Hegemony, 21/22 May 2005*, King's College London, London, UK, London Water Research Group.

Cascao, Ana (2007) Ethiopia - Challenges to Egyptian Hegemony in the Nile Basin. *Water Policy* (forthcoming) (Special Issue on Hydro-Hegemony).

Chapagain, A.K. and A.Y. Hoekstra (2004) *Water Footprints of Nations, Volume 1: Main Report*. Value of Water Research Report Series No. 16. Delft, Netherlands, UNESCO-IHE Delft.

Chomsky, Noam (1992) *Manufacturing Consent - Noam Chomsky and the Media*, Video documentary produced on DVD by Zeitgeist Video, Necessary Illusions Productions Inc., Mark Achbar and Peter Wintonick.

Chomsky, Noam (1993) The Israel - Arafat Agreement. *Z Magazine* (October 1993).

Cohen, Amiram (2004a) Kinneret Committee to meet over opening of Degania Dam. *Ha'aretz*. Tel Aviv, Israel, 1 February 2004.

Cohen, Amiram (2004b) Paritzky: Sea of Galilee pumping must continue over Passover. *Ha'aretz*. Tel Aviv, Israel, 17 March 2004.

Cohen, Amiram (2004c) Turkish water deal signed. *Ha'aretz*. Tel Aviv, Israel, 5 March 2004.

COHRE (2005) *Ruling Palestine: A History of the Legally Sanctioned Jewish-Israeli Seizure of Land and Housing in Palestine*. Jerusalem, The Centre on Housing Rights and Evictions + BADIL Resource Centre for Palestinian Residency and Refugee Rights, May 2005.

Conca, Ken (2006) *Governing water: Contentious Transnational Politics and Global Institution Building*. Cambridge, MA, USA: Massachusetts Institute of Technology Press.

Cronon, William (1992) A Place for Stories: Nature, History and Narrative. *The Journal of American History* 78 (4): 1347-1376.

Daily News (2005) Jewish Settlers poison Palestinian Village Water Supply. *Daily News Internet News source*. palestine-info.co.uk,

Daoudy, Marwa (2005a) Turkey and the Region: Testing the Links Between Power Assymetry and Hydro-Hegemony. *Presentation given at First Workshop on Hydro-Hegemony, 21/22 May 2005*, King's College London, London, UK, London Water Research Group.

Daoudy, Marwa (2005b) *Le partage des eaux entre la Syrie, l'Irak et la Turkie - Negociation, securite, et asymetrie des pouvoirs*. Paris: CNRS Editions.

Dellapenna, Joseph W. (2003) Water Rights and International Law. *In*: Nicholson, E. and P. Clark, *The Iraqi Marshlands: A Human and Environmental Study*. London, UK: Politico's.

Dery, David and Ilan Salomon (1997) "After Me, The Deluge": Uncertainty and Water Policy in Israel. *Water Resources Development* 13 (1): 93 - 110.

Dietz, Thomas, Elinor Ostrom and Paul C. Stern (2003) The Struggle to Govern the Commons. *Science* 302 (December 2003): 1907-1912.

Dillman, Jeffrey D. (1998) Water Rights in the Occupied Territories. *Journal of Palestine Studies* 19 (1): 46-71.

Dinar, Ariel (2003) Preventive diplomacy, international relations, conflict resolution and international water law: implications for success and failur of the Israeli-Palestinian water conflict. *International Journal of Global Environmental Issues* 3 (2): 188 - 225.

Dombrowski, Ines (1998) The Jordan River Basin: Prospects for Cooperation Within the Middle East Peace Process. *In*: Scheumann, W. and M. Schiffler (eds), *Water in the Middle East: Potential for Conflicts and Prospects for Cooperation*. Heidleberg, Germany: Springer.

Dreizin, Jossef (2004) Desalination in the Middle East Region. *Israel/Palestine Center for Research and Information Water for Life Conference October 2004*, Antalya, Turkey, 12-14 October 2004.

Dunleavy, Patrick (2003) *Authoring a PhD - How to Plan, Draft, Write and Finish a Doctoral Thesis or Dissertation*. Hampshire, UK: Palgrave Macmillan.

el Khairy, Omar (2006) 'Power is always negotiated between the dominant and the subordinate'. Discuss. Essay prepared for MA on Migration and Diaspora Studies. School of Oriental and African Studies, London.

el Musa, Sharif (1996) The Land-Water Nexus in the Israeli-Palestinian Conflict. *Journal of Palestine Studies* 25 (3).

el Musa, Sharif (1997) *Water Conflict - Economics, Politics, Law and Palestinian-Israeli Water Resources*. Washington DC, USA: Institute for Palestine Studies.

el Musa, Sharif (1998) Towards a Unified Management Regime in the Jordan Basin: The Johnston Plan Revisited. *Yale F&ES Bulletin* Bulletin 103.

Evans, Graham and Jeffrey Newnham (1998) *Dictionary of International Relations*. London, UK: Penguin Books.

EWOC (2002) *Water and Wastewater Situation in the West Bank Governorates During and Following the IDF Re-occupation March, April 2002 - Draft Interim Report.* Jerusalem, Emergency Water Operations Centre (USAID, UNDP, Oxfam), June 2002.

Falkenmark, M. (2001) The Greatest Water Problem: The Inability to Link Environmental Security, Water Security and Food Security. *Water Resources Development* 17 (4): 539-554.

Fanon, Franz (1986 [1952]) *Black Skin, White Masks.* London, UK: Pluto Press.

Fanon, Franz (1990 [1963]) *The Wretched of the Earth.* London, UK: Penguin Books Ltd.

Farber, Efrat, Avner Vengosh, Itai Gavrielli, Amer Marie, Thomas D. Bullen, Bernhard Mayer, Ran Holtzman, Michal Segal and Uri Shavit (2004) The origin and mechanisms of salinization of the Lower Jordan River. *Geochimica et Cosmochimica* 68 (9): 1989-2006.

Feitelson, Eran (2000) The Ebb and Flow of Arab-Israeli water conflicts: are past confrontations likely to resurface? *Water Policy* 2000 (2): 343-363.

Feitelson, Eran (2002) Implications of shifts in the Israeli discourse for Israeli-Palestinian water negotiations. *Political Geography* 21 (2002): 293-318.

Feitelson, Eran (2004) The New Water Geography. *Lecture given at the IPCRI 'Water for Life' Conference 12-14 October 2004,* Antalya, Turkey, 12-14 October 2004. Israel/Palestine Center for Research and Information.

Feitelson, Eran (2005, pers. comm.) *On Israeli and Palestinian Water Discourses.* Personal communication with author, Jerusalem, 6 September 2005.

Feitelson, Eran (2005a) Political Economy of Groundwater Exploitation: The Israeli Case. *Water Resources Development* 21 (3): 413-423.

Feitelson, Eran and Marwan Haddad (2000) *Management of Shared Groundwater Resources: The Israeli-Palestinian Case with an International Perspective.* Ottawa, Canada: International Development Research Council and Kluwer Academic Publishers.

Fischhendler, Itay (2004) Legal and Institutional adaptation to climate uncertainty: a study of international rivers. *Water Policy* 6 (4): 281-302.

Fischhendler, Itay (2005) Spatial Adjustment as a Mechanism for Resolving River Basin Conflicts: The US-Mexico Case. *Political Geography* 25 (5): 547-573.

Fischhendler, Itay (forthcoming-a) Institutional conditions for IWRM: the Israeli Case. *Accepted to Ground Water.*

Fischhendler, Itay (forthcoming-b) Ambiguity in Transboundary Environmental Dispute Resolution: The Israel-Jordanian Water Agreement. *Journal of Peace Research.*

FO 371/104953 (1953) *On Jordanian Plans to Develop the Yarmouk Plans.* Correspondence between Palestine Electric Corporation and UK Government, and between Jordanian Government and UK Government, UK Foreign Office Archives FO 371/104953 - 1532/15-19.

FO 608/274 (1920) *Peace Conference (British Delegation) - Eastern Mission (Turkey), Files 76-91.* Correspondance between British Foreign Office and World Zionist Organisation regarding control over the Litani and Yarmouk Rivers, UK Foreign Office Archives FO 608/274.

FOEME (2006a) Promotional Brochure Promoting Solid Waste Symposium. *Symposium on Solid Waste Polluting the Mountain Aquifer, 31 January 2006*, Jerusalem, Friends of the Earth Middle East.

FOEME (2006b) A Master Plan for Saving Water for Domestic Use in Israel. *Good Water Neighbours Bulletin, Friends of the Earth - Middle East* 2006 (30).

Frederiksen, H.D. (2003) water: Israeli Strategy, Implications for Peace, and the Viability of Palestine. *Middle East Policy* X No. 4 (Winter).

Frey, Frederick W. (1993) The Political Context of Conflict and Cooperation Over International River Basins. *Water International* 18 (1): 54-68.

Frey, Frederick W. and Thomas Naff (1985) water: An Emerging Issue in the Middle East? *Annals of the American Academy of Political and Social Science* 482 (November 1985).

Frisch, Hillel (2002) Water and Israel's National Security. *Efficient Use of Limited Water Resources: Making Israel a Model State*, Ramat Gan, Israel, A Project of the Begin-Sadat Center for Strategic Studies, Bar-Ilan University.

Galnoor, Itzhak (1978) Water Policymaking in Israel. *Policy Analysis* 4 (3).

Gibran, Kahlil (1965) You Have Your Lebanon and I Have My Lebanon. *In: The Treasured Writings of Kahlil Gibran*. Edison, NJ, USA: Castle Books.

Gleick, Peter (2004a) *Water Conflict Chronology - Introduction*, Pacific Institute, August 2003.

Gleick, Peter (2004b) *Water Conflict Chronology*, Pacific Institute, August 2003.

GOP (1947) *Memorandum on the Water Resources of Palestine*. Presented by the Government of Palestine to the United Nations' Special Committee on Palestine in July, 1947. Jerusalem, Government Printer, Government of Palestine.

Gramsci, António (2003 [1935]) *Selections from the Prison Notebooks*. Hoare, Q. and G. N. Smith, London: Lawrence and Wishart.

Greco, Francesca (2005) The Securitization of the Disi Aquifer: A Silent Conflict between Jordan and Saudi Arabia. *Presentation given at First Workshop on Hydro-Hegemony, 21/22 May 2005*, King's College London, London, UK, London Water Research Group.

Gregory, Derek (2004) *The Colonial Present*. Malden, USA: Blackwell Publishing.

Gyawali, Dipak (2002) Nepal-India Water Resource Relations. *In*: Zartman, W. I. and J. Z. Rubin, *Power & Negotiation*. Ann Arbor, MI, USA: The University of Michigan Press. 129-154.

Haddad, Marwan (2004) Politics and Water Management. *Presentation given at the IPCRI 'Water for Life' Conference 12-14 October 2004*, Antalya, Turkey, 12-14 October 2004. Israel/Palestine Center for Research and Information.

Haddad, Marwan (2005, pers. comm.) *On the History of Israeli-Palestinian Water Conflict*. Personal communication with author, Nablus, West Bank, 18 September 2005. Telephone conversation. 18 September 2005.

Haddadin, Munther (2001) *Diplomacy on the Jordan: International Conflict and Negotiated Resolution*. International Development Research Centre and Kluwer Academic Publishers.

Hajer, Maarten A. (1997) *The Politics of Environmental Discourse: Ecological Modernization and the Policy Process*. Oxford, UK: Oxford University Press, Oxford Scholarship Online.

Hanafi, Sari and Linda Tabar (2004) Donor assistance, rent-seeking and elite formation. *In*: Khan, M., *State Formation in Palestine*. London, UK: RoutledgeCurzon.

Harel, Amos (2002) Israel Bans Palestinians from Drilling for Water. *Ha'aretz English Language Daily*. Tel Aviv, Israel, 23 October 2002.

Hartmann, Elizabeth (2002) Strategic Scarcity: The Origins and Impact of Environmental Conflict Ideas. Development Studies Institute. Ph.D. Thesis. London School of Economics, London, UK: 376.

Harvey, David (2005) *The New Imperialism*. Oxford, UK: Oxford University Press.

Hays, James B. (1948) *T.V.A. on the Jordan - Proposals for Irrigation and Hydro-Electric Development in Palestine*. Washington, DC, USA, A Report Prepared Under the Auspices of the Commission on Palestine Surveys, Public Affairs Press, assisted by A.E. Barrekette, with an introduction by Walter C. Lowdermilk.

Heyns, Piet (2005) Managing a Hydropower Impasse on the Kunene River. *Presentation given at First Workshop on Hydro-Hegemony, 21/22 May 2005*, King's College London, London, UK, London Water Research Group.

Hobbes (1996 [1651]) *Leviathan*. Oxford World's Classics. Oxford, UK: Oxford University Press.

Homer-Dixon, T. (1999) *Environment, Scarcity, and Violence*. Princeton, NJ, USA: Princeton University Press.

Horrocks, Chris (1999) *Introducing Foucault*. Cambridge, UK: Icon Books Ltd.

Horta, Korrina (2007) Resisting hydro-hegemony in southern Africa: The Lesotho Highlands Water Project. *Presentation given at the Third International Workshop on Hydro-Hegemony, 12 and 13 May 2007*, London School of Economics, London, UK, London Water Research Group.

HSI (2004) *Development of Utilisation and Status of Water Resources in Israel (Annual Hydrological Report) 2003*. (Hebrew), Jerusalem, Hydrological Service of Israel.

Hutchings, Kimberley (2005) Review of Lukes' power: A Radical View. *Millenium: Journal of International Studies* 33 (3).

IC (2006) *Nasrullah's Speech of September 24, 2006*, Informed Comment: Thoughts on the Middle East, History and Religion, Global Americana Project.

ICBS (2004) *Agriculture in Israel - The Industry Account, Area and Livestock, Price Index of Output and Input 2001-2003*. Jerusalem, Israel Central Bureau of Statistics, September 2004.

ICBS (2005) *2005 Statistical Abstract of Israel*. Jerusalem, Israel Central Bureau of Statistics, 2005.

ICRC (1994) *Handbook of the International Red Cross and Red Crescent Movement - International Humanitarian Law*. Geneva, Switzerland: International Committee of the Red Cross.

IMFA (1999) *The Water Issue in the West Bank and Gaza*. Tel Aviv, Israel, Israel Ministry of Foreign Affairs Archives, 24 June 1999.

IMFA (2002a) *Cabinet Communique - 16 September 2002*. Tel Aviv, Israel, Israel Ministry of Foreign Affairs Cabinet Secretariat Archives.

IMFA (2002b) *Cabinet Communique - 13 October 2002.* Tel Aviv, Israel, Israel Ministry of Foreign Affairs Cabinet Secretariat Archives.

IMFA (2002c) *Cabinet Communique - 23 October 2002.* Tel Aviv, Israel, Israel Ministry of Foreign Affairs Cabinet Secretariat Archives.

IMFA (2004a) *Comparison of GNP capita in dollars.* Tel Aviv, Israel, Israel Ministry of Foreign Affairs Cabinet Secretariat Archives, 1 January 2004.

IMFA (2004b) *Armed Forces - Number of Forces.* Tel Aviv, Israel, Israel Ministry of Foreign Affairs Cabinet Secretariat Archives, 1 January 2004.

IMG (2004) *IMG Damage Assessment and Reconstruction Management in the West Bank and Gaza Strip Database.* Jerusalem, International Management Group, European Commission Representative Office in the West Bank and Gaza Strip, 2004.

IMOA (2001) *Israel Agriculture - Facts and Figures, 2nd edition*, Israel Ministry of Agriculture and Rural Development, Foreign Trade Center, December 2001.

Ishaq, Jad (2005) Roots of Water Conflict in the Eastern Mediterranean. *Presentation given at Palestine Academy for Science and Technology "Water, Values and Rights" Conference 2-4 May 2005*, Ramallah, West Bank.

IWC (1969) *Water Extraction in Israel, 1963-1967.* Tel Aviv, Israel, Israel Ministry of Agriculture, Water Commission, Water Allocation Department, January 1969.

IWC (1970) *Water in Israel, Consumption and Extraction, 1962-1968.* Tel Aviv, Israel, Israel Ministry of Agriculture, Water Commission, Water Allocation Department, March 1970.

IWC (1978) *Water in Israel: Consumption and Extraction, 1962-1976.* Tel Aviv, Israel, Israel Ministry of Agriculture, Water Commission, Water Allocation Department, 1978.

IWC (2002a) *Transitional Master Plan for Water Sector Development in the Period 2002 - 2010, Executive Summary.* Tel Aviv, Israel, Israel Ministry of National Infrastructures, Water Commission, Planning Division, June 2002.

IWC (2002b) *Water in Israel: Consumption and Production, 2001.* Tel Aviv, Israel, Israel Ministry of National Infrastructures, Water Commission, Demand Management Division, December 2002.

IWC (2004) *Supply of Water to the Palestinian Authority from the Desalination Plant at Hadera.* Tel Aviv, Israel, Israel Water Commission, prepared by Tahal Engineering Consultants, January 2004, January 2004.

IWL (1966) *Helsinki Rules on the Uses of Waters of International Rivers.* Helsinki, Finland, International Water Law.

Jägerskog, Anders (2001) The Jordan River Basin: Explaining Interstate Water Cooperation Through Regime Theory. *SOAS Water Issues Study Group, School of Oriental and African Studies / King's College - London* (Occasional Paper 31).

Jägerskog, Anders (2002) The Sanctioned Discourse - A Crucial Factor for Understanding Water Policy in the Jordan Basin. *SOAS Water Issues Study Group, School of Oriental and African Studies / King's College - London* (Occasional Paper 41).

Johnston, Eric (1955) *Johnston Allocation of Jordan River Waters 9/30/55 ('The Johnston Plan').* U.S. National Archives and Records Administration, College Park Maryland. NND927340, declassified 9/30/04.

Jones, Steve (2006) *Antonio Gramsci*. Routledge Critical Thinkers. Oxon, UK: Routledge.

Jridi, Aida (2002) *The Development of the Jordanian Jordan River Basin: The Main Historical Steps*. Montpellier, France, Ecole nationale de genie rural, des eaux et des forets, centre de Montpellier (Engref), October 2002.

JVL (2006) Modern Israel and the Diaspora. *Jewish Virtual Library , A Division of the American-Israeli Cooperative Enterprise*.

JWC (2001) *Joint Declaration for Keeping the Water Infrastructure out of the Cycle of Violence*. Dated 31 January 2001, Erez Crossing, Gaza, (Message from the Joint Water Committee communicated by the Israeli Prime Minister's Media Advisor, Israel Ministry of Foreign Affairs Cabinet Secretariat).

Kahhaleh, Subhi (1981) *The Water Problem in Israel and Its Repercussions on the Arab-Israeli Conflict*. I.P.S. Paper Number 9. Beirut, Lebanon, Institute of Palestine Studies.

Kaufman, Edward, Joe Oppenheimer, Aaron Wolf and Ariel Dinar (1997) Transboundary Fresh Water Disputes and Conflict Resolution: Planning an Integrated Approach. *Water International* 22 (1): 37-48.

Kay, Paul A. and Bruce Mitchell (1998) Performance of Israel's Water System under a New Master Plan: Post-audit and Implications for the Future. *Water Resources Development* 14 (1): 107-119.

Keating, Michael, Anne Le More and Robert Lowe, Ed. (2005) *Aid, Diplomacy and Facts on the Ground: The Case of Palestine*. London, UK, Chatham House.

Keohane, Robert. O. (1980) The Theory of Hegemonic Stability and Changes in International Economic Regimes, 1967-1977. *In*: Holsti, O. R., R. M. Siverson and A. L. George, *Change in the International System*. Boulder, CO, USA: Westview Press. 131-161.

KFW (2000) *Jenin Water Supply Project - Conceptual Report*, engineering report prepared by Schneider & Partner and Hijjawi Engineering Center for Kreditanstalt Fuer Wiederaufbau, January 2000.

Khan, Mushtaq (2004a) Evaluating the emerging Palestinian state: 'Good governance' versus 'transformation potential'. *In*: Khan, M., *State Formation in Palestine: Viability and governance during a social transformation*. London, UK: RoutledgeCurzon.

Khan, Mushtaq, Ed. (2004b) *State Formation in Palestine: Viability and governance during a social transformation*. London, UK, RoutledgeCurzon.

Kibaroglu, A. (2002) *Building a Regime for the Rivers of the Euphrates-Tigris Rivers Basin*. International Water Law and Policy Series. Brill, Netherlands: Brill Academic Publishers.

Kinnarty, Noah (2002) An Israeli View - If only there were quiet, the Palestinians have numerous opportunities. *Bitter Lemons On-line Journal 29 (August)*.

Kiser, Stephen D. (2000) *water: The Hydraulic Parameter of Conflict in the Middle East and North Africa*. INSS Occasional Paper 35. Colorado, USA, United States Air Force Institute for National Security Studies, September 2000.

Laboud, W. (1998) *Jenin - Past and Present*. Jenin, West Bank, Municipality of Jenin Water Department, August 1998.

Lasensky, Scott (2005) Chequebook diplomacy: the US, the Oslo process and the role of foreign aid. *In*: Keating, M., A. Le More and R. Lowe, *Aid, Diplomacy and Facts on the Ground: The Case of Palestine*. London, UK: Chatham House.

Lautze, Jonathan, Meredith Reeves, Rosaura Vega and Paul Kirshen (2005) Water Allocation, Climate Change and Sustainable Peace - The Israeli Proposal. *Water International* 30 (2): 197-209.

Lindemann, Stefan (2005) *Water regime formation in Europe: A research framework with lessons from the Rhine and Elbe river basins*. From conflict to collective action: Institutional change and management options to govern transboundary watercourses. Berlin, Germany, Forschungsstelle für Umweltpolitik.

Lonergan, Steve and David Brooks (1994) *Watershed: The Role of Fresh Water in the Israeli-Palestinian Conflict*. Ottawa, Canada: International Development Research Council.

Lowi, Miriam (1993) *Water and Power - The Politics of a Scarce Resource in the Jordan River Basin*. Cambridge, USA: Cambridge University Press.

Luft, G. (2002) *The Wazzani River Dispute: More Tension Along the Israel-Lebanon Border*, Peace Watch 397 (20 September 2002).

Lukes, Steven (2005 [1974]) *power: A Radical View - 2nd edition*. Hampshire, UK: Palgrave MacMillan.

Lukes, Steven (2005b) Power and the Battle for Hearts and Minds. *Millenium: Journal of International Studies* 33 (3): 477-493.

Lustick, Ian S. (2002) Hegemony and the Riddle of Nationalism: The Dialectics of Nationalism and Religion in the Middle East. *Logos* 1 (3 (Summer 2002)): 18-44.

Ma'an (2006) *Israel Threatens to Cut Water Supplies to Palestinian Areas Due to Debt*. Ma'an News Agency, 17 October 2006, Ramallah, Palestine.

MacDonald, Alan (2002) *A brief summary of the hydrogeology of the West Bank*. Draft Working Paper British Geological Survey: SUSMAQ Project.

Madhoun, Fayek (2005) Drinking Water Quality: Evaluation of Chloride and Nitrate Concentration of Well Supplies in the Gaza Governorates (1990-2002) - Palestine. *Water for Life in the Middle East: 2nd Israeli-Palestinian International Conference*, Antalya, Turkey, 20-12 October 2004, Israel/Palestine Center for Research and Information.

Malanczuk, P., Ed. (1997) *Akehurst's Modern Introduction to International Law - 7th Edition*. London and New York, Routledge.

Markel, Doron (2004a) *Monitoring and Managing Lake Kinneret and its Watershed, Northern Israel - a response to environmental, anthropogenic and political constraints*, Unpublished.

Markel, Doron (2004b) *Monitoring and Managing Lake Kinneret (Sea of Galilee) and its Watershed, Northern Israel - a response to environmental, anthropogenic and political constraints*. Powerpoint presentation.

Mason, S., C. Bichsel and T Hagmann (2003) "Trickling-Down or Spilling-Over ?" - Exploring the links between international and sub-national water conflicts in the Eastern Nile and Syr Daria Basins;. *ECPR Joint Sessions of Workshops Edinburgh, Workshop 9: "Geography, Conflict and Cooperation"*, Edinburgh, 28 March - 2 April 2003.

Maternowzki, Eileen (2006) *On the Wazzani Springs Dispute.* Personal communication with author, via email, May - June 2006.

McCaffrey, Stephen (2005) Water Conflict and International Law. *Paper submitted to Palestine Academy for Science and Technology "Water, Values and Rights" Conference 2-4 May 2005*, Ramallah, West Bank.

McLean, Iain and Alistair McMillan (2003) *Oxford Concise Dictionary of Politics.* Oxford, UK: Oxford University Press.

Medzini, Arnon (2001) *The River Jordan: Frontiers and Water.* London, UK: School of Oriental and African Studies.

Medzini, Arnon and Aaron Wolf (2004) Towards a Middle East at Peace: Hidden Issues in Arab-Israeli Hydropolitics. *Water Resources Development* 20 (2): 193-204.

Mekoroth (2005) *Palestinian Authority West Bank Water Consumption Water Bill, July and August 2005.* (internal Mekoroth/WBWD correspondence) Ramla, Israel, Mekoroth.

Messerschmid, Clemens (2003) Protecting the Mountain Aquifer - A Missed Opportunity. *Open Letter to Friends of the Earth Middle East,* In response to FOEME conference "Protecting the Mountain Aquifer", Israel 2003, 19 January 2003.

Messerschmid, Clemens (2004) Structure of the Joint Water Committee. Ramallah, West Bank, 27 May 2004. Email correspondence.

Messerschmid, Clemens (2005) Till the Last Drop... The Palestinian Water Crisis in the West Bank, Hydrogeology and Hydropolitics of a Regional Conflict. *In*: Khatib, I., K. Assaf, D. Clayes and A. al Haj Daoud, *Water Values and Rights.* Ramallah, Palestine: Palestine Academy Press.

Messerschmid, Clemens (2007) *Separating the Waters, Parts 1 and 2.* Ramallah, West Bank, Electronic Intifada, 1 June 2007.

Mimi, Ziad and Bassam Sawalhi (2003) A Decision Tool for Allocating the Waters of the Jordan River Basin Between all Riparian Parties. *Water Resources Management* EWRA 17 (6): 447-461.

Naff, Thomas and Ruth Matson (1984) Middle East water: The Potential for Conflict or Cooperation. *In*: Naff, T. and R. Matson, *Water in the Middle East - Conflict or Cooperation?* (Westview Replica Edition) Boulder, USA: Westview Press.

Nassar, Yasser (2002) *Virtual Water Trade as a Policy Instrument for Achieving Water Security in Palestine.* Gaza City, Unpublished.

Nassereddin, Taher (2005, pers. comm.) *On the History of Cooperation through the JWC.* Personal communication with author, Ramallah, West Bank, 5 September 2005. 5 September 2005.

Nembrini, Pier Giorgio (1995) Do Water Production and Treatment Facilities Need Greater Protection in Armed Conflicts? *Water and War - Symposium on Water in Armed Conflicts*, Geneva, Switzerland, International Committee of the Red Cross.

Newman, A. (2004, pers. comm.) *On current water issues.* Personal communication with author, Tel Aviv, Israel, 9 September 2004.

Newman, David (2002) The Wazzani and Our Water Problem. *The Jerusalem Post.* Jerusalem, 18 September 2002.

Newton, Joshua (1999) *Thoughts of Resolution: The Israeli-Palestinian Joint Water Committee*, Israel/Palestine Center for Research and Information / Friends World Program, Long Island University.

NSU (2004) *Negotiations and the Peace Process - Borders*. Ramallah, West Bank, Negotiations Affairs Department, Palestine Liberation Organisation.

NSU (2005a) *Israel's Wall*. Ramallah, Palestine, Negotiation Support Unit, Negotiation Affairs Department, Palestine Liberation Organisation.

NSU (2005b) *The West Bank - Gaza Water Link - Concept Paper*. Confidential. Ramallah, West Bank, Negotiation Support Unit, Negotiation Affairs Department, Palestine Liberation Organisation, February 2005.

NSU (2005c) *The West Ghor Canal - Concept Paper*. Confidential. Ramallah, Palestine, Negotiation Support Unit, Negotiation Affairs Department, Palestine Liberation Organisation, September 2005.

Nye, Joseph (2004) *Soft Power*. New York, NY, USA: Public Affairs, a member of the Perseus Book Group.

Ohlsson, Leif and Anthony Turton (1999) The Turning of a Screw: Social Resource Scarcity as a Bottle-neck in Adaption to Water Scarcity. *SOAS Water Issues Study Group, School of Oriental and African Studies / King's College - London* (Occasional Paper 19).

Onishi, Kayo (2005) Hydropolitics of China and Downstream Countries in the Mekong River Basin. *International Symposium on the Role of Water Sciences in Transboundary River Basin Management, 10-12 March 2005*, Ubon Ratchathani, Thailand.

Oslo II (1995) *Israeli-Palestinian Interim Agreement on the West Bank and the Gaza Strip*. Washington, D.C., 28 September 1995.

Oxfam (2003) *Forgotten Villages: Struggling to survive under closure in the West Bank*. Oxfam Briefing Paper No. 28. Oxford, UK, Oxfam International.

Oxfam (2003b) *Palestine village encases spring in concrete to thwart further settler attack*. Oxford, UK, Oxfam Great Britain, November 2003.

Oxfam (2006) *Assessment Report - Gaza, September 2006 (External Version 16 October 2006)*. Oxford, UK, Oxfam Great Britain.

PASSIA (2004) *Diary 2004*. Jerusalem: Palestinian Academic Society for the Study of International Affairs.

PCIIWS (2002) *The Parliamentary Committee of Inquiry on the Israeli Water Sector*. headed by MK David Magen, Jerusalem, Israeli Knesset, June 2002.

Pearce, Fred (2004) Israel lays claim to Palestine's water. *New Scientist*, 27 May 2004,

Pearce, Fred (2006) *When the rivers run dry: What happens when our water runs out?* London, UK: Eden Project Books.

PENGON (2003) *The Wall in Palestine - Facts, Testimonies, Analysis and Call to Action*. Jerusalem, Palestinian Environmental Non Governmental Organisation Network.

PHG (2004a) *The Impact of the Wall's First Phase on Water*. Ramallah, Palestine, Palestinian Hydrology Group.

PHG (2004b) Halmish Settlers are stopping supply of water to Bani Zeid Algharbyh. *Water and Sanitation Hygiene Monitoring Project, Palestinian Hydrology Group*. Ramallah, West Bank, 23 August 2004.

PHG (2006) *Water for Life 2005: Continued Israeli Assault on Palestinian Water, Sanitation and Hygiene During the Intifada.* Ramallah, West Bank, Palestinian Hydrology Group - Water, Sanitation and Hygiene Monitoring Program, supported by the European Commission Humanitarian Aid Department (ECHO) and Oxfam-Great Britain, April 2006.

Phillips, David (2004, pers. comm.) *On Israeli Tactics at the JWC.* Personal communication with author, Ramallah, West Bank, 13 September 2004. 13 September 2004.

Phillips, David, Shaddad Attili, Stephen McCaffrey and John Murray (2005) The Jordan River Basin: 1. Clarification of the Allocations in the Johnston Plan. *Submitted for publication to Water International.*

Phillips, David, Shaddad Attili, Stephen McCaffrey, John Murray and Mark Zeitoun (2005) The Water Rights of the Co-riparians to the Jordan River Basin. *paper submitted to Water Values and Rights Conference May 2005*, Ramallah, West Bank and Gaza City, Gaza Strip, Palestine Academy for Science and Technology.

Phillips, David, Marwa Daoudy, Joakim Öjendal, Anthony Turton and Stephen McCaffrey (2006) *Trans-boundary Water Cooperation as a Tool for Conflict Prevention and Broader Benefit-sharing.* Global Development Studies No. 4. Stockholm, Sweden: Ministry of Foreign Affairs.

PWA (2003a) *Water Needs for Un-Served Communities in West Bank 2003.* Ramallah, West Bank, Palestinian Water Authority, 2003.

PWA (2003b) *Water Projects Status and Donations in the Northern and Southern Governorates.* Ramallah, West Bank, Palestinian Water Authority, December 2003.

PWA (2004a) *Leakage Control Report*, Palestinian Water Authority, World Bank.

PWA (2004b) *The Annexation and Expansion Wall: To Control the Palestinian Water Resources.* Ramallah, Palestine, Palestinian Water Authority.

Reisner, Marc (1986) *Cadillac Desert - The American West and its Disappearing Water.* New York, USA: Penguin Books.

Renger, Jochen (1998) The Middle East Peace Process: Obstacles to Cooperation over Shared Resources. *In:* Scheumann and Schiffler, *Water in the Middle East: Potential for Conflicts and Prospects for Cooperation.* Heidleberg, Germany: Springer.

Rook, Robert E. (2000) An American in Palestine: Elwood Mead and Zionist Water Resource Planning 1923-1936. *Arab Studies Quarterly* 22 (1): 71-90.

Roy, Sara (1995) *The Gaza Strip: The Political Economy of De-Development.* Washington, DC, USA: Institute for Palestine Studies.

Said, Edward (1996) *Peace and Its Discontents: Essays on Palestine in the Middle East Peace Process.* Vintage.

Schiff, Ze'ev (2005) Gaza sewage could cripple desalination facility. *Ha'aretz Daily (English).* Tel Aviv, Israel, 16 September 2005.

Schnell, Izhak (2001) Changing Territorial Concepts in Israel: From besieged nation-building to globalisation (Introduction). *GeoJournal* 53: 213-217.

Schwarz, Rolf (2004) *The Israeli-Jordanian Water Regime - A Model for Resolving Water Conflicts in the Jordan River Basin?* Occasional Paper No. 1. Lausanne, Switzerland, Programme for Strategic and International Security Studies.

Scott, James C. (1985) *Weapons of the Weak: Everyday Forms of Peasant Resistance.* London: Yale University Press.

Segal, R., Weizman, E. (2003) *A Civilian Occupation: The Politics of Israeli Architecture.* Tel Aviv, Israel: Babel.

Selby, Jan (2003a) *Water, Power and Politics in the Middle East - The Other Israeli-Palestinian Conflict.* London, UK: I.B. Tauris.

Selby, Jan (2003b) Dressing up Domination as 'Co-operation': The Case of Israeli-Palestinian Water Relations. *Review of International Studies* 29 (1): 121-138.

Selby, Jan (2005) Joint Mismanagement: Reappraising the Oslo Water Regime. *Water for Life in the Middle East: 2nd Israeli-Palestinian International Conference,* Antalya, Turkey, 20-12 October 2004, Israel/Palestine Center for Research and Information.

Sengupta, Somini (2002) In Israel and Lebanon, Talk of War Over Water. *New York Times.* New York, USA, 10 October 2002.

Shamir, Uri (2004) *Testimony to the Committee on International Relations of the US Congress House of Representatives on 05 May 2004, "Water Scarcity in the Middle East - Regional Cooperation as a Mechanism Towards Peace".* Washington, DC, USA.

Shawi, M. (2003, pers. comm.) *On water stoppages in Jenin.* Personal communication with author, Jenin City, West Bank, September 2003. September 2003.

Sherman, Martin (1999) *The Politics of Water in the Middle East - An Israeli Perspective on the Hydro-Political Aspects of the Conflict.* London, UK: Macmillan Press Ltd.

Sitton, Dov (2001) Development of Limited Water Resources: Historical and Technological Aspects. *Jewish Virtual Library.*

Snowdon, Peter (2006) Drying Up Palestine. Video documentary on the DFID-funded SUSMAQ Project in Palestine, UK Department for International Development.

Sobelman, Daniel (2002) Both sides get belligerent on Wazzani River dispute. *Ha'aretz.* Tel Aviv, Israel, 23 September 2002.

Sobelman, Daniel and Uri Ash (2002) Sharon Warns Against Diversion of Water Sources in Lebanon. *Ha'aretz Daily (English).* Tel Aviv, Israel, 11 September 2002.

Soffer, Arnon (2002) *Mapping Special Interest Groups in Israel's Water Policy.* Efficient Use of Limited Water Resources: Making Israel a Model State. Ramat Gan, Israel, Begin-Sadat Center for Strategic Studies, Bar Ilan University Department of Political Science.

Soffer, Arnon (2005, pers. comm.) *On Israeli Water Use - Past, Present, Future.* Personal communication with author, Haifa, Israel, 2 September 2005. 2 September 2005.

Stiglitz, Joseph E. (2002) *Globalization and its Discontents.* London: Penguin Books.

Stork, Joe (1983) Water and Israel's Occupation Strategy. *Middle East Research & Information Project - MERIP Reports* 116 (July-August 1983): 19-24.

Strange, Susan (1982) *Cave! Hic Dragones:* A Critique of Regime Analysis. *International Organization* 36 (2): 479-496.

Strange, Susan (1987) The Persistent Myth of Lost Hegemony. *In:* Tooze, R. and C. May, *Authority and Markets - Susan Strange's Writings on International Political Economy.* Hampshire, UK: Palgrave Macmillan.

Strange, Susan (1994) Who Governs? Networks of Power in World Society. *In*: Tooze, R. and C. May, *Authority and Markets - Susan Strange's Writings on International Political Economy*. Hampshire, UK: Palgrave Macmillan.

SUSMAQ (2001a) *Sustainable Management of the West Bank and Gaza Aquifers - Final Report*. Ramallah, West Bank, Sustainable Management of the West Bank and Gaza Aquifers, Working Report, Water Resources and Planning Department, Palestinian Water Authority, August 2001.

SUSMAQ (2001b) *Data Review on the West Bank Aquifers*, Sustainable Management of the West Bank and Gaza Aquifers, Working Report SUSMAQ-MOD #02 V2.0, Water Resources and Planning Department, Palestinian Water Authority, August 2001.

Swyngedouw, Erik (1999) Modernity and Hybridity: Nature, Regeneracionismo, and the Production of the Spanish Waterscape, 1890 - 1930. *Annals of the Association of American Geographers* 89 (3): 443-465.

Tagar, Zecharya, Tamar Keinan and Gidon Bromberg (2004b) *A Seeping Time Bomb: Pollution of the Mountain Aquifer by Sewage*. Tel Aviv, Israel, Friends of the Earth Middle East, February 2004.

Tahal (1959) *The Jordan Project Planning Report, submitted by Tahal Water Planning for Israel, Ltd.* Jerusalem, Jerusalem Academic Press (a.k.a. "The Seven Year Plan"), 1959.

Talhami, Michael (2005) Water resources of Palestine in the period 1993 to 2003 (Oslo): Sustainability and security of use and management. Essay prepared for Water and Water Policy Class, Department of Geography. King's College London, University of London, London, UK.

Thomas, Martyn D. (2004) Water Consumption and Scarcity in Israel 1948 - 2002. Environment, Politics and Globalisation. Master's Thesis. King's College London, London, UK.

Trottier, Julie (1999) *Hydropolitics in the West Bank and Gaza Strip*. Jerusalem: PASSIA - Palestinian Academic Society for the Study of International Affairs.

Trottier, Julie (2003) *Water Wars: The Rise of a Hegemonic Concept - Exploring the Making of the Water War and Water Peace Belief within the Israeli-Palestinian Conflict*. Paper prepared for the Green Cross International project *From Potential Conflict to Co-operation Potential*. Geneva, Switzerland.

Trottier, Julie (2007) A wall, water and power: the Israeli 'separation fence'. *Review of International Studies* 33: 105 - 127.

Turton, Anthony (1999a) Water Scarcity and Social Adaptive Capacity: Towards an Understanding of the Social Dynamics of Water Demand Management in Developing Countries. *SOAS Water Issues Study Group, School of Oriental and African Studies / King's College - London* (Occasional Paper 9).

Turton, Anthony (1999b) Water Demand Management (WDM): A Case Study from South Africa. *SOAS Water Issues Study Group, School of Oriental and African Studies / King's College - London* (Occasional Paper 4).

Turton, Anthony (2000) Precipitation, People, Pipelines and power: Towards a 'Virtual Water' Based Political Ecology Discourse. *SOAS Water Issues Study Group, School of Oriental and African Studies / King's College - London* (Occasional Paper 11).

Turton, Anthony (2003) The political aspects of institutional developments in the water sector: South Africa and its international river basins. Department of International Politics, Faculty of Humanities. Ph.D. Thesis. University of Pretoria, Pretoria, South Africa.

Turton, Anthony and Nikki Funke (2007) Hydro Hegemony in the Contexst of the Orange River Basin. *Water Policy* (forthcoming) (Special Issue on Hydro-Hegemony).

Turton, Anthony and Richard Meissner (2002) The hydrosocial contract and its manifestation in society: A South African case study. *In*: Turton, A. and R. Henwood, *Hydropolitics in the Developing World: A Southern African Perspective.* Pretoria, South Africa: African Water Issues Research Unit.

Twain, Mark (2004 [1916]) *The Mysterious Stranger and Other Stories.* Penguin Books.

UN ILC (1997) *Convention on the Law of the Non-navigational Uses of International Watercourses,* United Nations International Law Commission, 1997.

UNDP (2006) *Human Development Report 2006 - Beyond Scarcity: Power, Poverty and the Global Water Crisis.* New York, USA, United Nations Development Programme.

UNEP (2003) *Desk Study on the Environment in the Occupied Palestinian Territories,* United Nations Environment Program.

Unicef (2006) *Reservoir Repairs and Reconstruction in South Lebanon.* Tyre, Lebanon, Minutes from Meeting of 2 October, Unicef Water and Sanitation Humanitarian Relief Coordination Cluster.

US Embassy (1965) *Report on Meeting to address response to Israeli Security and Water Security Concerns.* Tel Aviv, Israel, US Embassy in Israel telegram to US Department of State, Washington, 26 February 1965 (published by the Jewish Virtual Library as "The United States Hears Israeli Concerns on Security and Water Rights").

USAID (2002a) *West Bank Integrated Water Resources Management Plan.* Tel Aviv, Israel, United States Agency for International Development and the Palestinian Water Authority, prepared by CH2MHill.

USAID (2002b) *Baseline Water Resources Evaluation Draft Report January 2002.* Tel Aviv, Israel, United States Agency for International Development and the Palestinian Water Authority, prepared by CH2MHill., January 2002.

USAID (2005) Website for the West Bank and Gaza. *United States Agency for International Development.*

USAID (2006) U.S. Overseas Loans and Grants [Greenbook]. *USAID.*

Van Aken, Mauro (2003) *Facing Home: Palestinian Belonging in a Valley of Doubt.* Maastricht: Shaker Publishing.

Vengosh, Avner, Wolfram Klopmann, Amer Marei, Yacov Livshitz, Alexis Guttierez, Mazen Banna, Catherine Guerrot, Irena Pankratov and Hadas Ranaan (2005) Sources of salinity and boron in the Gaza Strip: Natural contaminant flow in the southern Mediterranean coastal aquifer. *Water Resources Research* 41.

Warner, Jeroen (2004a) Mind the GAP - Working with Buzan: the Illisu Dam as a security Issue. *SOAS Water Issues Study Group, School of Oriental and African Studies / King's College - London* (Occasional Paper 67).

Warner, Jeroen (2004b) Water, Wine, Vinegar and Blood.   On politics, participation, violence and conflict over the hydrosocial contract. *Proceedings from Water and Politics Conference, 26-27 February 2004, Ch. 3*, Marseilles, France, 15 March 2004. World Water Council.

Warner, Jeroen (forthcoming) Hydro-Hegemony as a Layered Cake - The Case of Turkey. *Water Policy* (submitted as part of a Special Issue on Hydro-Hegemony).

Waterbury, John (2002) *The Nile: National Determinants of Collective Action.* Ann Arbor, MI, USA: Yale University Press.

WBWD (2003) *Water Facilities for WBWD Water System (map).* Ramallah, West Bank, West Bank Water Department.

Wester, Philippus and Jeroen Warner (2002) River basin management reconsidered. *In*: Turton, A. and R. Henwood, *Hydropolitics in the Developing World: A Southern African Perspective.* Pretoria, South Africa: African Water Issues Research Unit, Council for Scientific and Industrial Research.

Williams, P. (2001) *Water Usually Flows Downhill: the Role of Power, Norms and Domestic Politics in Resolving Transboundary Water-Sharing Conflicts.*, University of California Institute on Global Conflict and Cooperation, Working Paper 1998.

Wolf, Aaron T. (1995) *Hydropolitics Along the Jordan River.* United Nations University Press.

Wolf, Aaron T. (1998) Conflict and Cooperation along international waterways. *Water Policy* 1 (1998): 251-265.

Wolf, Aaron T. (2000a) "Hydrostrategic" Territory in the Jordan Basin: Water, War, and Arab-Israeli Peace Negotiations. *In*: Wolf, A. and H. Amery, *Water in the Middle East: A Geography of Peace.* Austin, USA: University of Texas Press.

Wolf, Aaron T. (2000b) From Rights to Needs: Water Allocations in International Treaties. *In*: Feitelson, E. and M. Haddad, *Management of Shared Groundwater Resources: The Israeli-Palestinian Case with an International Perspective.* Ottawa, Canada: International Development Research Council.

Wolf, Aaron T., Ed. (2002) *Conflict Prevention and Resolution in Water Systems.* The Management of Water Series. Cheltenham, UK, Elgar.

Wolf, Aaron T. (2004) *Freshwater Transboundary Dispute Database.* Corvallis, OR, USA, Oregon State University.

World Bank (2002) *Physical and Institutional Damage Assessment, West Bank Governorates, March-May 2002 - Summary Report*, International Bank for Reconstruction and Development, 23 May 2002.

World Bank (2003) *27 Months of Intifada, Closures and Palestinian Economic Crisis.* Jerusalem, International Bank for Reconstruction and Development, May 2003.

World Bank (2004) *Infrastructure Assessment - West Bank and Gaza.* Jerusalem, International Bank for Reconstruction and Development, June 2004.

Yitzhak, Yoav (2004) Water Commission: Disengagement Will Entail Huge Investment in Water - Decision-making on the Disengagement Plan has not taken this into account. *Globes On-line.*

Yoffe, Shira B., Aaron T. Wolf and Mark Giordano (2001) Conflict and Cooperation over International Freshwater Resources: Indicators and Findings of the Basins at Risk. *Journal of American Water Resources Association* 39 (5): 1109-1126.

Zaslavsky, Dan (2002) *Water as a Metaphor.* Haifa, Israel, Technion - Israel Institute of Technology, Faculty of Agriculture.

Zeitoun, Mark (2007) Complicity when the dam breaks. *International Herald Tribune.* Paris, France, Opinion, 6 April 2007,

Zeitoun, Mark and Jeroen Warner (2006a) Hydro-Hegemony: A Framework for Analysis of Transboundary Water Conflicts. *Water Policy* 8 (2006): 435-460.

Zisser, E. (2002) Israel and Lebanon: The Battle for the Wazzani. *In*: Heller, M., *Tel Aviv Notes - An Update on Political and Strategic Developments in the Middle East, No. 50,*. Tel Aviv, Israel: Moshe Dayan Center for Middle Easter and African Studies / Jafee Center for Strategic Studies, Tel Aviv University. October 2002.

Zolo, Danilo (2005) The Right to Water as a Collective Right. *paper submitted to Palestine Academy for Science and Technology "Water, Values and Rights" Conference 2-4 May 2005*, Ramallah, West Bank.

Index